FROM POVERTY BAY TO
BROADWAY

FROM POVERTY BAY TO BROADWAY
THE STORY OF TOM HEENEY

Lydia Monin

Hodder Moa

National Library of New Zealand Cataloguing-in-Publication Data
Monin, Lydia.
From Poverty Bay to Broadway : the story of Tom Heeney / by Lydia Monin.
ISBN 978-1-86971-125-2
1. Heeney, Tom, 1898-1984. 2. Boxers (Sports)—New Zealand
—Biography. 3. Boxing. I. Title.
796.83092—dc 22

A Hodder Moa Book
Published in 2008 by Hachette Livre NZ Ltd
4 Whetu Place, Mairangi Bay
Auckland, New Zealand

Text © Lydia Monin 2008
The moral rights of the author have been asserted.
Design and format © Hachette Livre NZ Ltd 2008

All rights reserved. No part of this publication may be reproduced or transmitted in any form or by any means, electronic or mechanical, including photocopying, recording, or any information storage and retrieval system, without permission in writing from the publisher.

Ernest Hemingway letter on page 233, dated 10 March 1936, to Bob Considine, published in the *Washington Herald*. Reprinted with the permission of Scribner, an imprint of Simon & Schuster Adult Publishing Group, on behalf of the Hemingway Foreign Rights.

Designed and produced by Hachette Livre NZ Ltd
Printed by 1010 Printing International Ltd., China

Front cover image: Getty images

Contents

Acknowledgements	6
Key Characters	7
Introduction	9
A Sportsman's Death	13
Young Blood	18
What a Warrior He'd Have Made	32
The Ugliness of Fear	49
A Bushwhacker on the Town	59
The Courage of a Colonial	63
My None Too Brilliant Career	72
Looking for Another Dempsey	90
A Ring of Gold in Filth and Slime	108
The Path to Logical Contendership	125
Heeneyville, Formerly Gisborne	138
Taming the Unarmed Killer	158
The Rocking Statue of Pain	172
From Tiger to House Cat	189
Under a Tottering Tower	203
Eight and Two and You're Out	210
Fading with the Platinum Blondes	218
Boxing with Hemingway	227
Epilogue	240
Bibliography	245
Index	249

Acknowledgements

Thanks, once again, to Andrew for everything. Many thanks to Mum, Dad, Peter and Paul for their help and hospitality on Waiheke Island; and to Andria, Dermot, Lyn and Len for putting me up in the UK.

A big thank you to Mario Castricone for his tireless efforts to unearth fascinating material about Tom's life. Many people kindly contributed stories, letters, interviews, articles, images and other assistance, including 'Papa' Tom Heeney, Gerry Heeney, Ron Palenski, James J. Houlihan, Mike Edwards, Eric Hoggins, Mike Parker, Dave Cameron, Hugh Griffin, John Jones, Rev. Stephen Donald, Hank Kaplan, Christine Dekker, Liz Griffin, John Heeney, Tom Heeney (Hastings), Jim Benson, Pat Benson, Paul Hodges, Howard Kleinberg, Enrique Cirules, Paula Longhi. Special thanks to Roberta Van Anda for all her help in New Jersey.

Thanks to the following institutions: National Library of New Zealand, Alexander Turnbull Library, Archives New Zealand, Tairawhiti Museum, Auckland City Libraries, University of Auckland Library, Auckland Archives of Sisters of Mercy, Auckland Catholic Diocesan Archives, Kippenberger Military Archive and Research Library, Royal Humane Society of New Zealand, Queensland State Archives, New York Public Library, District of Columbia Public Library, Library of Congress, National Archives and Records Administration, John F. Kennedy Presidential Library and Museum, *Kansas City Star*, *Miami Herald*, Middletown Public Library, Port Washington Public Library, Manhasset Public Library, Monmouth County Historical Association Library and Archives, Newark Free Public Library, North Hempstead Town Hall, *Boston Globe*, British Library, Trinity College Library Dublin, National Library of Ireland.

The author also gratefully acknowledges the assistance of the New Zealand History Research Trust Fund.

Key Characters

Baer, Max, World Heavyweight Champion 1934–35, fought Tom in 1931, 1932
Bell, Colin, Australian boxer, fought Tom in 1921, 1922
Carroll, Sir James, Acting Prime Minister of New Zealand, 1909, 1911
Carroll, Lady Heni Materoa, Sir James Carroll's wife
Delaney, Jack, World Light Heavyweight Champion 1926–27, fought Tom in 1928
Dempsey, Jack, World Heavyweight Champion, 1919–1926
Dominey, Fred, Tom's New Zealand trainer
Gallico, Paul, journalist, novelist and short-story writer
Gibbons, Tommy, leading American boxer, used Tom as a sparring partner, 1924
Harvey, Charlie, Tom's American manager
Heeney, Eliza, Tom's mother
Heeney, Hugh, Tom's father
Heeney, Jack, Arthur and Pat, Tom's brothers
Heeney, Marion (née Dunn), Tom's wife
Hemingway, Ernest, journalist, novelist and short-story writer
Hennessey, Jimmy, Tom's American trainer
Madden, Bartley, Irish-born boxer, fought Tom in 1926
Maloney, Jimmy, leading American boxer, fought Tom in 1927, 1929
McCleary, Brian, New Zealand boxer and All Black, fought Tom in 1923
McGeehan, Bill, writer
Mortimer, Bernard and John, Tom's British managers

Pegler, Westbrook, writer
Rice, Grantland, writer
Rickard, Tex, boxing promoter
Risko, Johnny, Austrian-born boxer, fought Tom in 1927, 1931
Runyon, Damon, journalist and short-story writer
Scott, Phil, British Heavyweight Champion 1926–31, fought Tom in 1924, 1926
Sharkey, Jack, World Heavyweight Champion 1932–33, fought Tom in 1928
Tunney, Gene, World Heavyweight Champion 1926–28, fought Tom in 1928
Uzcudun, Paulino, Spanish boxer, fought Tom in 1927
Whitaker, Cyril, New Zealand boxer, fought Tom in 1923

Introduction

'Fight fans are not sure whether, under international law, Heeney's victory will not cause this country to revert automatically to the status of a British colony,' reported the *New Yorker*. Boxing mattered back in those days — back when prizefights were patronised by conmen, racketeers, gangsters and their molls; back when charm, notoriety and style were what mattered most; back in the roaring twenties. When Jack Dempsey beat Jess Willard for the heavyweight championship on 4 July 1919 it heralded the arrival of sport as entertainment for the masses in a prosperous, post-war America. The 'celebrity' was born and sportsmen were idolised. Into this world stepped Tom Heeney of Gisborne, and through a potent mix of doggedness, brute strength, an inhuman capacity to absorb punishment, and the good fortune to be in the right prize ring at the right time, Tom got his shot at the title.

Tom Heeney became New Zealand's first global sporting hero and a member of the smart set in 'Jazz Age' New York. It was 1928 and heavyweight champion Gene Tunney had been guaranteed five million bucks in today's money to defend his title. Tunney could pick his own opponent; he chose Tom and life would never be the same again. Nobody had wasted much ink on the 'Hard Rock from Down Under' before that day, but now there were tickets to sell and Tom Heeney needed a story. The fight crowds had an insatiable appetite for lurid accounts of a prizefighter's past and Tom came from a distant land so there was no danger of friends and family spoiling the illusion by telling the real story.

> What a past that man has to look forward to! The whole underside of the world is the backdrop for his reminiscences. Kangaroo breaker in his native New Zealand, pearl diver in the Japan Sea, pantryman

> to the cannibal king of the Solomon Islands, first white man to enter the forbidden city of Lhasa, python strangler in the Carnatic, scaler of Mount Everest, all-conquering Don Juan of Polynesia, original discoverer of the dinosaurs' eggs in the Gobi, personal bodyguard to the Mikado, founder of the Chinese Republic, two-fisted scourge of the Indian Ocean — every section of the lower half of the planet must yield touches of colour to the lives of Heeney.
>
> With two hundred million square miles of Down Under to contribute purple patches to the Heeney cycle, the publishing houses will have no difficulties with the new champion. If Heeney does not confess freely, the most mellifluous confessors in the country will be found to confess for him. If he does not reminisce fluently, the best talent in that field will be signed up to recollect for him. Heeney may not know it, but he has a past coming on that will stun him. He has a childhood, boyhood, and youth approaching that ought to raise his opinion of himself several hundred per cent.
>
> *New Yorker*, 2 June 1928

In the end there were no literary agents scrambling to sell Tom's autobiographies and biographies, the 'wild flights of imagination' the *New Yorker* described. Just as the Wall Street Crash ended the Jazz Age, the Tunney–Heeney fight was the end of boxing's golden era. 'It was borrowed time anyhow,' wrote F. Scott Fitzgerald, 'the whole upper tenth of a nation living with the insouciance of grand dukes and the casualness of chorus girls.' The exploits of prizefighters just didn't seem that important any more.

So Tom's story was forgotten and, over time, scattered across continents in old newspapers, letters, scrapbooks, archives and in the memories of friends and family and a few boxing old-timers. Tom didn't enter the prize ring to 'save his second cousin Elaine from being left at the church by Lord Spanyan', he didn't 'fall in with the fast set of the Sydney waterfront', he hadn't 'routed the kangaroo rustlers', and he didn't 'win the war'. But the real story of Tom's life *is* truly remarkable. From a labourer's cottage in Gisborne, Tom journeyed into the golden age of boxing and was there when it all imploded, sitting on the challenger's stool at the Yankee Stadium one sultry July evening in 1928.

There's an old saying that there's a broken heart for every light on

INTRODUCTION

Broadway, and Tom's time along the Great White Way ended with a succession of beatings by younger men. Yet Tom's capacity to take a right hook was matched by his ability to take life's blows. He killed a man with one punch, left another for dead on the canvas, found himself broke and lonely thousands of miles from home, and within a year or so of winning a small fortune the Depression took it away. But just like he did in the ring, Tom always came back fighting.

Tom Heeney scrapped through the tough times and created a new life for himself outside the ring. Unlike so many prizefighters, his story didn't end in misery and hardship after he'd gone 'down the toboggan slide' as the boys would say. And in a time when prizefighting, outside the ring at least, was at its dirtiest, 'Honest Tom' stayed honest to the end. 'That,' wrote boxing scribe Paul Gallico, 'makes the chances a thousand to one that they ever get up to a shot at the heavyweight title.'

This, finally, is Tom's story.

A Sportsman's Death

A couple more bouts and Cyril Whitaker was through with the ring. He was getting married the following week. But sitting in his corner Cyril looked nervous. He seemed gentlemanly, not your typical pug.

He lived in New Plymouth but hailed from Southland, and down south everyone knew the Whitaker boys. Five of nine brothers played rugby for Southland. A sixth, one of two killed in action, was a champion pole-vaulter. Cyril rowed and played tennis. He worked in the mines on the West Coast and played rugby against the Springboks in 1921 when he was awarded a gold medal for being the best forward in the local team. He was a clean, fast, scientific boxer and was 'a man of singularly fine character, and one of the "whitest" men who ever entered the boxing arena'. He was just the kind of person the game needed, for a man could be given no finer requiem than the words he 'died a sportsman'.

A fairly even fight was expected with a knockout unlikely. Tickets were cheaper than usual and the Town Hall in Auckland was packed. They had travelled from opposite coasts of the North Island: the clever boxer from the west, Cyril Whitaker, and a heavy hitter from the east, Tom Heeney. It was 15 three-minute rounds for a purse of £150 to be split £90 to the winner and £60 to the loser.

Dugald Keith Hagen, a Northern Boxing Association doctor, examined the men beforehand. Cyril had been complaining of headaches after being kicked in the head during a game of rugby, but this only emerged later. He had trained at the Donovan Bros' gym in Parnell while Tom sparred down the hill at Stewart Smith's gym in Customs Street, where he showed he could 'snap in heavy punches'. Both were fit, but the doctor judged Cyril to be in better condition. At six foot Cyril was taller and had a longer reach, but stripped in their corners it was clear that Tom was more powerfully built.

Police Sergeant Alfred Ernest Rowell inspected both the ring and the gloves. Percival Greenhough of the Boxing Association helped put up the ring. Association Chairman James Wilson Russell oversaw the arrangements for the contest. They were all at ringside to see the fight. Below the heavy sail canvas sat a layer of felt and below that was a layer of seagrass matting, because a boxer had injured his head in an accident down south. They wore eight-ounce gloves, two ounces heavier than the minimum. Tom's trainer thought they were larger than usual and Tom also noticed the difference. The preparations were complete and the fight began.

At the gong both men attacked, Cyril getting in first with a straight left. Tom swung short lefts and rights in the clinches, which became increasingly frequent.

'Break, lads!' referee Frank Burns said repeatedly. Burns had refereed more than a thousand fights.

The second round was similar. They sparred for an opening and clinched with short-arm jolts. Burns demanded they separate. Cyril used his straight left to Tom's face. But Tom wasn't ruffled. 'As they warmed to their work it was apparent that Whitaker, although having the advantage in height and reach, was handicapped by a certain natural nervousness, his opponent's imperturbable style contrasting sharply with the New Plymouth man's facial expression,' wrote a ringside scribe.

In the third Cyril flinched after a heavy blow to the abdomen but leapt back, driving Tom to the ropes with five left-right-left blows. Tom responded and went after Cyril in the middle of the ring. An exchange of blows ended when a thudding straight right sent Cyril crashing to the canvas. The Southlander stayed down.

'One — two — three — four . . .'

He raised himself to rest on his knee.

'. . . five — six — seven — eight — nine . . .'

Cyril struggled to his feet. Dr Hagen thought he had recovered and seemed none the worse. But one commentator wrote that he probably 'never knew what he was doing afterwards, and gave that impression to the ringsiders from the manner he went for the clinch and hung on'. Cyril was pummelled with right and left swings and stinging uppercuts. He couldn't retaliate and just before the gong took a heavy right to the body. He walked to his corner and looked sick as he sat down.

But Cyril wasn't ready to give up. 'Not for long was the groggy look on his mobile face, for early in the fourth Whitaker made a vicious lunge with his quick left, and Heeney was pleased to skip out of range,' wrote one scribe. Cyril made a remarkable recovery and outboxed Tom in the next few rounds. The crowd roared its approval when he broke away from a clinch early in the fifth and shot out straight lefts to Tom's face. Retaliation came in the form of a heavily planted right cross to the body. Whitaker grunted.

'Stand off him!' the crowd yelled at Cyril.

At the opening of the sixth the men fell into a clinch once more. They broke and Tom swung a left to Cyril's face. Cyril lunged in, but Tom held him off before swinging two rapid lefts. A right swing just missed Cyril's head at the sound of the gong. After more clinching in the seventh a blow from Tom fell harmlessly off Cyril's shoulder and Tom took a jolt to the head without flinching.

Walter Howard of the Gisborne Boxing Association thought Tom was content just to evade Cyril. But if Tom wanted to go easy on his opponent, the crowd wasn't having it.

'Go it, Gisborne!'

'Go for him, Tom!'

Halfway through the bout the boxers talked to each other. 'Why don't you turn it up?' Tom asked Cyril. Cyril looked towards his seconds.

Tom cut and closed Cyril's right eye in the eighth. By the ninth Tom was boxing fiercely; in the tenth Cyril found a new reserve of energy and opened with a blow to the nose followed by one to the jaw. Tom responded with a wide toothy grin. More clinching followed, and Tom drove in a right uppercut, just missing his opponent. Cyril landed a straight left, only to be caught by a heavy blow to the body at the bell.

The crowd clapped at the end of the eleventh, in which both men 'mixed it fairly freely'. Early in the twelfth Tom's eye was closed but his trainer would later claim he had a sparring mark over his eye that Cyril hadn't even found. After a clinch Cyril broke away to smash Tom with a right downward blow and Tom swung a right and left. A heavy left to Cyril's face drew blood and he hung on. Tom was now punishing Cyril.

After the 'Devil's number' went up a heavy right to Cyril's jaw sent him reeling and he stopped the same punch a moment later. As he was hit the rubber 'bite' for his teeth spun out. He looked really tired now. A body blow made him wince as the gong sounded to end the fourteenth.

'How do you feel Whitaker — are you all in?' the referee asked.

'No, I'm quite all right; don't stop the fight.'

Sergeant Rowell thought Cyril couldn't win but didn't believe his condition was bad enough for him or the Inspector of Police to stop the fight.

And so the last round began. Cyril leapt at Tom and sent him to the corner. But he was tired and was punished with a vicious right to his right eye. He reeled on the ropes and covered up. Tom was going for a knockout. Cyril stumbled, the referee stepped between them and stopped the fight. Burns thought Cyril would be knocked out and he didn't want that after 'a good fight'. The stoppage surprised Boxing Association Chairman Russell.

Burns held up Tom's arm while Tom held up Cyril. The boxers shook hands and the audience cheered. But it had been a poor fight. 'As a display of scientific boxing, the contest was disappointing, neither of the boxers exhibiting any evidence of science,' reported one newspaper. 'It was characterised by wilful and extravagant slogging, with repeated clinching for safety and frequent requests from the referee to "break away."' The amateur bouts that had opened the tournament were cleverer and much more interesting. 'The big fight was anything but spectacular,' wrote another, 'both men slogging away in monotonous style for fourteen rounds.' Cyril was applauded for his grit and determination. 'It is extremely doubtful if any other heavyweight in the country could have stood up to the punishment which Whitaker was subjected to at the hands of Heeney, and seldom has a gamer display been witnessed in

Auckland than that for which the Taranaki man was responsible in their hard fought battle,' said one critic.

The crowd dispersed. Cyril walked over to the ropes, picked up his protective dental plate and reached his corner. Sergeant Rowell left the ring area, as did Dr Hagen, who said he would've examined the fighters before leaving if he'd thought it necessary. Cyril sat down in his chair and spoke to his seconds as his gloves were being taken off. Greenhough helped him with his gloves.

'Hard luck, Whitaker!' he commiserated.

'Hard luck, but it was a good fight!' Cyril replied. Or perhaps he said 'a fair fight'. Greenhough wasn't sure.

Cyril started for his dressing room. He walked across the ring and Greenhough held the ropes apart for him. As he stooped down to get through the ropes he leaned forward and collapsed. The 24-year-old was carried to the dressing room unconscious.

Cyril Whitaker would never know what happened next: the calling of the doctor; the rush to Auckland Hospital; the emergency brain surgery; the remarkable but fleeting improvement in his condition; and finally the slide into death the following night. Neither would he know he had died at the hands of a man who'd be fêted by writers and movie stars, whose name would be writ large on Broadway and who would come within one murderous right hook of being heavyweight champion of the world.

Young Blood

The journey ended on the morning of 1 February 1878. It had begun almost three months earlier in Plymouth when 21 married couples, 72 single men, 51 single women, 15 boys, nine girls and six babies boarded the *Carnatic*. They endured 11 nauseating days as their barque was battered about the English Channel by severe gales before she was finally able to get away from land. There followed a monotonous and cramped voyage broken only by the sight of a few icebergs. The *Carnatic* was signalled as she made her way towards Lyttelton. Her passengers were about to begin a new life in the New World.

At 3.30 p.m. the *Carnatic* was anchored off Diamond Harbour. After the health and immigration inspection, reporters were shown around the ship. The compartment for the single women, mostly domestic servants, was 'fairly lighted, and clean and tidy'. The married couples' area was also in good condition and the single men's quarters were in 'a tolerable state of cleanliness and order'. The men were farmhands and mechanics. Half the single women and most of the single men were Irish. These were children of the famine generation, drawn to New Zealand through various emigration schemes. The colony desperately needed men to work and women to marry them, and during the great influx of the 1870s and early 1880s more than a fifth of the country's settlers were Irish. The single men on the *Carnatic* were 'a good, strong, useful looking lot of young fellows, and well suited for the country'. One of them was a very strong but small-framed farmer's son from County Derry, with just four coppers in his pocket. His name was Hugh Heeney.

Fifty of the immigrants boarded the morning train to Timaru and Ashburton, while the rest went by a later train to the barracks at Addington. Hugh Heeney spent a year in Ashburton before working his way north. In his first job, milking, he earned 12s 6d a week, but later found work that offered 6s a day. He travelled up the country and settled in Gisborne, nestled on the shores of Poverty Bay and isolated by high ranges to the south and west. The land to the north was little more than wilderness with muddy tracks and unbridged river crossings. There were few metalled roads. The harbour was the best way into Gisborne, but at certain times of the year, when seas ran high, ships couldn't even land their passengers.

Poverty Bay might have been called Endeavour Bay. It was the first place James Cook landed in New Zealand before he circumnavigated and mapped the country. The crew of the *Endeavour* badly needed wood and water, but they clashed with Maori resulting in several deaths. The crew found no fresh water, barely any timber, and only a few ducks to eat. 'At 6 a.m. we weighed and stood out of the Bay, which I have named Poverty Bay, because it afforded us no one thing we wanted,' Cook wrote.

Gisborne developed as a port town, offering a trading station and shelter for ships in search of timber, flax, oil and whalebone. But land disputes between settlers and Maori had resulted in a series of bitter wars. The land on which Gisborne was built, bounded on the east by the Turanganui River and on the north by the Taruheru River, was bought by the Crown in 1868. This was the year of the infamous Poverty Bay Massacre in which Te Kooti and his force killed 60 residents, Maori and Pakeha, and much of the land held by the 'Native rebels' was taken. The township comprised then a few stores, a hotel, a courthouse and a scattering of buildings close to the mouth of the Waimata River. There were about 150 Pakeha in the district and some 500 Maori. In the early 1870s whares, houses and huts were mostly built on sleds because of the uncertainty over land ownership. When an owner demanded rent the house was pulled to the next section and so on. But by the time Hugh

Heeney arrived in Gisborne there were permanent houses, several hotels, and a public board looked after streets and footpaths. The main thoroughfare, Gladstone Road, was lined with poplar trees, and bullock carts were pulled through the dust in summer and the mud in winter.

Hugh found work milking and blacksmithing, and then became the licensee of the Pakirikiri Hotel. He later worked in a brewery where he would win bets by hoisting a 52-gallon barrel of beer onto a truck, a feat that normally required three men. He worked for Messrs D.J. Barry Limited for 17 years, rising to become second only to the brewery manager. He was capable, conscientious and popular. In the early 1880s Hugh bought land in Kaiti separated by ti-tree and scrub from Gisborne. This was a time when settlers throughout New Zealand bought bush-covered land and cleared it, chopping firewood outside the back door if necessary. The land was there to be tamed. Manliness, strength, adaptability, self-sufficiency and being skilled with a hammer and saw were the virtues required of pioneer males. And every good pioneering man needed an equally robust partner. Hugh found one in Elizabeth Coughlan.

Eliza was Irish too, but she'd lived for a couple of years in Queensland after arriving in Townsville in 1878. Mrs Heeney, a local newspaper would write many years later, 'represented the spirit of old Ireland as exemplified by bold and impulsive men and women in every part of the world'. The daughter of a labourer, she ran away from County Cork after a family argument. She made her way to England by selling a turkey and then made enough money to emigrate to Queensland, where a brother lived. There were five deaths during the three-month journey on the *Sir William Wallace* and just about everyone on the ship was in poor health by the time they got to their destination. But Eliza's constitution was remarkable and she survived the journey untroubled. She landed in Australia without hat, boots or food, and found work as a cook on an up-country station even though she didn't know one end of a kettle from the other. An argument with a 'black tracker' working on the station led to her premature departure. She was so worried about the tracker finding her she was carried on the shoulders of European friends for miles. When her brother died Eliza moved to New Zealand, where she had a relative in Tolaga Bay, and ended up in Gisborne. 'Miss Coughlan took service with prominent families here and for several years survived the consequences of a number of scrapes into which her Irish devilment led her. These incidents became family lore in later years, after she married Mr Hugh Heeney and settled down to married life.'

The wedding was on Saturday 23 February 1884, the day when Thomas Roe was fined five shillings for keeping an unregistered dog, when the Maori Haka Troupe performed for a second night in Parnell and Boylan's Hall, and when the local newspaper reported how 'mean fruit thieves' had 'pillaged and destroyed in a manner worthy of barbarians in war time'.

Streets and houses grew around the Heeney property. The town and suburbs merged and the population increased from 3826 in 1896 to 5687 in 1906, and to 8196 in 1911. The country's first freezing works was built and a combination of great weather and soil was ideal for orchards. Extensive bush clearing began in the early 1880s and by December 1907 the smoke was so dense some days that Kaiti Hill was obscured.

The Heeney family grew as Gisborne grew around them. Eliza bore 10 children: Mary, Patrick, Nellie, Thomas, Hugh, John (Jack), Francis (Frank), Arthur, Thomas and the youngest, Patrick. She reared the children, milked the cows, made butter, baked bread and sewed clothes for her burgeoning brood. It was a hard, basic existence and the family was touched by tragedy. The first Pat died of rheumatic fever and the first Tom died a child. And in January 1903 there was a terrible accident. On this particular summer's day 13-year-old Hughie was out with three of his brothers and two Griffiths brothers, all younger than him. They watched while he cooled off in a waterhole. He got into deep water and drowned, apparently unable to swim. The second Tom was born on a chilly autumn day, 18 May 1898, and was destined to become an international celebrity in a far-off land.

Hugh Heeney raised his sons in a town where children created their own fun. Sports were a way of keeping the boys entertained, under control, and most importantly, at home at night. Hugh always had a rugby ball, a cricket bat and ball and a pair of boxing gloves. 'That was all the interest he showed in us boys,' Tom recalled. 'He wanted us to know how to fight.' Boxing, Hugh thought, was 'the greatest body-building exercise in the world' and it was one of the first things he wanted them to learn. After dinner and homework the Heeney boys and neighbouring children would gather in the 'gym', an old barn, to box and wrestle. Hughie — as his children always called him — kneeled to face the smaller boys. 'I was about five when he put the gloves on me,' Tom said. 'As soon as we could defend ourselves he taught us how to hit by allowing us to take free blows at his jaw and none of us ever made him wince.' Hugh was not one of life's spectators: 'I remember in the good old days having my amateur gym nearly full of an evening many a time, and everybody in the place had the gloves on during the evening. No onlookers — all active participants in the fun and sport and body building, and character-improving. Looking on only makes you a loafer.'

'Boxing in good spirit knocks all the viciousness and meanness out of a man. I know it,' Hugh wrote. 'You will find in all men — among Irishmen especially — at times a perverseness or pigheadedness or cocksureness, to a greater or lesser degree. In some it is scarcely noticeable; in others it is, and can quickly grow into a vice if not checked. In some it's more or less self-contained — a sort of mental thought: "By Jove, I'm a good sort of chap; there are few can touch me." In others it is more manifest, and often develops into swaggering swashbuckling. That's why you ought to make 'em box. Taking and giving good, clean, healthy blows will soon make them realise that there are other fellows in the world just as good as they are.' He thought the sport gave men clean, bright eyes and clear skin. It was healthy for mind and body. 'Most vices — this is my theory — arise either from ill-health or from being cooped up — either mentally or physically — so that a man cannot let off steam naturally. It is natural for a man to let off steam, just as natural as it is for an engine to do so. Coop him up, or let him coop himself up, in mind or body or soul, and an explosion is bound to come, with disastrous results.'

As cities and towns developed in New Zealand, men like Hugh sensed that pampering and luxury would sap virility and the pioneering spirit would be lost. Hugh embodied the old spirit. He enjoyed the open air and said his wife would have been miserable in a town. 'In the cities you are continuously breathing air that has already been breathed. In the tram cars, in the crowded streets, in the big buildings, in the theatres and picture show, the air is nearly always stale. It's been breathed before, often several times over. The lungs don't get the oxygen; the blood does not get recharged.'

But how could Hugh not have a passion for fighting? He was, in birth and at heart, an Irishman. Ireland was the home of vicious faction fighting as a way of sorting out disputes, and the Irish dominated bare-knuckle and gloved boxing in America. New Zealand too, laid claim to a great heavyweight champion of the day, Bob Fitzsimmons. But Hugh's adopted country was developing a passion for another sport: rugby. 'The character of the Pakeha male stereotype in New Zealand was forged by the interaction of two powerful traditions: the desire to keep alive the muscular virtues of the pioneer heritage, and the concern to contain that masculine spirit within respectable boundaries. The purest expression of the stereotype has been found in rugby football and the rituals which have come to surround the game,' wrote Jock Phillips in *A Man's Country?*. Rugby was seen as embodying values of courage, pluck, endurance and a sense of fair play — many of the same attributes Hugh saw in boxing.

Hugh liked sports, even if it meant the odd stray ball flying through a window. 'Young blood is naturally gregarious, and the association of young animal spirits knocking themselves about in their games — they never suffer serious hurt — is building up strong bodies for them.' Tom boxed, played rugby and was a good runner. He also went pig-sticking, where a specially bred thick-necked dog ran down wild boars and often the pig's sharp tusk would fatally spear the dog in its stomach. But of all the sports Tom tried, swimming was his passion and he was happiest at Waikanae Beach, in the centre of town. Even after he'd travelled extensively Waikanae Beach would remain for him the best beach in the world.

Tom got into plenty of scrapes and that's where Mrs Heeney's brand of discipline came in. Eliza believed in corporal punishment, the 'a-good-beating-never-hurt-anyone' school of thought. 'As a youngster, Tom wasn't so bad as boys go. All boys are young animals that have to be led, not pushed. But you've got to be firm with them often enough, otherwise they'll kick over the traces,' she wrote. Tom would later attribute his toughness to the many 'hidings' he received as a child. Eliza wrote of the time she sent him to Gisborne with a shilling to get a stick of tobacco for his father:

> He came back with half a stick and no change. He wouldn't tell me what he'd done with the other sixpence. I said: 'Tom, what will you do — tell me or take a thrashing?'
> 'Take a thrashing,' he said.
> I knew as well as he did that he had bought some cigarette

tobacco for himself. At his age it would be either that or a present for a girl — and that, with Tom, was quite out of the question. Tom, at twelve, could no more talk to a girl, let alone make advances, than he could fly.

Eliza didn't tolerate backchat. 'I gave her some lip one day, and how I regretted it afterwards,' Tom recalled. He was chased out of the house and down the road.

'Will ye stop?' his mother demanded.

Tom halted long enough to 'hand out more freshness'. He then outran his mother and stayed out all day. When darkness fell he edged his way back to the house. He sent in his younger brother Pat to see how angry their mother was.

'She's waiting for you, Tom, with a quince stick, a nice thin one that will bend but not break.'

Tom found some thin quince sticks of his own and stuffed them into his stockings to pad his legs.

'Tell her I'm coming,' he said to Pat.

'I'm sorry I did that,' he told his mother and got a 'terrific beating'.

Tom was threatened with no supper but knew no matter how much his mother beat her children she always fed them. Another beating followed when the boys wanted a tent. There was no money, so they improvised and made one from sacks.

'You'll not be sleeping out there,' said Eliza.

Tom and two brothers ignored her warning and sneaked a mattress outside, 'happy as larks'. They got drenched by heavy rain during the night and in the morning a neighbour alerted Eliza. 'There was a wild chase after us — we with our little shirts flying in the breeze, for pyjamas were unknown. A good hiding was given to the ones she caught.'

Not even a friend of the Heeney boys managed to escape the legendary wrath of Mrs Heeney. Con Dooling regularly came over on Friday nights to spend the weekend at the Heeney house. One night the boys were in the bedroom but not in bed. They were 'buck-jumping', leaping against each other from the beds. Con crashed into the window, glass shattered and he cut his face. The Heeney boys ducked under the bed when they heard their mother coming up the stairs. 'She was in a rage, and a big woman she was whose backhand wallop would knock you flat,' Tom recalled. 'She had grabbed a mop and in the dark she let out with the handle, landing on poor Con, who was sitting on the bed, the only one to be found. He never gave a whimper to let her know who it was, but the next morning he departed and that was his farewell visit to our house.' In one version of the story still told within the Heeney family Con fled in the middle of the night. Tom and the others were sorry that their friend, who would later lose his life in the war, had suffered a beating from Mrs Heeney.

The pioneers believed in hard work. Tom and his brothers shined their father's heavy muddy boots with hard blacking polish on Saturdays. Hughie inspected the work when he got home in the evening. If there was a problem he punished the culprit and Tom admitted it was usually him. But he only ever received one 'thrashing' from his father. 'My mother gave me at least 12,000,000 wallopings, all of which I deserved; but my father gave me only one.' Tom said his father's idea was to give a child 'one good licking' at an early age that he'd never forget.

Tom's younger brother Pat, the baby of the family, was the 'curly-headed boy'. Tom was the closest in age and became the younger boy's favourite. He refused to go to bed at night without Tom, who was annoyed he had to leave his older brothers playing about the house 'and turn in with little Pat'. One day Tom took little Pat out for a 'walk', determined to break the bond.

> I got him up the road, a sandy surface it was, out of earshot from my mother. Then I began to wallop him. I got him down in the sand, which filled his mouth and ears, and was hiding him plenty when suddenly I was lifted off my feet by the back of the neck to look into the angry face of my father. In my plan I had forgotten that it was noon hour and he would be coming home from work.
>
> He hurled me into the house. I looked out of the window to see him carefully selecting a switch from a quince tree in the yard, and a good thick one it was, too!
>
> Then he came in and beat me about the legs as hard as ever a kid got licked. There seemed no end of it until my mother interfered. That was a surprise, as she had given me millions of whippings and nothing ever stopped her once she was under way.

> For days after I had welts on my legs as big as a razor strop and even in bed I would roll and toss at night, they were so sore. But it served the purpose — for I never forgot it.

Hugh Heeney thought school days were important for 'expansion, growth and development' but that his boys were better off without homework. It was a typical attitude. 'Faced with the extreme nature of his environment, the colonial male held intellectual skills and booklearning in low regard. His own masculinity was bound up with physical prowess and his versatility made him suspicious of undue specialisation and the technical learning which might underpin it,' wrote Jock Phillips.

When he was six Tom attended Saint Mary's Catholic School on Childers Road. Catholic communities had their own schools that reinforced the Irish identity. The Irish faced suspicion and prejudice both over religion and the stereotype that they were a drunken and disorderly rabble. But this strengthened them. From 1904 to 1912 St Mary's was run by the Auckland Sisters of Mercy and then the Sisters of Saint Joseph took over. Classes were taught in an old convent on Lowe Street and in a hall in Childers Road. There was a two-tiered structure, with more 'elite', fee-paying students taught in the convent while the 'parochial' or 'parish' pupils were taught in the hall. Out back was a dirt playground where a high fence separated the boys and girls. Tom walked a mile and a half to the school — unless he could get a ride on the horse-drawn bus for the children who went to the public school. They could ride the bus for nothing but for Tom and his like who went to the Catholic school, the fare was a penny. Tom and his brothers only had three pennies a week between them, so they would leap on the tail step of the bus and hang on.

'Whip behind,' the kids on the bus yelled to the driver when they spied the hangers-on.

'Out would come the long lash with a terrific swish and off we would jump but not before we grabbed one squealer by the collar. If we got him down from the bus before the stinging lash got too hot, the kid was sure of a fine belting,' Tom recalled.

Tom, like Hugh before him, wasn't one for the books. He was always in trouble and bragged that he averaged a fight a day and was never happy unless he got it. He was bigger than most of the other boys and became a ringleader but not a bully. One day he and half a dozen other boys 'played the wag' from school and went to Waikanae Beach. Dean Lane told Hugh what happened the following day and Hugh wrote the story.

> Next day a little urchin knocked timorously at the Dean's door just before school opened.
>
> 'Well,' said the Dean, recognising the youngster as one of the pupils who had been missing the previous day.
>
> 'Pl-pl-please, Sir, Tom Heeney wants to see you, and please, Sir,' stammered the youngster, 'and please, Sir, he has said to me to ask you not to do anything to me, please, Sir, until he has seen you.'
>
> 'Very well,' said the Dean, 'I will see Tom Heeney,' and he got up, expecting to find Tom Heeney waiting at the door.
>
> 'Please, Sir, he's not at school, Sir.'
>
> 'Well, young man, where *is* he?'
>
> 'Please, Sir, he's over there, Sir. I'll show you.'
>
> And so the master followed the boy, and the procession of two proceeded across two wide paddocks until it came to a high corrugated iron fence, and here it halted, and the diminutive leader of the procession beat a hasty retreat. And the voice of Tom Heeney arose from the other side of the fence: 'Please, Sir, I was responsible for the boys playing the wag yesterday, and, please, Sir, if you promise not to punish them, I will come straight on into school.'
>
> The Dean, who has an Irish sense of humour, appreciated Tom's strategic position, and, being of opinion that the cause of discipline in this case would not be prejudiced if he acceded to this somewhat high-handed request, was content to graciously consent thereto.

Nevertheless, the Dean 'boxed Tom's ears' on many occasions, as did Mother Liguori, another of Tom's teachers. One night Mrs Heeney rang the doorbell and asked to see her. In her memoirs Mother Mary Bernard Towers told of how, trembling at the prospect of meeting an irate parent, Mother Liguori went into the parlour. 'Ah now, Sister,' said Eliza, 'I want to give you a pound to buy a decent cane, and give it to him well!'

Tom Heeney came to embody the stereotypical 'pioneer man'. He was physically hard, loved the outdoors, kept his emotions to himself, was loyal, humble, conscientious and upright. He came to be known as 'Honest Tom'. But as a boy he and a group 'copped' a Maori canoe one day.

> Two of us took a ride down the river, sailing along pleasantly until a shot was fired from the bamboo trees on the bank. Then stones began to sail by and it became too hot for us. The Maoris [sic] were on the bank heaving rocks our way. We paddled in towards the shore and leaped out in the muddy water that came up to our shoulders.
>
> Then the bloomin' idiots tried to force us in again to bring in the canoe. What we told them didn't make for good relations. But it was some time before we got up our courage to go home and get the hiding that was due to us for the wet clothing.

And there was greyhound coursing for hares — with other people's dogs. On Friday night Tom and others would untie a few dogs from properties in town and keep them overnight. Early on Saturday the dogs were raced over the hills on the scent of the hares until they caught their prey. When they'd had enough the boys released the dogs, which returned to their owners. 'It always gave us a good laugh when people would tell how every Friday their dogs disappeared only to return on Saturday night,' Tom recalled.

One night after a dance in Gisborne Tom and two friends started for home on a horse they'd found grazing near the hall. Tom and one of the friends knew how to ride bareback but the other had never been on a horse. 'Hit him on the head,' Tom shouted to the boy in front in the darkness. The more the horse was hit the faster it galloped. 'The fat fellow had a terrible time rolling like a ship in a storm, and it was all I could do to hold him on.' At a sharp bend in the road the horse turned suddenly, throwing the boys into a ditch. 'I was on the bottom and my thumb was sticking straight up. When the fat fellow landed on it I thought it was broken but when we got unpiled I gave it a yank and it snapped back. For months afterwards that thumb would slip out even in bed if it touched a blanket.'

During the heat of the summer when the fruit trees bloomed Tom roamed the countryside, swam in the river behind the brewery where his father worked, and raided an orchard on the opposite bank. When the owner tired of chasing the young thieves he gave them one apple and one pear tree to pick but they still couldn't resist giving his other fruit trees 'a trim for good luck'.

The only thing Tom liked about school was rugby. He'd stay behind and play most nights and this meant ignoring his chores at home. But for Tom, the chance to play rugby was worth whatever punishment came his way. Instead of sulking after 'receiving just chastisement' his father wrote, he happily helped out as if nothing had happened, overfeeding the pigs and fowls. Every Saturday afternoon he would get to play against the region's public schools. The headmaster of Te Hapara School, Frank Faram, always brought oranges. Tom was impressed. 'Oh, that's the school I want to go to,' he told his mother. Tom said he nagged his mother so often that she finally gave in and let him swap schools.

Another pupil at the school was future sports writer and broadcaster Wallie Ingram. He remembered an incident involving Tom and a tomahawk:

> We had a big 'scrub paddock' near the school, a five- or six-acre paddock full of tall manuka, containing the greatest array of 'forts' kids had anywhere. To find them was an art on its own. Frequently these forts were guarded by lads armed with tomahawks and on one occasion Tom was caught by the guards, who decided to 'execute' him. He was told to put his head on a post-top while Basil Middleton, one of the bigger pupils, 'chopped it off'. Always big-hearted, Tom obliged, but at the last fraction of a second he pulled his head away — and the tomahawk blade embedded itself in the post! 'You fool,' said Tom. 'I didn't think you would do it!' 'You fool,' said Basil. 'I thought you'd pull your head away!'

One day a girl intercepted a note with a poem she wasn't meant to see. She took it to the teacher, who dismissed the class but ordered the boy who'd last handled the note to stay and get 'six of the best'. While the teacher fetched the strap Tom told the boy to hide outside while he took his place. The teacher ignored Tom's defence of his fellow pupil, so Tom picked him up, carried him along the corridor and dumped him in a basin of water.

Ingram told of the way Tom donned gloves and sparred with another boy when the headmaster was away but didn't hit him because he didn't want to hurt him. He also ordered another pupil to return some stolen thrush chicks to their nest.

Hugh insisted Tom attend a Catholic school and wasn't told that his son had gone to Te Hapara for three months. He was livid, but Tom soon left Te Hapara anyway. There are different versions of the incident that led to his departure. Tom said he didn't mind the beatings from Faram because he liked him, but he had no affection for the assistant headmaster. To 'celebrate' the last day of term a group of pupils threw stones on the roof and smashed windows with books. The assistant headmaster was swinging his strap. Tom swung his pack of books at the teacher's head. 'Down they came on top of his dome,' Tom boasted, 'and down he went to the floor. I jumped on him and punched him as hard as I could. We wrestled and fought, he trying to hold my arms and get a sock at me. It was a wild scene with all the kids dancing around shouting "Kill him, Tom, kill the bloater", and the poor women teachers crying their eyes out. It was a tough fight, and I think about a draw.'

Another version of the story goes that there was a broken window and a pupil had been collared for the offence. Tom believed this to be an injustice, so he lunged at the teacher and knocked him to the ground. The teacher ordered other pupils to hold Tom down while he gave the young Heeney 'the soundest thrashing that he had ever had'. 'This episode I didn't like too much,' wrote his father. 'It looked as if Tom were getting too big for his boots.' Tom went home crying. 'Well, Tom,' his mother told him, 'if you got a hiding, you must have deserved it. And even if you didn't deserve it, well, there's not much satisfaction in letting everybody know that you didn't like it.' Tom refused to go back — ever.

'Well, Tom, if you won't go back to school, you'll go to work,' Eliza told him.

The next day she found him a job as a blacksmith's assistant. It paid four shillings a week.

'I'll start next week,' Tom said.

'You'll do nothing of the sort. You'll start tomorrow morning or else go back to school.'

Tom took the job but hated it. It was too hard and he arrived home in tears.

'Tom,' his mother said, 'it's either work or school.' Tom went back to work. Desperate to leave the blacksmith's shop, he responded to an advertisement in the paper a fortnight later. 'Boy wanted to learn plumbing trade,' it read. 'Must be strong and willing. — Apply Ed. Martin, Gisborne.'

'Ted' Martin recalled the essence of his first conversation with Tom.

'How old are you?'

'Fifteen.'

'Just left school?'

'No. I've been working a fortnight.'

'Where?'

'At a blacksmith's.'

'Why did you leave him?'

'I haven't yet. But I'm going to. He rouses too much.'

The job was with Messrs Martin and Swain in Gladstone Road. It was rumoured that his new employer 'had an early demonstration of Tom's fistic prowess', but Tom was good friends with Martin, who, according to Hugh, said that his young recruit was 'a good, honest, conscientious worker, who never skimped his job, but put the whole of his attention on the work in hand'. The pair once put a ton of iron on a roof in four hours, a Poverty Bay record according to Martin. Tom's father proudly wrote that Tom 'wasn't a bit like an ordinary plumber's assistant, because he was never called back to a job after he left it'. There's a story that Tom was called to work on a swimming pool in which a team was playing a game of water polo. Instead of waiting for them to finish, Tom went to work, water gushed everywhere and the players were left waist-deep in water. Tom didn't panic. He suggested they switch to basketball and left.

Tom worked for Messrs Martin and Swain until he left New Zealand. He was the only child of the family not to complete standard six. But he'd learnt the lesson his parents wanted to instil in all their boys: 'Let them learn to take life's hard knocks and smile when it hurts most.' Barely into his teens, Tom's childhood was over and events were occurring half a world away that would soon bring about the end of a much broader age of innocence. A war was looming to which tens of thousands of young New Zealand men, asked to undergo the ultimate test of courage and masculinity, would willingly answer the call. And when it was over few families would be untouched by grief.

What a Warrior He'd Have Made

Frank Heeney left the trenches at 10 minutes past six on the morning of Wednesday 13 September 1916. A bullet ripped into him just above the heart. A stretcher was scrambled. His sergeant and good friend asked how he felt. 'I am pie-oh, Bill,' he said as his life ebbed away. Frank was carried just 150 yards before he died. There lay the body of the biggest, strongest Heeney boy — the one who could've been the best boxer.

The battle had begun two and half months earlier with the slaughter of 20,000 men on one day. Now every dawn at the Somme signalled another day of stalemate. The men lived in the awful stench with the rats and the lice and the mud. Frank's friends erected a cross. They nailed a board onto a German rifle and cut his name, number and 'RIP' into it. Later, lying injured in an English hospital, Frank's sergeant wrote to Mrs Heeney. Frank died gallantly doing his duty, he was liked and respected and he suffered no pain. 'That was a soldier's death. Poor Frank!' wrote Eliza.

Tom heard the news of his brother's death on a sweltering hot day after he'd been swimming in the surf. Frank had promised his mother many times to have a photograph taken. But he never did. So Eliza gathered her other children and placed them in front of a camera.

New Zealand Governor Lord Liverpool announced the outbreak of war on the steps of Parliament to nearly 15,000 people on 5 August 1914. That evening an even bigger crowd marched through the streets of Wellington. King George V had declared war on behalf of New Zealand and the other lands in the Empire. New Zealanders regarded Britain as 'Home' and were tied to the mother country politically, economically and emotionally. They were quick to offer support. A telegram from the Governor to the King read, '. . . come good or ill, [New Zealand], in company with the other Dominions and Dependencies of the Crown, is prepared to make any sacrifice to maintain her heritage and her birthright'. The Great War took over 120,000 New Zealand men from a total population of just over a million into service and almost half would be killed or wounded.

Applications for enlistment poured in at Gisborne and the district provided more than its quota of volunteers. There were stories of men riding continuously for 48 hours to join up. Tom's older brothers Jack, Frank and Arthur signed up and 17-year-old Tom begged his parents to let him go too. At first they refused, but were about to change their minds when the news came of Frank's death and Tom wasn't allowed to go. 'I'm strong enough even if I'm not old enough. Why can't you let me go? Why, I feel like a shirker staying here at home,' pleaded Tom. He was underage but saw posters urging young men, especially single ones, to join up. 'Shirkers' were vilified and grotesquely caricatured in cartoons. They were labelled cowards, not worthy to call themselves men.

Tom had undergone compulsory military training at a territorial camp in Hastings where his boxing skills were called upon. There was a rivalry between Hawke's Bay and Poverty Bay, and Hawke's Bay said they had a boxer who could defeat anyone their rivals put up. Tom was selected to represent Poverty Bay with £30 staked on him to win. But come fight night Tom was nowhere to be found. He was tucked up in bed and had forgotten about the bout. He was dragged to the ring, won in two rounds and trundled back to bed.

Jack and Frank were promising boxers. Jack won the amateur welterweight title and was selected to take part in the Australian–New Zealand tournament in Sydney. The tournament was abandoned when more serious fighting half a world away became the priority. Frank won the Gisborne Boxing Association's lightweight championship in July 1914. He was the best boxer in the family but Jack was the keenest —

he read up about the big fights and was the first to box seriously. Tom followed Jack's lead. He made his first appearance as an amateur in July 1915 in Whinray's Hall. Jack was the star attraction and had been matched against the welterweight champion of Auckland. Tom recalled it was carnival week and he was at the races. A lad came running up to him. 'Your brother Jack wants to see you.' There was a fighter that couldn't make the weight limit and Jack told officials Tom would substitute.

'Is the fellow I'm to fight young?' Tom asked Jack.

'No, he's an old bushwhacker.'

'Well, then count me out.'

But under pressure from Jack, Tom finally agreed. 'When I walked into the dressing room I had my first glimpse of the bushwhacker. His muscles were knotty and he was hard and hairy as a baboon. I guess I got white, and know I would have walked out on the show if Jack hadn't been with me.' Tom looked nervously around the hall. It wasn't just his opponent that scared him but the glimpse of his father in the crowd. He hadn't told his parents he was fighting. 'Old Hughie' wanted his boys to be able to box but didn't want them to fight competitively. When Tom knocked his opponent out in the third round, however, 'Old Hughie' couldn't help but be pleased. For his trouble Tom took home a gold watch and some money thrown into the ring by a spectator with the words, 'to buy yourself some ice cream, laddy'.

Tom continued to impress on the rugby pitch and in 1917 he represented Poverty Bay. Then, aged 19, he finally persuaded his parents to let him go to war. 'He seemed to be so miserable, that in the end I finally consented, and so he went,' wrote his mother. 'He was a big lad for his age, and looked like a man, but he was only a boy, and I knew it — hoping against hope that he would have better luck than poor old Frank.' Tom recalled that he had tried to join up but every enlistment officer turned him down, 'even if I told him I was fifty'. Then he went with his father for a few drinks in a café and capitalising on Hugh's jovial mood pulled out the paper for his father to sign, which he did. His mother's name was already on it.

On Thursday 10 January 1918 a plumber, 5 ft 9½ ins tall, with light brown hair, blue eyes and a fair complexion, enlisted in the New Zealand Expeditionary Force. Tom was passed as medically fit for active service.

But this wasn't his first attempt to pass the medical examination. About six weeks earlier he'd tried to enlist but was diagnosed with 'Valvular Disease Of Heart; (Aortic Stenosis); Heart action intermittent'. Aortic stenosis is an abnormal narrowing of the aortic valve. Tom was determined to go to war and concealed his apparent heart condition the second time around.

Just a couple of weeks after he enlisted, Tom earned a medal. His act of bravery wasn't on the Western Front but Waikanae Beach. The drama began on a Sunday afternoon. At about 1.30 p.m. Elizabeth Galloway left her home on Ormond Road with Vera Rhodes and Vera's sister Elsie. She told her father she was going to the beach to bathe. He said she told him she could swim and he told her several times not to go too far out. The girls arrived at Waikanae Beach at around a quarter past two. There was a heavy swell and a strong undertow and earlier a young woman had got into difficulty and had to be helped ashore. The trio changed into their bathing costumes and went into the water. They walked in up to their waists, Elizabeth not venturing quite as far out as the other two. 'After paddling for a few minutes my sister Vera put her hand on my shoulder and I found that the undercurrent was taking us out. We all called out for help but no notice was taken for some little time,' Elsie said. The girls were swept off their feet and out to sea.

Tom was walking along the beach when he heard someone calling out, but didn't pay much attention. Then he was told of the girls' plight. Tom headed into the surf while a group of men ran to get the lifeline. 'The first one I came into contact [with] was Miss Galloway,' Tom recalled. 'She was floating on her back with her head underneath the water, and appeared to be unconscious. I caught hold of her and took her ashore. I had to bring the body in about 40 yards.' In the meantime Elsie was rescued by Eric Robinson, the son of Gisborne's town clerk. When she got to the beach she saw Elizabeth being carried in by Tom. Vera, who couldn't swim, was still in the water.

The lifeline reached the water's edge. 'I started out again but was called back by someone to put the lifeline on,' said Tom. 'After I had put it on I went out after the other one. I went out about 30 yards and picked up the other girl. She was conscious and said she was done. They pulled us ashore then with the lifeline, which was attached to me. In pulling they pulled the line too quick and pulled us under, with the result that I was sick.

I then went along to Mrs Warren's place and dressed. When I brought the second in I saw people, including Doctor Kahlenberg, working at artificial respiration with Miss Galloway. I was a bit sick at the time and not able to render any further assistance.' People watching the drama confirmed Tom was so badly knocked about while he was being hauled in that he was violently sick on reaching the shore. Two doctors were unable to revive Elizabeth on the beach and she was pronounced dead. 'Eyewitnesses of the sad occurrence speak most highly of the conduct of the lad Heeney, which is deserving of warm commendation,' reported the *Gisborne Times*.

The coroner's inquest was held the following day. Tom, Elizabeth's father, Elsie May Rhodes and Constable Fischer gave statements to the coroner, who returned a verdict that Elizabeth was accidentally drowned. The *Poverty Bay Herald* reported that the coroner 'added a rider to the effect that Heeney's action was deserving of great credit, and he would bring it under the notice of the Humane Society'. Senior Sergeant Clarkson endorsed the coroner's remarks, adding that 'Heeney went into the water at great personal risk without the lifeline'.

A man told a reporter that he and four friends, namely W. Whitely [sic], W. Robinson, T. Ingram [sic], McDonald and another friend known as 'Chum', were diving off a log when they noticed the three girls in trouble about 200 yards away. McDonald couldn't swim so the other four set off without him. They reached the girls 200 yards outside the breakers. Miss Galloway was 'floundering and apparently done' when seized by Ingram, who got her as far as the breakers. She began struggling and he lost and reclaimed her three times. Ingram, now exhausted, saw Tom, who took her while Ingram went ashore for the reel. In the meantime Robinson had taken Elsie ashore but Whitely and 'Chum' were unable to get Vera, so Tom, with the help of the lifeline, rescued the older Miss Rhodes.

Tom disputed the story. He hadn't seen anyone near Vera or Elizabeth. And then the argument about who had been the greater hero that afternoon intensified, in a letter to the editor.

> Sir — In reference to the recent Waikanae beach fatality, published in your last issue, we, the undersigned, while very much regretting to have to again refer to the unfortunate accident beg to flatly contradict Mr Heeney's statement. We were in the water when

the young ladies first appeared in difficulties, and there was no sign of Mr Heeney in the water at that time. We, the undersigned, immediately proceeded to the rescue, and we had to go considerably beyond the breakers to reach the young ladies, and it was not until we had brought them back to the breakers that Mr Heeney came upon the scene, and we think that, in fairness to all, the praise (if any be needed) should be fairly apportioned. — Yours faithfully,

T. Ingham
E.D. Robinson
E. Ellery
W.E. Whitely [sic]

The Royal Humane Society of New Zealand decided on who deserved what. Tom and Robinson were awarded bronze medals while William Eugene Whiteley, Thomas Ingham and Robert Henry Eric Ellery were presented with certificates.

Tom was an unwilling hero. 'The only time I have known him get angry in his life was at the persistence of those who wanted to hold a public demonstration and present Tom's medal to him. He wouldn't hear of it for a moment,' wrote his father. A compromise was suggested: he could be given the medal in a semi-private presentation. That too was rejected. In the end the medal was posted to him.

Summer turned to autumn and Tom began his army service on the second day of April 1918. After a spell at Trentham Military Camp he sailed for England. He had a stretch in the guardhouse — one of several — for 'sassing' an officer and was then made to work in the laundry, but afterwards it was learned he played rugby and he was given a place on the camp football team. Then he was allowed to eat steak and onions, had sheets and didn't have to get up until seven in the morning. But he said when an officer once wanted to make him a 'non-com' he refused as he wanted to remain a plain old private.

He was still in England undergoing final training when the Armistice came. Tom said he was so sick of soldiering by then he went down to London on 'French leave' and Jack, who was training for a fight there, arranged for his brother to be transferred to help him train. But Tom wanted an even easier job and went to the colonel's office. When asked what he was doing there he said he didn't know; he had been transferred and was just following orders. 'The colonel scratched his head, looked up at me as if I were going to prison the next minute. Then he spoke up. "Well, there's a boat leaving tomorrow for New Zealand. Get that!"'

Tom returned to New Zealand aboard the *Raranga* in March 1919. The ship developed a problem and put into Newport News for a few days. Tom was with a group of Anzacs walking along the road when a member of the Military Police instructed them to move over to the other side of the road. 'It don't look to me as if this side was wearin' out. What's the use of goin' over?' Tom asked. The MP told them to move over again. When they didn't he reached for his gun and threatened to use it. They did as they were told, having realised the American soldiers were 'pretty tough fellows'. Tom was officially discharged on 27 May 1919 after serving 127 days in New Zealand and 294 days abroad.

Tom returned to Gisborne and to his job as a plumber with Martin. In the evenings he sparred with Jack, who was now a professional fighter. Professional boxing developed in New Zealand largely as a way of helping to fund amateur boxing, but the post-war years saw more professional fighting than ever before and the twenties would be the country's best boxing era. It was still a relatively new sport in terms of formal organisation: the New Zealand Boxing Association was formed in 1902, the first legal professional contest was held a few years later, and early in 1908 rules were introduced covering the conduct of professional bouts. Those who controlled boxing in the early 1920s talked of the need to preserve the dignity of the sport, to foster amateur boxing, the 'clean, manly sport that strengthened the moral fibre of the lads', and urged that the sport should be 'governed by high minded principle and directed in a channel of justice'.

Not like the display given by pupils from an amateur boxing school one Saturday night in Gisborne. Two drunks — who it was said should've climbed into their beds rather than a boxing ring — scrapped before the men in collars and ties and high-heeled boots came on. One took exception to some ringside remarks, left the ring, went over to the person who'd offended him and said: 'Who's fighting this d--- fight, you or me? So keep your bally mouth shut.' He went back into the ring, got a bloody nose and went to his corner to have his gloves taken off, much to the audience's amusement. The crowd also found it very funny when one of the spectators was challenged to get into the ring and said he couldn't as he was barred by the Gisborne Boxing Association; and they clapped and laughed some more when a right hook and a short left uppercut sent a boxer into a half flip, landing on his shoulder and head as he fell.

Boxing struggled for respectability everywhere and Gisborne was no different. The sport was regarded as depraved and degrading, especially when money was involved. But in the United States a change was taking place. Before the war, boxing was considered a brutal and uncivilised sport followed only by the rough, the uncouth and the uncultured. It was mostly illegal before 1917. But during the war it kept men fit and broke the monotony of military drill. Before America entered the war a sergeant was teaching Canadian recruits how to use the bayonet when he realised that the basic foot, hand and body movements in bayonet fighting were the same as those used in boxing. General John J. 'Black Jack' Pershing, who commanded the American Expeditionary Force, thought it was important for soldiers to know how to use their fists.

During the war, training camps were set up at home and abroad. Professional boxers like Freddie Welsh, Mike Gibbons, Benny Leonard, Packy McFarland and 'Battling' Levinsky became instructors. Special training was offered in gymnasiums and tournaments were organised. Future champions were groomed and an audience was cultivated that would attend boxing in tens of thousands. A tall, rather shy youth from New York, Gene Tunney, donned the gloves while a United States Marine private in a camp in France. He won the light heavyweight championship of the American Expeditionary Force in 1919. Millions of men were introduced to sport during the war, fuelling the development of a national sports culture.

Prior to the war it was mostly men who attended prizefights. But when Jack Dempsey knocked out Jess Willard to become the world's heavyweight champion in 1919 women had a special section in the audience. There were still pockets of resistance, but even conservative newspapers like the *New York Times* labelled boxing's opponents as 'half a century behind the times'. This was the beginning of the golden twenties, with New York at its heart. The Georges Carpentier–Jack Dempsey fight in June 1921 generated the first million-dollar gate. Promoter Tex Rickard proclaimed, '. . . the best people in the world are here today. And this is just the beginning.'

In New Zealand too, boxing became more popular and respectable and purses rose, but there were no golden gates. Tom's first professional fight in February 1920 was for £75 and expenses and he was still working as a plumber. The previous month Tom had driven his first car, an old 'Henry', to Hastings to see American Jimmy Clabby fight Tommy Uren. A boxer due to fight Brian McCleary in a heavyweight contest had failed a medical and Tom was asked to substitute. Tom protested that he wasn't in training and had no gear, but finally agreed to an exhibition of four rounds. He stepped into the ring in trousers, shirt and stockinged feet. The referee declared a draw.

Tom claimed he turned professional by accident and that it was only because he looked impressive enough against Jack that he was allowed to join him in the professional ranks. He saw it as a sideline, 'which soon became nearly as important as his swimming', recalled Hugh. Tom later blamed swimming for hindering his boxing as it built up the wrong muscles. But there was at least one reason Tom wanted to make money from boxing: the porridge he had to eat for breakfast as a child. His father was working so he got the bacon and eggs, he explained. 'My father knew how much I loved his breakfast so he used to leave me some and I'd lick the plate up. We were hungry kids, darned hungry. And that's why, I say to this day, boxing is a great sport for elevating you when you are down. People will always pay to see two men put up a good scrap. That is some of the real good that comes out of boxing. Well, I grew up looking for bacon and eggs so after a couple of neighborhood scraps, I turned professional and never have been hungry for breakfast again.'

Tom debuted against Bill Bartlett, a tall, tough Murchison man. The fight was for 15 three-minute rounds at the Opera House. A large crowd including a number of women filed into the ornate building that had gone up eight years earlier on the corner of Childers Road and Peel Street. The use of a concrete mixer — a first in Gisborne — provoked a labourers' strike of several days, but the finished building was admired for its elegant fittings and furnishings, a turquoise blue velvet pile carpet, its ventilation, fireproofing, electric lights and separate seats throughout. Bill Bartlett was well known in Gisborne as he'd fought there before. A request was made that there be no 'barracking' for either contestant.

Alan Maxwell's first impression of Tom was of a 'big, loose-limbed lad with an easy smile and the chewing gum habit'. The referee, a former New Zealand lightweight champion, thought Tom's physique suited that of a prizefighter but that his personality seemed too good-natured. He was clearly nervous during the uninspiring fight that generated 'just a trickle of excitement' in the third when Bartlett caught him on the top of his head with a right and then rushed in and Tom slipped onto his right knee. In the same round, Bartlett protested that Tom had used the illegal 'rabbit-killer blow' and Tom was cautioned for hitting on the back of the neck. In the fifth Tom pretended to walk away but stopped suddenly to plant a violent right on the shoulder of his opponent. But by the eighth the crowd became restless, urging the men 'to put more ginger into it'. 'Put on the Maori boy again,' someone shouted, in reference to 'the amusement occasioned by an earlier contest in which a half-caste was one of the principals', wrote a local reporter.

Despite Tom's inexperience Bartlett gave up at the end of the eighth. He called the referee to his corner and threw in the towel. 'It was by no means a one-sided "battle",' wrote an observer, 'but Heeney's more rugged condition was beginning to foreshadow a verdict that was inevitable.' Tom 'came in for rounds of plaudits unparalleled in the history of boxing contests locally', and he had to shake so many hands it was a few minutes before he could escape to his dressing room.

'I'm too old and must give in to youth. Youth wins,' conceded Bartlett. He thought Tom would be unbeatable in the Dominion. But the general feeling was that Tom won because of ruggedness not ability. Even his father admitted that: 'As in practically all Tom's fights in New Zealand, Tom's victory was due to his strength and determination rather than to any skill as a boxer.'

At the Gisborne Boxing Association's second tournament of the year Tom met George Modrich for a purse of £70. Modrich was taller and slightly heavier. Once again Maxwell refereed. Among the spectators were the Minister of Public Works and future prime minister Gordon Coates, and Sir James Carroll, who was watching Tom's fledgling career with interest. Sir James was an enormously charismatic politician and a superb orator with a passion for sport. The son of a Sydney-born Irish father and a Maori mother, he became the first Maori to win a general seat when he took Waiapu (later the electorate of Gisborne) in 1893. Sir James married Heni Materoa, who also became hugely influential in the district and was regarded as a 'Mother to the Maori people'. He had long campaigned for closer ties between Maori and Paheka.

Folklore suggests that Irish Catholics got on better with the Maori than any other Pakeha group. This has been attributed to the notion of both peoples being downtrodden; to the similarity between the clachan and the marae; and to an underlying emotional parallel between Irish-Catholic emigration and the erosion of Maori property in the 1860s and beyond. In the days of colonisation the identification of the Irish with the Maori was a British ploy to denigrate the Irish, whose repression they considered crucial to maintaining the Empire. Irish nationalists, who lauded what they considered to be heroic Maori resistance against the British, reversed this and celebrated the comparison. In a speech endorsing Home Rule for the land of his paternal ancestors, Sir James suggested that Saint Patrick was in fact a Maori who, after casting out the snakes from New Zealand, decided to repeat the trick in Ireland.

The Carrolls straddled the two cultures in Gisborne and their home was always full of people. They had no children of their own but raised those of relatives. Sir James loved boxing and in his younger days it was said he 'accounted for a Pakeha braggart in great style'. He was awarded a medal for a 75-yard sprint and was a champion at putting the 16-lb shot and wrestling. And he was fond of tossing the caber. So it was hardly surprising that he befriended Tom. 'None knew Tom Heeney better than Sir James Carroll,' Lady Carroll would write. 'What a splendid type is Tom,' said Sir James. 'A big man, a very giant, splendid in physique, and yet how light on his feet. And how he enjoys boxing! What a warrior he'd have made in the old days! And how unruffled! Nothing upsets his quiet control. He is the smoothest tempered boxer that ever stepped into a ring.'

There wasn't much lightness of feet on the night Tom met Modrich, however, and by the fourth round it was more of a wrestling match. 'Seeing that the Heeney–Modrich match was much marred by continual clinching and wrestling the boxing authorities would do well to take steps to prevent a repetition of this state of affairs,' one commentator complained. Tom got the decision after 15 rounds. The clinches weren't his fault, he said. Modrich admitted the better man won but pointed out he'd broken his nose while sparring a month previously and it was on his mind throughout the bout.

Tom was given a shot at the New Zealand heavyweight title against Aucklander Albert Pooley in only his third professional fight. Nine days earlier Jack had become middleweight champion of New Zealand. 'Gisborne can now claim to being the best boxing town in the Dominion,' wrote 'Old 'Un' in the *Gisborne Times*.

> Lin Robinson, featherweight professional champion, Jack Heeney, middleweight professional champion, and Des Lawless, amateur welterweight champion, comprise a trio record which cannot be claimed by any other town in the Dominion. It only needs Tom Heeney to beat Pooley tonight and bring the heavyweight championship here and then 'Old 'Un' thinks it could be said without contradiction that there is no town in the world, certainly none the size of Gisborne, that could lay claim to such a proud fistic record.

It was another struggle between experience and youth at the Opera House, which was filled almost to capacity. The title fight was over 15 rounds for a purse of £150. The taller Pooley, weighing 12 st 3 lb, entered the ring first. Tom, weighing 12 st 10 lb, more heavily built and about six years younger, followed with his brothers Jack and Artie and his trainer Fred Dominey. Dominey became Tom's trainer without any written agreement. 'We were friends and everything was based on mutual trust,' he said.

Just after the gong sounded and before a punch had been thrown one of the stays of the ring gave way and the contest was stopped while it was fixed. So went the report the following day. Years later, after Tom had become famous, the tale of the broken stay became the story of the imploding ring. 'The most exciting part of the bout was when the ring collapsed,' Tom apparently said. 'It was set up on a platform in an open-air theatre. The screws holding the braces to the floor broke in the middle of a slugging bout, the whole thing went down, and both of us were thrown out of the ring. We were only on a half-minute when it collapsed and the crowd ran for safety. When it was fixed we carried on with the battle. I had coaxed my sister to attend her first prizefight. When the smash-up came, she thought it was me being knocked out, and dashed for home. That was her first and last appearance at a prizefight.'

The fight resumed. Pooley was the aggressor in the first and bored in. Referee Maxwell had to call 'break' about half-a-dozen times. For the first few rounds Pooley kept Tom away with a straight, accurate left. Tom was backed onto the ropes and looked anxious and said afterwards he knew Pooley was going for a knockout. By the sixth he thought the danger had receded and knew he needed to become aggressive to win. He changed tactics. He kept moving in and Pooley began to tire towards the tenth. With a 'grandstand finish' Tom won on points and became the new heavyweight champion of New Zealand. The match was 'a very clean and interesting tussle, fought out in a manly manner, by a narrow margin,' reported one scribe. There were now two boxing champions in the Heeney household. In February 1921 Pooley tried and failed to get the title back from Tom, who won again on points. Tom smiled and said he could have gone on for longer and that if there hadn't been so much hanging on he would've done even better. Pooley said if he didn't get another fight within a month he'd probably retire.

Tom's first fight away from Gisborne was in Te Karaka against a man who had already beaten his brother, the middleweight champion of New South Wales Jack Cole. Tom had left home to work in Wanganui and after six months had a fair bit of money after getting lucky at 'hazards'. His father had warned him against gambling as the result of a bad experience on his way to New Zealand, he said. In a card game on the first day on board ship Hugh lost the shilling his father had given him. Tom returned to Gisborne and bet £200 on his brother Jack to beat Cole. When Cole won, Tom was home and broke and decided to stay put.

Cole was a lot lighter than Tom but ranked among the best Australians. The fight was held under electric light in what was said to be one of the largest marquees erected in New Zealand, specially brought down from Auckland. Te Karaka had a population of about a hundred, yet up to 1500 crammed into the tent. The ring was about three feet off the ground, giving everyone a clear view. So eager were the organisers to make sure every detail was right a rehearsal was held the previous night.

Referee Bert Lowe, a former champion from Gisborne, handed down an extremely unpopular decision. He gave the fight to Tom but Cole thought he'd won easily and even the *Gisborne Times* reported that 'over practically the whole of the journey, Cole did the forcing', his defence could hardly have been better and that he 'proved himself a master of ringcraft'. Tom's supporters swarmed around him while a dumbfounded Cole stood in the middle of the ring. Impartial observers were very surprised and what Cole's supporters said 'could not be represented in any family journal'. Cole was the favourite and a lot of money had gone on him. A number of punters who'd bet heavily were said to have agreed in a private meeting not to pay out. There were stories that people who had bet on Tom refused to pick up their winnings. A few days later Tom's father sued Cole for £30 in respect of a dishonoured cheque. Cole had stopped the payment because he was unhappy with the decision. Hugh was non-suited and Cole was granted £2/10/- in costs.

Tom was the heavyweight champion of New Zealand but he was still playing rugby. After the war he represented Poverty Bay again and in 1921 he was selected for the Hawke's Bay-Poverty Bay XV to play the touring Springboks at McLean Park in Napier. On a fine day on a dry ground in front of some 8000 people the visitors won by 14 points to 8. 'Tom played a wonderful game for his side — he was always a trier,' wrote his father. 'Naturally, the forwards were the mainstay of the team, and every man of them played magnificently,' observed a local newspaper. 'M. Brownlie and McNab, two of the biggest and strongest, were delightful to watch. In splendid condition, they followed up and worried the Springboks in the tight and in the loose from start to finish. Kirkpatrick in the tight work and Heeney in the line-outs were invaluable.' After the match both teams dined at the Caledonian Hotel and among the numerous toasts and speeches mention was made of the good play of the combined forwards and of the side giving the visitors one of the hardest games of the tour.

Tom's boxing career reached a turning point in October 1921 when he fought Colin Bell. The bald-headed, burly old Australian heavyweight champion was lured to Gisborne by the Boxing Association for a purse of £225 plus expenses. Gisborne was brimming with visitors and those who couldn't cram into the Opera House for the big fight peered through the windows. Tom looked boyish against his older opponent who was as 'bald as a billiard ball'. He seemed unsure how to keep Bell away and was troubled with half-arm punches about the body while in the bear-hug clutches of his opponent. Whenever Tom landed he was warmly applauded and about halfway through the fight when he staggered Bell with a right uppercut the applause was deafening. But Tom slipped further and further behind on points before someone yelled, 'Stand off and box him, Tom!' — so he did, narrowly missing out on the decision when Maxwell declared the bout a draw. On his return to Sydney, Bell's manager Jack Clarke said: 'Colin won every round of the match. Heeney is a very second rate boxer. Over there you've got to knock 'em out to win, and win to get a draw.' The fight encouraged Tom to make boxing his career. He talked things over with Jack, 'and we both figured that carrying my gloves to Australia was the next logical step to take'.

More than 50 of Gisborne's leading businessmen and sports enthusiasts gathered at the Cosmopolitan Club on the eve of Tom's departure in December 1921. The Mayor, who'd known Tom since he was a boy, presided. He understood Tom was going to Australia and perhaps later to England and America. It was difficult to say what he was capable of, as he had never really been tested in New Zealand. Above all, he said, Tom was a trier. Then an address was read:

> Presented to Tom Heeney by His Worship the Mayor on behalf of the sporting community of Gisborne.
>
> We, the undersigned, wish in this small way to show our appreciation of your true sportsmanlike attitude during your career as a boxer, and in this city. We feel that we are losing one of our mainstays in professional boxing in New Zealand and hope that you will have a brilliant and prosperous career in Australia or any part of the world you may visit.
>
> On behalf of the citizens of Gisborne we have great pleasure in signing our names:
>
> G. Wildish, Mayor; W. Lissant Clayton, Patron; B.H. Aislabie, Chairman; M.W. Craig, Secretary.

Tom was given a wallet of banknotes. Poverty Bay Trotting Club member Arthur Webb said Tom had set out in search of adventure and all he had was a pair of hands, but with those hands he planned to fight his way through the best in the world until he reached the top. One speaker said Tom had three assets: health, strength, and the most important asset in a boxer, brains. He hoped Tom would return to Gisborne after a successful career in the ring and 'take unto himself a lassie'. That got a laugh. Tom thanked everyone for the gift and kind words. He assured them he would 'play the game' and always put up a straight fight wherever he was.

In the year or so he was away, Tom got nine fights, mostly in Queensland. In his first, against Max Gornik at Brisbane, he 'slashed and ripped his opponent unmercifully' and then got one of the smallest amounts for a win he'd had, about £34. It was given to him in two-shilling pieces in a canvas bag as two shillings was the price of admission.

Then there was a rematch with Colin Bell. Con Sullivan promoted the match on Saint Patrick's Day 1922 at Mackay, further up the Queensland coast, for the Australasian championship, the Australian heavyweight title and the 'Referee' belt, organised by W.F. Corbett of the sports paper *The Referee*. A close fight over 'twenty rounds of slashing attacks' in front of 2500 people ended with Bell's victory. At the beginning of the nineteenth Bell was heard to remark: 'That old nut of yours is very awkward.'

Next up was Jim Flett, a Sydney man who stood about 6 ft 3 ins. Both men were suffering from boils due to the heat and it was suggested neither was in the best form. Tom got the decision and described Flett's style as 'any old way to hit the other man'. A win on points over Jack Leahy followed and then another match with Bell. Tom wanted to meet Bell in three-minute rounds but the Australian continued to insist on 20 two-minute rounds. He won again. The decision was booed by three quarters of the spectators and Sullivan cabled 'Old 'Un' of the *Gisborne Times* that such a terrible decision made him feel like giving up promoting boxing matches. Bell's manager Jack Clarke thought Bell won the two fights in Australia against Tom because he was too clever. Dominey claimed Bell wouldn't have gone the distance with Tom in three-minute rounds.

Tom talked about the fights with Bell as the hardest of his career. Years later, when his best fighting days were over, he remembered the pain the Australian had inflicted — although over time the three fights seemed to have merged into one. He talked of a bout with Bell in the tropical heat of Australia that ended in a draw. He first remembered it as a 20-, then as a 15-, round fight, but one that felt like it went 40 rounds. 'But, doggone, you know, he broke two of my ribs, gave me a cauliflower ear of tremendous proportions and I'll be doggoned, he rammed my front teeth completely through my lip by -----, it was the worst 15 rounds of my whole life. Awful!'

When Bell pulled out of a match with Tom Batho at Ayr, Tom filled in. Batho's seconds threw in the towel after a few rounds. Back in Mackay, Tom drew with Charlie Taylor. While he was in Mackay the Gisborne Boxing Association wrote to him asking whether he'd return to fight Australian Jim Baillie, with £25 for expenses. He replied he'd meet Baillie but only for £50 expenses. The Association decided not to offer more. Tom made so little money in Queensland he cut sugar cane to fund his trip back to Sydney. But he couldn't get a match so he moved on to Adelaide, fighting Ern Waddy to a tedious draw. On his return to Sydney he fought Melbourne heavyweight Jack Complin. He won in the ninth but it was a poor fight and he went back to Gisborne.

His performances in Australia suggested Tom would be nothing more than a useful heavyweight. He seemed muscle-bound and was sometimes too tired to train properly. 'Tom never really had the killer instinct,' said Dominey. 'It depended on how the other fellow was treating him how Tom would go but I am sure that in his time in New Zealand and Australia there would have been no boxer who would have gone more than five rounds with him when he was really roused.'

When Tom returned to New Zealand in 1923 he set out to get his old title back. It was now held by the same man he'd fought with stockinged feet in Hastings, Brian McCleary. McCleary had won it in a bout against Cyril Whitaker. Whitaker applied to the Northern Boxing Association in April asking to be matched with any heavyweight and mentioned that he'd be especially interested in meeting Tom. It was a logical match for Tom: a victory over the leading contender would bring him closer to the championship. And so the ill-fated meeting with Whitaker was arranged.

Hugh and Eliza Heeney.

The house where Tom was born.

A family portrait. Back row: Arthur, Jack, Nellie, Frank. Middle row: Eliza, Hugh. Front row: Tom (age 7), Pat.

Hugh's 'gym' where he taught his boys to box.

Left: St Mary's School, Gisborne.

Below: The workshop where Tom learnt the plumbing trade.

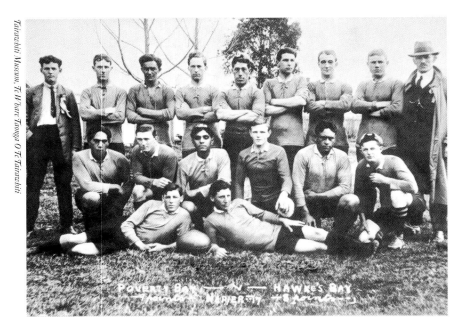

Above: Tom (back row, second from right) represents Poverty Bay, 1917.

Left: Tom serves his country during the First World War.

Courtesy of Mike Edwards

Jack (left) encouraged Tom's early fights.

Tom promised always to put up a straight fight wherever he was.

A promotional card introduces Charlie Harvey's new fighter.

One of Tom's managers, John Mortimer.

Boxing promoter, Tex Rickard.

Weighing-in before the Sharkey fight.

Charlie Harvey looks on as Tom reads about his victory over Delaney.

The Ugliness of Fear

Cyril Highton Whitaker died of a brain haemorrhage. The bleeding started after he had been hit by Tom Heeney. According to the coroner, 'there was no doubt the rupture was sustained during the boxing match, which had been conducted in accordance with the regulations and which appeared to have been a perfectly clean fight'. It was just one of those occurrences that happened from time to time. No witness at the inquest was concerned about the way in which the fight was conducted. No one thought the fight should have been stopped earlier. Sixteen pages of evidence led to the usual conclusion when a boxer died: nobody was to blame.

'Both contestants were physically fit for the contest,' stated the Northern Boxing Association doctor Dugald Keith Hagen.

'I have seen thousands of fights and can say that nothing unfair occurred throughout the contest,' declared Association Chairman James Wilson Russell.

The bout was 'not as severe as some heavyweight fights I have seen,' insisted Honorary Secretary of the Association Roderick Murray Carter.

'The fight was absolutely clean and fair,' maintained referee Francis Burns.

'It was a clean fight fought in an exceptionally good spirit,' affirmed Sergeant Alfred Ernest Rowell.

Tom stayed in Auckland for the inquest and was portrayed as a victim of the terrible events that night. 'The result was most distressing to Tommy Heeney, who is one of the most amiable and even-tempered heavyweights who ever stepped into the ring,' wrote one newspaper. It was not unusual for a boxer to collapse after a hard fight but usually they recovered. It was thought Whitaker would be well in the morning. A story later emerged that he had complained of severe headaches since being kicked in the head playing rugby. So was Tom merely the unfortunate fighter selected by fate to deal the lethal blow?

Nobody blamed Tom for Whitaker's death, except Tom. Guilt threatened to end his career. 'It wouldn't have taken much for me to quit at that point,' Tom recalled many years later. 'But I knew I had burned my bridges. It was either continue fighting or return to plumbing.' Tom was a fighter from a small town in a small country with a trainer who'd been his childhood friend. A man had died at his hands and Tom was left alone, without a manager or adviser to help settle his conscience and ease his guilt. The maiming or killing of an opponent, wrote S. Kirson Weinberg and Henry Arond in the article 'The Occupational Culture of the Boxer', 'is quickly rationalized away by an effective trainer or manager in order to prevent an access of intense guilt, which can ruin a fighter. The general reaction is that the opponent is out to do the same thing to him and that this is the purpose of boxing: namely, to beat the opponent into submission.'

The quickest way to win a fight is to knock a man unconscious, and what some see as entertainment others see as uncivilised brutality. It was in the interests of everyone involved with boxing to portray Whitaker's death as brave and honourable. They didn't want a grieving public to blame the sport. Calls to ban prizefighting could follow. It was better to ensure people grieved in the same way they might grieve over a soldier killed in battle. A soldier's death isn't pointless. It is sacrificed to a greater cause. And so Whitaker died an honourable death on the front lines of a sport he loved.

Boxers, friends and supporters deluged Whitaker's family with sympathy messages and a fund was set up to buy a headstone for his grave in Southland. The Gisborne Boxing Association sent a letter to Cyril's parents:

Dear Sir and Madam, — The committee and members of the Gisborne Boxing Association deeply deplore the loss of your son, Cyril, at Auckland, following an operation.

Everyone feels that no words can convey the depth of sympathy that is felt in your bereavement at the loss of so gallant and honourable a sportsman, who left scarcely any style of sport untouched, and touched nothing that he did not adorn.

We can only hope that God, in His infinite mercy, will in time soften the grief that you feel in this hour of your great tribulation. I have the honour to remain,

Sir and Madam,
Yours in sorrow,
Harold Carr,
Hon. Secretary.

Meanwhile, plans were made for Tom's next fight. He'd had several offers across the Tasman, but the Gisborne Boxing Association asked W.F. Corbett of *The Referee* to find an Australian opponent to come to New Zealand. Gordon Coghill wasn't available because he'd just opened a business at Bondi; his brother Les accepted the offer but was then beaten in another match and injured his fist; Ern Sheppard's mother was ill; Fonce Mexon didn't appeal to Corbett; Australian heavyweight champion Ern Waddy was too busy; Blackie Miller was away. Tom was matched with Jim O'Sullivan but the Auckland heavyweight cancelled because of stomach problems and lumbago. Australian Jim Flett was keen to meet Tom again so he was cabled and came over to Gisborne. Flett was down three times in the ninth and his seconds threw in the towel. Tom was faster, lighter on his feet, and his blows had more sting.

Next up was New Zealand heavyweight titleholder Brian McCleary in Christchurch for a purse of £200. The Dunedin-born champion was a light heavyweight but was regarded as one of the cleverest boxers in the country. Tom was to be his last opponent, as he didn't want to jeopardise his chances of selection for the upcoming All Black tour of England. There was a long-standing rivalry between Auckland and Christchurch, and ahead of the fight an argument broke out between the *Auckland Star* and the Christchurch *Sun*.

> How sensitive those Christchurch folk are. Thus does a writer in the *Sun* of that city wax indignant over a paragraph which appeared in this column recently. 'An Auckland writer laments that Tom Heeney is to meet Brian McCleary in the latter's own town, Christchurch. He says that it is a great pity they could not have met anywhere else, as nobody in the Cathedral City wants to see McCleary get a beating. It is admitted that the Southerner will have a tough proposition in Heeney, but a fight is not over until the count is taken by one of the boxers, or it goes the full number of terms. Apart from that, the opinion expressed is not very complimentary to Christchurch followers of the game. They are not so one-eyed as to begrudge a better man his win, even though he comes from far afield.' Well, well, we are glad to hear that, now.
>
> *Auckland Star*, as reprinted in the *Gisborne Times*, 23 July 1923

Twelve hundred spectators gathered under the curved, corrugated-iron roof of the King Edward Barracks. In the early rounds, McCleary, a stone and a half lighter than Tom, piled on the points. 'From the moment the pair got into their stride as it were, in the matter of pure out and out boxing, McCleary undoubtedly stood out well in front,' reported a Christchurch newspaper. 'He was faster in attack and active as a cat on his feet. Time and again he eluded the grim but slower moving Heeney. Smack would go a fast left with just sufficient force to rock Heeney's head and provided just that fractional moment of relief to escape from the threatened danger.' But Tom gradually wore the champion down. 'Tom had fought with even more than his usual aggressiveness — whether it was that McCleary had beaten his brother Jack, or that he felt more than usually fit, or because their previous "meeting" had been such an even affair, there is no means of knowing,' recalled Hugh Heeney.

By the fourteenth McCleary was very tired. One scribe said he hadn't properly recovered from a severe bout of influenza and should never have been in the ring. He'd also played a gruelling inter-island rugby match in the mud in Wellington the previous week. With about a minute to go in the fourteenth the fight came to a dramatic end. Tom worked McCleary to the ropes and struck him with a right hook and left to the jaw. McCleary fell to the canvas. When he arose Tom knocked him down again. McCleary was obviously beaten, but the referee climbed through the ropes, waved Tom back and allowed the fight to continue. At the count of nine McCleary struggled up. Tom came in with a left and right to the jaw of his groggy opponent and McCleary went down again. This time he couldn't move.

McCleary's seconds tried to revive him. But just as he seemed about to wake up he would lapse back into unconsciousness. He was taken to Lewisham Hospital, fighting for his life.

Tom regained the title — but was criticised for his behaviour in and out of the ring. He'd tried to goad McCleary into a brawl. 'He would not do anything, except move round the ring out of reach. In fact, on thinking the matter over since,' Tom apparently said with a smile, 'I reckon that that night McCleary ran over sixteen miles. I had trained for a boxing match not for a marathon, and felt quite fagged next day from the continued use of unresponsive muscles. However, it is all finished now, and I'm looking for a challenger to the title, but no more marathons please!'

'Is that generous to a defeated foe who was lying unconscious for nearly two weeks after the fight?' queried 'Spearmint' in the *Auckland Truth*. 'Heeney forgot to tell the Gisborne people that McCleary was giving him nearly two stone, which made it a ridiculous match. The verbose individual forgets the lashings he has received at different times and proof of what a wonderful (?) fighter he is can be gained in the fact that he could not beat an old man like Colin Bell.'

'And so, with regret, we read remarks attributed to Heeney on his return to Gisborne, which with us finally places Heeney in the class to which we suspected he belonged,' wrote a Christchurch *Sun* correspondent. The remarks were made while McCleary, 'battered into unconsciousness by the smashing blows of Tom Heeney', was still in hospital. The *Auckland Star* wrote that McCleary fought on 'doggedly, reeling groggily, literally "out" on his feet in the fourteenth term, only to be battered into unconsciousness, and several weeks in the hospital as the result of Heeney's merciless punishment'.

Tom denied the comments and thought about instructing a solicitor to get the error retracted. Instead, he wrote to McCleary refuting the remarks. But the 'marathon' furore, the accusation he'd unnecessarily punished McCleary, and Whitaker's death caused Tom 'many painful moments'. He was deeply hurt by the attacks on his sportsmanship.

His reputation as a fighter, however, was intact and he was now considered practically invincible. But he no longer had the heart for boxing and he dwelt upon Whitaker and McCleary and the allegations that he was unsportsmanlike. 'His battle with Brian McCleary was a tremendous affair — a willing, doughty go, and in the heat of battle each took and gave a vast amount of punishment,' wrote his father. 'Brian was in hospital for many weeks afterwards, and there was not a sorrier man than Tom. For many months he was not the same man. He didn't put the vim, the force, the dash, into his work.'

Jim O'Sullivan should have been an easy win. The 35-year-old former King Country bushman had fought just two professional contests. Surely he wouldn't last more than six rounds? For 30 seconds Tom and O'Sullivan waited for a good opportunity to get in the first punch. The last time Tom was in the Auckland Town Hall with referee Frank Burns, Whitaker was in the opposite corner. Suddenly, Tom rushed in sideways, head bowed, and the men exchanged body blows. But Tom was slow and lifeless. O'Sullivan seemed overawed by Tom's reputation until he realised the Gisborne man wasn't such a big threat after all. By the tenth, Tom's supporters were getting frustrated.

'Put him to sleep, Tom! Time's up!'

But the knockout never came. The crowd roared when O'Sullivan was declared the winner and the new champion was carried around the ring.

'He lost because he was *afraid*,' remembered Hugh Heeney. 'Not afraid of O'Sullivan, not afraid of physical hurt — Tom is the last man on earth to show any symptoms of physical fear; we all know that, but afraid to let loose the physical force that is pent up within him, lest in doing so he might cause hurt, as he did to McCleary. The result was that he was not the same old tearing, vital, swift-moving Tom Heeney that we all know in the ring. He was hesitant, let the other man carry the fight to him, and the result was that he lost on points.'

Ernest Hemingway wrote about the way Max Baer fought with fear in a bout with Joe Louis. Fear, he said, 'is a very ugly thing. All human beings have it just as all human beings perform natural functions. But children are trained not to perform these functions in public and fighters are trained not to be frightened while fighting. If they know their trade they have something else to think about. If they do not know their trade and are frightened while fighting, they have no business being fighters anymore than a game-cock that runs has any business being a game-cock.' Hemingway thought Baer might have been afraid of death, as he had killed one of his opponents. 'If that was what he was afraid of, that makes it, somehow, even worse as a spectacle. That sort of fear ought not to be sold as a public entertainment: not even at twenty-five dollars a seat.'

'Spearmint' hinted that O'Sullivan's victory was a moral one. 'We said a few weeks ago, after Mr Heeney's very rude remarks about Mr McCleary that Jim O'Sullivan was the only man in sight who could give him a go for the title, and Jim did — and he got away with it on his merits.'

It was the only fight Tom would ever lose in New Zealand. He proved not only that he still possessed a knockout punch but that Jim Savage from Wanganui couldn't have been more inappropriately named. Savage was from England and had once gone 12 rounds with Bombardier Wells. He wanted his first fight in New Zealand to be against the best heavyweight. He lasted two and a half minutes. 'Savage is the biggest dud that this country has ever seen — and we have had some beauties — and if he gets another match in the Dominion this writer will eat a set of gloves,' proclaimed 'Spearmint'.

Tom was rematched with O'Sullivan during race week in November in Gisborne. McCleary had recovered, and even wanted another match with Tom. O'Sullivan demanded £200 win, lose or draw but settled on £150. For Tom, this match wasn't about the money, it was about getting his title back, and he trained harder than he ever had. A bearded Tom looked 'somewhat dour and determined' on the morning of the fight said Alan Maxwell, who'd been brought up from Wellington as O'Sullivan feared a local referee would be biased.

The fight was sold out and hundreds were turned away, forced to gather outside to await the news. Betting was heavy, slightly favouring Tom. The applause as O'Sullivan entered the ring became a roar when Tom arrived with Artie, Jack and Fred Dominey. The early rounds were full of clinching and wrestling. The referee gave one, two and four to Tom. Round three was a draw and the fifth proved to be the last. The pair clinched and when they broke an old cut above Tom's left eye had opened up. He had to keep wiping away the blood and got angry. 'The mishap also had the effect of inducing Heeney to put his utmost vim into the contest,' wrote one scribe. 'But as Heeney rushed in O'Sullivan would pole out his left. On more than one occasion the injury received further attention, increasing the flow of blood.'

'Go for it, Jim; he's not up against Savage now!' shouted an O'Sullivan supporter.

'Get to him, Tom!' cried the locals.

Tom rushed with punches to head and body. O'Sullivan was hurled onto the ropes in front of the press table and went down on his right knee. As he arose Tom was about to rush in again. O'Sullivan went down without being hit. Tom stopped and the hall erupted. Maxwell tried to separate the fighters as they 'were walking into one another in the excitement'. He grabbed O'Sullivan, whose hand went up in the air. Later, Maxwell explained he'd placed his hand on O'Sullivan's shoulder with the intention of disqualifying him and it was O'Sullivan who lifted the arm. But the crowd thought Tom had been disqualified. They booed, stamped, and some applauded. Men clambered over seats, cursing Maxwell. The ring filled with officials, seconds and spectators. Maxwell tried to speak but was shouted down. O'Sullivan went to his corner to be congratulated. Blood gushed down Tom's face as he stormed around the ring. 'Blinded, baffled, and bewildered, Heeney was the embodiment of rage, and men drew back from the ropes as he passed, with the respect that would have been shown to an uncaged tiger.'

Maxwell headed towards the footlights to offer an explanation. But when he got there the curtain was falling. It was raised again and he put his hand up to speak but it was no use. Looking around, he beckoned Tom over. He grabbed him around the waist, swung him about to face the crowd, raised his hand and announced, 'The winner'. The booing and hissing became cheers of 'Good old Tom!' Now O'Sullivan's supporters went wild. The curtain fell and rose and rival supporters shouted and jostled. Both boxers wanted the fight to resume.

Maxwell was hoisted onto the press table and said he had no option but to disqualify O'Sullivan.

'You mean he slipped down,' someone countered.

O'Sullivan's chief second Charlie Peoples got up and protested that Maxwell had held up his man's hand as the winner. 'Heeney had to stroll away, because an elderly ringsider who claimed that the referee had given the fight to O'Sullivan by holding up that boxer's hand had reached the stage when he said that he reckoned that he was as good as Heeney ever was; and it was with difficulty that blows were not struck to settle numerous other arguments within and outside the theatre,' reported a journalist. Finally the lights were dimmed and the police arrived.

Could O'Sullivan's protest be considered when new rules stated a referee's decision was final? Were the new rules in force? If the referee believed O'Sullivan had gone down purposely to avoid more punishment was disqualification the only option?

Tom and O'Sullivan met for the third time on, appropriately enough, Boxing Day 1923 in the Palmerston North Opera House. 'In this battle Heeney held the upper hand from the start, and he handed O'Sullivan a lacing which put the Aucklander out of the game for good,' wrote Maxwell. For seven rounds Tom punished O'Sullivan severely, and in the eighth broke his nose. O'Sullivan dropped under a storm of punches but at the count of eight he was saved by the bell. When the ninth began he staggered forward with his smashed-up face but collapsed under a rain of blows. He tried valiantly to get to his feet but his legs failed him and he was still on his hands and knees at 'ten'. O'Sullivan told Tom he thought Tom must have been just kidding in the first two fights. So said Dominey. The story goes that Tom had bet £100 on himself in the previous meeting but O'Sullivan hadn't honoured the bet. So before this fight he went to O'Sullivan's hotel room and threatened to 'thrash him' if he didn't pay up.

In 1923 Tom killed one man in the ring and almost killed another, won his title back, lost it, then regained it amid chaos and controversy. But when the year ended Tom was unquestionably champion again. He had returned to his old self.

Tom was sunbathing on Waikanae Beach the following February when a little girl ran up to him to say someone was drowning. There was a high north-east sea outside Poverty Bay that was breaking heavily at Young Nick's Head. Huge waves crashed onto the beach and there was a strong and dangerous backwash. It was a treacherous sea for all but the strongest swimmers.

Arthur Neill had arrived at around three o'clock. Julian Syret was in the water when he saw Neill wade in. He called out to him not to go too far out. Neill didn't respond. Syret continued swimming with his friend Miss Green and the next thing he remembered was a cry for help. Neill was in trouble. The teenager looked as if he didn't know how to swim and was trying to paddle in the heavy breakers. Opposite the Grey Street entrance to the beach, separated from the rest of the swimmers, Neill was swept out by the undertow. Syret and Green tried and failed to reach him. Green went ashore to get a lifeline while Syret attempted again to find Neill but he'd disappeared.

Tom led the rescue party. Taking the lifeline manned by Syret and three others he made a 'gallant attempt' at rescue but was battered by the big waves, swept along the beach and covered by floating seaweed. He got close to where Neill was last seen and the reel was run right out, but there was no trace. He came out of the water exhausted. A launch was sent to the area but the sea was so rough the vessel couldn't approach the beach and had to return. A constable patrolled the shore in case the body was washed in by the high tide. Many of those on the beach went back to town without going into the surf.

The *Gisborne Times* reported Tom's courageous efforts to save Neill's life, and there was another story in that day's paper that related to Tom. Eight months after Cyril Whitaker's death a polished grey granite memorial stone, 'subscribed by boxers and sportsmen of the Dominion as a tribute to his great sporting spirit and fine character generally', was to be sent south and set upon a concrete base, bringing its height to over six feet. There it would stand, a permanent reminder from the boxing world that Cyril Whitaker lost his life as a gallant and brave soldier of the ring.

A Bushwhacker on the Town

Tom needed to move on again and 'the Homeland' beckoned. Former amateur lightweight champion turned referee Earl 'Mick' Stewart had recently returned from England where he'd seen Joe Beckett and other leading British heavyweights like Phil Scott, and he was sure Tom could beat them.

Stewart made a special trip to Tokomaru Bay to referee what would be Tom's last title defence, against Ern Young, a handsome 21-year-old from Wanganui. It was an easy win in the fourth round when Young's seconds threw in the towel.

Stewart thought Tom could succeed in the Old Country and he recommended the services of Bernard Mortimer. 'For your information,' Stewart wrote, 'Mr Bernard Mortimer is a very influential man and a member of the National Sporting Club. This gentleman brought out Joe Beckett, England's heavyweight champion. Beckett, as you know, is not a good champion, but his success was mainly due to Mortimer's judicious matching . . . I wish you to understand that Mr Mortimer is not a boxing manager in the sense that we know them in this country, but must be viewed rather as a keen sportsman, interested in boxing and all that goes with it.' Stewart cabled Mortimer:

> Tom Heeney, heavyweight champion, leaving six weeks hence. Would you be prepared to place him? Telegraph what are the prospects of matches at the present time.

Mortimer cabled back:

> Prospects exceptional. Empire championship should be easy for good man. Would welcome opportunity to handle Heeney.

So arrangements were made for Tom to travel to England with Fred Dominey. But there was a school of thought that Tom was merely a burly, strong second-rater who was likely to 'get his big "block" knocked off'. He had had no consistent expert training, just lessons from his father, then Jack, plus some advice from Jimmy Clabby. And he didn't take his training seriously enough. Tom was set on going, however, and a boxing tournament was staged in the training rooms in Gladstone Road as a farewell. Two hundred people turned up to watch a series of exhibition bouts and to hear speeches lauding Tom. Gisborne Boxing Association President W. Lissant Clayton felt sure Tom would distinguish himself and he spoke of Tom's reputation as a clean fighter. Clayton thought Tom needed an austere manager because he was too kind-hearted and too good-natured. He hoped Tom would feel his responsibility and refrain from England's national beverage. Clayton said he wouldn't be surprised if the name of Tom Heeney featured in press cable news in the near future.

The great speaker of the evening was Sir James Carroll. He said Tom carried with him to the Old Country the prestige of Poverty Bay and of New Zealand and the best wishes of the residents of Gisborne. Tom was more of a playful fighter than a serious fighter and he must drop all that now. Sir James wanted Tom to beat Georges Carpentier who was supposed to be the most alert, scientific and deft boxer for his weight the world had seen.

'Now, Tom, don't disappoint Gisborne. Don't bring sorrow and tears on the North Island. Steady yourself, Tom!' Carroll said.

There was applause and laughter.

'You must have someone to keep you right, keep you exercised, keep you trained. We all hope you will be in the credit side of our ledger as the result of your trip to the Old Country.'

Sir James urged Tom to be strong and to do his best for 'Maoriland'

and to win triumphs on her behalf. He said the occasion brought to mind his own youth when the boys around the pa loved boxing. Methods had changed but he couldn't help thinking the straight left was still the boxer's best friend. 'Mind you,' he added, 'I am not discounting the value of the right hook or the right swing in their proper place, but when you find yourself in any difficulty remember that the straight left can get you out of trouble easier than any other blow.' Sir James showed Tom how he thought the straight left should be used and how it should be followed by a right. He joked that he didn't think his own boxing days were over yet and promptly challenged Dr Scott or D.J. Barry to join him in the ring for three rounds.

The Mayor thought Tom would do a lot to advertise New Zealand and he felt sure Tom would 'make good' and return a greater champion.

Tom and Jack fought three rounds and then Ben Aislabie spoke. He said Tom had been a good friend to the Boxing Association and that they had never had the slightest trouble with him. Every 'sport' in Gisborne would anxiously await news of his first fight. Tom was always a 'home bird' and always hurried home as soon as a fight was over. Things would be different in England. Tom stood up and the spectators sang 'For He's a Jolly Good Fellow' followed by three cheers. He thanked everyone for the evening's entertainment and promised to do his best.

The New Zealand Boxing Council gave Tom a letter of introduction he could give to those in authority in English boxing circles:

> This will introduce to you Tom Heeney, holder of the heavyweight championship of New Zealand who is visiting England in the hope of being matched with men in his class. Heeney's performances in the ring, both here and in Australia, are as creditable to him as is his record outside his profession. The New Zealand Boxing Council is pleased at being able to say that Heeney has shown himself to be a clean, honest fighter, and having attained the greatest heights that are possible here he naturally turns to fields that offer advancement. He visits England accredited by the New Zealand Boxing Council, which recommends that he be given the opportunity to prove himself. — For the Council,
>
> W.G. Atack
> Hon. Secretary

And so Tom began his long journey to Britain for the second time. When he boarded a train bound for the capital at Napier he weighed 14 st 5 lb. During a stop at Woodville he decided to check his weight on the public weighing machine on the station platform. 'These New Zealand train journeys are a terrifying ordeal, we all admit, and we expect some shaking down, but this was beyond a joke,' Hugh Heeney wrote. To Tom's amazement he weighed a mere 7 st 4 lb. 'Struth!' he was heard to exclaim, 'I guess I'll have to fight Jimmy Wilde [world flyweight champion] instead of Joe Beckett!'

He lost something else on that trip too — a year from his age. On the train he thought about the fact that he was almost 26, and worried he might seem too old to be 'coming champion'. He might find it difficult to get matches. So he decided to say he was born in 1899 not 1898. A scribe who met Tom outside the New Commercial pub on Lambton Quay thought he looked like a 'bushwhacker' in town for the weekend. He was unshaven, his trousers bagged at the knees and he wore an 'old-time black slouch hat' pulled down at the front and back.

A small circle of well-wishers farewelled Tom Heeney on the 10,839-ton SS *Ruahine* that left Glasgow Wharf for Southampton and London via Panama on 13 May 1924. In the words of one journalist: 'It was a case of Nobody going to Nowhere, if not Oblivion.'

The Courage of a Colonial

Tom's mother wanted him to fight Phil Scott. 'That's the man I'd like to see Tom have a proper go at,' she declared.

Quite why Eliza wanted to see her boy bash the 'Tottering Tower of London' starts on a summer's day in 1924 with 60,000 people packed into Wembley Stadium. It was the biggest and most important boxing tournament in England for many years. This was the summer of Wembley's British Empire Exhibition, the largest and most ambitious exhibition that had ever been held anywhere. It may not have sparked a great Imperial revival as intended, but the extravaganza did provide some relief from the post-war gloom. London boomed as millions came from all over the globe to 'wemble'. That's where Tom first saw Phil Scott. 'If I cannot beat him then I reckon I am a dunce,' he said. Tom would spend the next two and a half years trying to beat Phil Scott.

Tom was due to fight at the Wembley tournament. He'd been matched with Australian George Cook but Cook developed a swollen arm. Tom's prospects in London looked good, though. He was taken on as a sparring partner to Tom Gibbons, the golf and ice cream-loving American who was at the tail end of his career but was a big name in the cash-rich golden era of boxing sweeping the States. Gibbons' training camp was luxurious, with music and dancing and billiard rooms; while outside stretched a nine-hole golf course and a score of tennis courts. It offered the comfort and opulence of an exclusive gentleman's club. A vast lamplit banqueting and dance hall had a table dressed with delicate napery at one end and a ring at the other. Chinese lanterns dangled overhead and expensive hangings adorned the walls. And so scruffy Tom Heeney entered the old-world opulence of the London Country Club at Hendon. It was there that British boxing writers got their first look at him.

He 'created a rather good impression among those who saw him, for he showed speed and hitting power and the ability also to take a punch', observed one. 'Indeed, he has quite a clever left hand and a very serviceable right. It was really a good workout between Gibbons and Heeney.' Olympic trainer Johnny Watson watched a few sparring sessions between the two Toms and thought the New Zealander was a powerful, rugged boxer whose best punches were a left hook and a right to the body. 'I like the look of him,' said boxing referee Eugene Corri, 'but until I have seen him box I cannot say whether he will rise to great heights in the ring. But I will watch his progress with more than ordinary interest.'

Tom also impressed Gibbons, who liked the New Zealander and admired his tenacity and spirit. British heavyweights had a reputation in America for doing no training, staying up late drinking and smoking — and still believing they were great champions. But Gibbons saw potential in Tom. 'Pack up and come to the States,' he advised. 'There is a lot of action there and you will chase a lot of those guys out of the ring.' Tom didn't know that he was being secretly tested. 'I thought at the time that Tommy was a hard one in the gymnasium but it was not until years later, when I was talking to Gibbons one day and I said to him, "Tommy, you sure were rough with me those days in London," that he said, "Tom, I was told by your manager to see if you could be hurt because he was thinking of trying you out in the US. I told him you were good enough and that I couldn't hurt you."' Fred Dominey said the idea of a trip to America had always been at the back of their minds and that Gibbons 'clinched it'.

But first Tom wanted to succeed in the Old Country. One of the best of Britain's few promising heavyweights at the time, the former fireman Phil Scott, won his fight at Wembley against another of Gibbons' sparring partners, Andre Anderson. Although Scott's extraordinary bravery would earn him a George Cross in the Second World War, during his boxing career he was known as 'Phainting Phil' the 'swooning swan'. Tom would later say that Scott was 'an artist at winning on fouls, which carries no credit with it'. Scott was certainly mediocre compared to the best Americans. Mortimer accepted an offer for a match with Scott and was prepared to back Tom against the Englishman for £100. London boxing arena, The Ring, bid for the match and at stake was the title of British Empire heavyweight champion, invented by the promoters to add interest to the bout. It was arranged for 22 September for £100 a side and a purse of £350: 75 per cent to the winner, 25 per cent to the loser.

When the doors opened, the seats filled up until there was standing room only. Then the standing room was bought up and many were turned away at the entrance. The All Blacks had a special block of seats. They were touring Britain, Ireland and France at the time and had come to be known as the 'Invincibles'. The team included Brian McCleary.

The octagonal building was designed without corners so there would be nowhere for the Devil to lurk, for The Ring used to be Surrey Chapel, also known as Rowland Hill's Chapel, after its former minister. Legend has it that Hill's wife had a passion for clothes unbecoming of a minister's spouse and that her husband would preach at her: 'Here comes my wife, with a whole wardrobe on her head and back.' Long deserted, the chapel became a warehouse and was eventually purchased by former British lightweight champion Dick Burge in 1910. It is said the arena wasn't named after a boxing ring but after a black kitten with a white ring around its neck that wandered into the building the day it was bought by Burge.

Two fit and healthy-looking men stepped onto the canvas. The pale, blue-eyed Scott was over 6 ft tall and possessed a 'most beautiful body', wrote one scribe. The gong sounded. And that's pretty much where it all started to go wrong for Tom. He opened fast, with hooks to the head, but Scott intercepted them and jabbed him with hard, straight lefts. In the second Tom was cautioned for holding before taking several punches to the jaw. He shook his head and threw a few slow hooks that Scott avoided. Tom tried to get out of the way by turning his head or body or seeking refuge at close quarters. In the early rounds he was lucky not to be knocked out.

'Heeney was revealed as a poor-class boxer, and seemingly a punchless one,' commented one reporter. 'His attacks carried no real sting; neither was he difficult to hit.' 'Heeney knows practically nothing about the game,' said another. 'He has a pathetic faith in his left swing, to which he clung throughout, despite innumerable failures to connect, but he made it clear he had no faith at all in any other punch, and save for an occasional right smash in the scrambling clinches and, say, for half-a-dozen right drives to the ribs, he never attempted any other blow.' Scott was also unimpressive. 'Again and again Scott threatened to drop his man, but that was as far as he got. It was a one-sided, but uneventful fight,' wrote one critic. 'Scott was so slow with his right that at least nine times out of twelve in the last fourteen rounds Tom was able to duck before the right started,' wrote another, and Scott's left 'might as well have been amputated'.

Tom lost on points, by a wide margin, in a tedious match. His reputation, it seemed, had been overstated. He 'may well be champion of New Zealand, but if he is, it can only be because New Zealand heavyweights are far inferior even to our own', wrote one critic. Eugene Corri said if Tom was the great forward he was supposed to be it was a pity he hadn't pursued a place in the All Black team. 'I am convinced that he will neither make fame nor fortune as a heavyweight here.' Tom was strong, and 'like all Colonials, he has abundant courage', but he didn't seem to have ever had a boxing lesson and was 'about as crude as they make them'. Even a New Zealander who'd seen the fight wrote home that Tom had overreached himself. Tom found Scott's height and stance awkward. He didn't like tall fighters who forced him up onto his toes to deliver a punch. He also thought he'd been overtrained and had left his energy in the gymnasium and on the road. Tom said when he first met Bernard Mortimer his manager thought all men should train the same. 'It did not take me long to find out that he was wrong.' Mortimer struggled to get Tom to train as hard as he wanted him to.

Tom should never have been advised to leave New Zealand, suggested one pundit. He should catch the first boat home. 'We in New Zealand were all disappointed with the result; but how must poor Tom have felt?' his father wrote. 'There seemed no definite prospect of his getting another match, but he stuck it out.' It cost money to sail home and Tom wanted another shot at Scott. So he stayed.

Late summer merged into autumn and then came the beginning of winter when the Thames snaked rough and grey through the city. The days shortened and in the darkness oblongs of light could be seen in the buildings high above the burning street lamps and the iron railings.

London in the 1920s was still the world's greatest city. The economy flourished, the suburbs grew and new roads were built to ease the congestion of the narrow streets. The whole of Regent Street was rebuilt to satisfy the demand for better shops. But Tom had no money for luxuries. He was homesick, cold, and only able to afford a fish-and-chip diet. He remembered London for the drizzle and the fog and places that were 'so expensive that if you order coffee and cough three times they take the gold out of your teeth'.

In early November Tom got a chance to 'make good' when he was matched with Belgian Frans Hendrickx and returned to The Ring. The fight was declared 'no contest' in the sixth of a scheduled 15 rounds because there was too much holding. Tom's prospects in London looked bleak. He talked about his fists not yet bringing him a reward big enough to satisfy a dock labourer. When he met a Gisborne journalist towards the end of the All Black tour he said all he wanted to do was to get another match with Scott, square the account and then return to his friends in New Zealand.

While Tom waited for Scott, he was offered a preliminary bout at the National Sporting Club: £25 to win, £10 to lose. He took it. 'That is the stuff that Tom is made of,' his father wrote. 'Where many another man would've given up in despair, he still stuck to it. For a champion boxer to be reduced to the ranks of the contestants in a preliminary — a stop-gap exhibition before the main attraction — that would've been the end of the career in the case of ninety-nine boxers out of a hundred. But not for Tom. He wouldn't come back to New Zealand a failure. He would stay there until he had made good. He owed it to his manager, he owed it to himself, he owed it to his friends, but, most of all, he owed it to New Zealand. *Their* representative would not cry "quits" after one inglorious defeat.' Tom rushed the ex-army man 'Trooper' Jim Young of Brixton with left and right swings. In the third he swung a right to his opponent's head, knocking him down. Young took three more counts before the end of the round. In the fourth he tried desperately to get back in the fight but was battered to the canvas for the full count.

The knockout boosted Tom's reputation with promoters and journalists. Maybe he hadn't been fully acclimatised when he lost to Scott? Gradually the story of how Tom could have been picked for the All Blacks became the story of how he'd worn an All Black jersey. Eugene

Corri changed his mind about Tom. 'Heeney was aggressive and walked right into his man and soon placed the contest to his credit. There was no clinching or holding, just good, straightforward fighting . . . I shall look to him to make a great name for himself in the ring.'

Tom's next match was a rearranged fight with George Cook. His manager wasn't that enthusiastic about it but Tom wanted to go ahead largely for the benefit of his opponent. Cook planned to go to America to fight but didn't have the money for the passage, so Tom took the fight to help him out. He trained at Alec Lambert's gym and despite a bout of flu was said to be doing good work. He was also sparring with Phil Scott to help the Englishman prepare for a contest. '[Tom] is a sportsman through and through. Read this,' wrote a *Boxing* scribe. 'While he was acting as sparring partner to Scott he nearly put the long fellow to bye-bye. I ran into [journalist] Norman Hurst and [Cook's manager] Charlie Lucas. "How's young Phil?" Norman asked. "Rotten," I said. "Tom Heeney nearly outed him this afternoon." "You George Bernard liar," said Hurst. "I have just left Heeney. In fact, we had a long chat, and he never said a word about it." How's that for real sportsmanship?' *Boxing* continued. 'Scott, if pressed, would readily confess that the New Zealander is a far better man than he appeared to be in their meeting at the Ring. Phil and Tom have had some hot turn-ups in the gym, and as a result of these Scott's opinion of Heeney now approximates very closely to that expressed by Tom Gibbons.'

A minute's silence fell over the spectators who gathered at Premierland in Whitechapel to see Tom and Cook on the evening of Thursday 12 February 1925. They remembered Charles Edward Sheppard and afterwards a collection was taken for funeral costs. The previous Sunday 21-year-old 'Teddy' Sheppard called into Premierland seeking work. A match was arranged that night with 18-year-old 'Pop' Humphreys. A doctor examined both bantamweights, who were friends. About 30 seconds into the sixth round the referee stopped the fight because he thought it was too much like an exhibition. 'That's enough,' he told the fighters. The men shook hands and Sheppard started for his corner. On the way he clutched his side, slowly sank to the floor and rolled over. The referee massaged the stricken fighter's heart in vain. Sheppard's second said he hadn't seen any foul blow or anger. Sheppard died as the result of 'a reflex inhibition of the heart as a result of a blow or blows'. The pathologist knew of the death of a man who had been knocked in the same spot by another man's elbow, and of similar deaths on the football field. Sheppard's death was found to be accidental, and the boxing business carried on.

Cook and Tom fought a close, gruelling match over 20 rounds, and when the referee gave the decision to the Australian the crowd was hostile. The scribes were divided. Tom 'appeared rather unlucky to lose the decision', commented one. Another supported Cook's victory, scoring the fight level at the end of 18 rounds and giving Cook the final two. Tom was hardly marked, whereas Cook looked like he'd been in a fight. Tom's showing was enough to revive Bernard Mortimer's chase of Scott. The following week he sent the *Sporting Life* a cheque for £100 and a challenge to the British heavyweight.

> Sir, — There is £100 of my money down for Tom Heeney to box Phil Scott. Do Messrs Rose [Scott's manager] and Ward [Scott's supporter] think my wagers will stop at £100, or that I am likely to forget that Scott will be a good favourite at about 2 to 1 on in a match with Heeney. The cut of the purse, 75 and 25 per cent, will suit Heeney.
>
> If Scott were champion of England — which he is a long way from being — I would put up the essential £200 side stake, but as he is what he is, I will not increase my side stake, but can assure Mr Ward that there will be as much money at the current odds behind Heeney as he will care to accept.
>
> In conclusion, you hold my side stake, and I leave your readers to read between the lines.
>
> Bernard Mortimer
> Southampton, Feb. 23, 1925

Charlie Rose replied with his own letter to the editor.

> Sir — Mr Bernard Mortimer supplies a very strong argument against a return match between Phil Scott and Tom Heeney. He says that Scott would be a good favourite at about 2 to 1.
>
> I leave the public to judge whether such a one-sided match is wanted from the sporting point of view.
>
> As to his cheap sneer about Scott and the championship, I would

most respectfully point out that if Scott 'is what he is,' Heeney is 200 per cent worse on Mr Mortimer's own showing. Also I will ask Mr Mortimer, as a business man, where he hopes an adequate purse will come from in the face of such unwise disparagement.

My last word is this: As the challenged party I claim choice of weapons, and if Mr Mortimer really wants the match he will have to put up at least £250 as a side wager.

If he refuses to do this your readers will not need to read between any lines, as he will have made it clear that he dare not risk his money on an equal basis.

C. Rose
London, Feb. 25, 1925

Tom tired of waiting for Scott. He hated the cold grey English climate and wrote home about the hand-to-mouth existence he was forced to lead because none of the leading fighters would meet him. Efforts were still being made to tempt him to cross the Atlantic. 'But next to Tom's sincerity and honesty, his outstanding quality is his loyalty,' his father wrote. 'I have an offer of my fare to America and a fight that will net me £750 with further prospects, but of course I wouldn't go there while my contract with Mr Mortimer lasts,' Tom wrote home. So Mortimer decided to send him somewhere that offered a better cut of the purses and a better climate. He accepted a match with South African heavyweight champion Johnny Squires in Johannesburg. Tom was to receive £200, win, lose or draw. A planned visit by Ted 'Kid' Lewis had fallen through so the Johannesburg promoter Starkey commissioned Norman Clarke, the secretary of the British Board of Control of Boxing, to select a new opponent. Clarke chose Tom:

> On the whole I feel that he is preferable to the others suggested. He is an honest, good-natured fellow, whom I have no hesitation in regarding as game and willing to give of his best — a thing I could not say to some of the others. Though not calculated to impress one in the gym, he is very strong, and for a big man, by no means slow, added to which he has a good right hand punch that always gives him a chance as long as he is on his feet.

Certainly he is a man one can always rely on to put up a fight, and not try and save his record by covering up, hanging on, etc., — and again, I could not say this of many others at present in this country.

If Squires is to give him weight and beat him, he will have to be a very useful man; to knock him out — a very good one.

When Harry Jacobs offered a £500 purse for a Heeney–Scott fight at the Albert Hall and £50 to each boxer for training expenses, the *Sporting Life* suggested that Scott's manager waive the minimum £250 side-stake condition. But Tom didn't want to let down the South African promoter. Mortimer sent a telegram to the *Sporting Life*:

> Pleased to accept Mr Jacobs' offer, but have accepted offer from South Africa. Sending Heeney away Friday on Edinburgh Castle. Return about ten weeks; ready for Scott then.

Jacobs' offer is the answer to Rose's letter.

Scott's backer visited the newspaper intending to cover the £100 deposited on behalf of Tom but he was too late. When Fred Dominey returned to Gisborne a few months later he faced a barrage of questions as to what was wrong with Tom 'at Home'. He thought Tom looked in good shape while training but couldn't strike his true form in the ring. He failed to get going with the Scott fight but he should have had the decision against Cook. And Dominey confirmed that Tom had indeed knocked Scott out during a sparring session.

My None Too Brilliant Career

'He acts younger and looks older,' wrote Paul Gallico of Tom and the grey hair around his temples. Tom had told Gallico he was 29. It was a spring day in 1928 and a group of men were gathered on the roof of Madison Square Garden. Above the arena was boxing promoter Tex Rickard, a newsreel photographer, sports writer Gallico, Tom and his managers. Tom and Rickard were filmed and afterwards the group relaxed and chatted.

Gallico saw Tom's large, powerful hands were covered in scars.

'Bottles!' explained the New Zealander. 'I was a rough 'un when a youngster. This here one,' he pointed to a mark that extended half an inch over a knuckle, 'I got runnin' away from six of 'em in South Africa. And believe me, when they come after you, you want to run.'

Gallico, who would later write such bestsellers as *The Snow Goose* and *The Poseidon Adventure*, once said he was a 'rotten novelist' and 'not even literary' but that he simply liked to tell stories. This is how he told the story of Tom running for his life in South Africa.

> They were all having a sort of party, it seems, about three years ago, and the place was Johannesburg, South Africa. The liquor ran out some time during the morning, and the party was not yet over. Tom

had had enough, but one of the men there was insistent they have some more and invited Tom to go with him to a place he knew and get some Tom went.

After considerable walking, they got to the place, and went in, down a long hall, and into a room, where two quart bottles of whisky were delivered to them, but for the first time Tom began to grow a little suspicious of his companion, and this suspicion waxed when the hall suddenly resounded to the tramp of heavy feet, and was confirmed when six tremendous Africans suddenly hove into view, headed their way. The Africans bore lead pipes, clubs, and the Johannesburg equivalent of sashweights.

Tom immediately slammed the door shut, and addressed himself earnestly to his companions who had lured him into a den in the coloured section of Johannesburg which, Tom tells me, is sudden death in many places. Our Tom had fifty-two quid in his pocket, and the Africans were coming to get it.

'Open the door, Tom,' said his pal, 'I'll be right behind you.'

At this juncture it became necessary for Tom to make several strong remarks to his companion, with the result that his friend suddenly curled up and went to sleep in a corner, taking no further interest in the proceedings.

The six Africans, however, were still interested, and promptly pushed down the door to find Tom waiting for them with a quart whisky bottle in each hand. These bottles were promptly awarded to the first two heads, leaving only four Africans, and in Heeney's hands remained only the two jagged bottle stumps.

Our Thomas is a former football player and a rough young fellow. Inflamed with righteous ire, and with a jagged bottle end in each hand, he was a lot rougher. 'Gangway,' called Thomas and waving his broken bottles, he charged.

He cut his way through, did our Thomas, but not before the enraged Africans banged him on the Stetson with their mallets, and slit him here and there with knives. Out into the open air went Thomas and after him the remainder of the Africans, shrieking for blood.

A large lady African, O, a tremendous lady African, attempted to intercept our Tom as he dashed for his life. Tom says that he still can make a mental picture of that lady African sailing through the air. On he dashed! 'And when I'm running away from something,' Thomas said, 'nothing can catch me!'

And then suddenly he found himself in a cul-de-sac — up a blind alley. No place to go, his bottle ends thrown away, and enraged Africans, in greatly augmented numbers, pounding down the road.

With our Tom, to think is to act. Ahead, houses; to the rear advancing Africans. Our hero took a running jump and dived head first through a window, where he landed, covered from head to foot with gore, in the bedroom of a gentleman and his wife. The latter took one look and fainted. The gentleman merely asked our Tom what he was doing there. Tom reported that he was there because he wanted to live a little longer, and explained. The gentleman thereupon produced a shooting pistol, the sight of which discouraged the Africans, and then he and Tom revived the lady and patched up Tom.

It seems that nobody knew the egg who had steered Tom into the Africans. He had just crashed the party. But anyway, that's how our Tom cut his hand.

Tom's arrival created a lot of interest in South Africa. He was written about as one of a new breed of boxer: men who took pride in their physical prowess and social skills. He wasn't like the crude and 'somewhat elemental' heavyweights of the past but a sturdy young man who had boxed himself from country to country.

The day before the fight with Johnny Squires the Johannesburg *Star* predicted Tom could be a stone and a half heavier than the South African. Neither Tom nor Squires scaled, but their weights were given as 13 st and 11 st 10 lb respectively. For the first couple of rounds Squires looked nervous while Tom was workmanlike. Squires settled in the second, although he walked away and turned his back to Tom near the ropes, who was 'on him like lightning' with a left to the head and a right to the body. However, Squires used a snappy left lead to good effect and in the fifth and sixth drew blood from Tom's nose. His speed made Tom appear slow. After the fifteenth Tom was increasingly aggressive with heavy body punches and swings to the face, and in the last couple of rounds he relentlessly battered his exhausted opponent in an attempt to knock him out. Despite doubling up and slipping momentarily to the boards, Squires, with blood streaming from his face, heard the final bell. Tom was announced the winner and the crowd rose to their feet to cheer both fighters.

A Squires–Heeney rematch was made for Cape Town. Tom almost lost the fight by being 'as docile as a lamb' and allowing Squires to amass points as he waited for an opportunity to knock him out. But in the fifteenth a powerful right he'd aimed at Squires' jaw caught the South African on the throat and in the seventeenth another punch landed on Squires' Adam's apple. He was struggling to breathe. By the eighteenth something was clearly wrong. As the gong sounded to end the round Squires retreated to his corner, ignored his seconds and continued over to Tom's corner. In a barely audible voice he said he couldn't go on. He was leading, just as he had been in Johannesburg before tiring in later rounds.

More fights were arranged and Tom delayed his return to London. He went sightseeing, attended South African club rugby games and was treated like a celebrity. He wrote about a Currie Cup match at Newlands for the *Cape Times* and his smiling face peered out from the newspapers. South Africans liked Tom and he liked them. 'I have been treated right royally,' he said during a visit to the office of the *Star* in Johannesburg, 'and if I had been the Prince of Wales the fine fellows I have met here could not have done more for me. Please tell them how I appreciate it.' Tom still struggled with public attention, however. At a boxing tournament he was introduced to the spectators and then the announcer said, 'And now Heeney will no doubt say "How do you do?"' 'How do you do?' said Tom, waving his hand and heading for his seat. 'Speech, Heeney,' the crowd chanted. 'I said exactly what I was asked to say,' Tom said as he sat down. 'He doesn't mind how many people are gazing at him while he's boxing, because all his attention is on the work in hand,' wrote his mother. 'But try to get him up in front of a crowd to make a speech. You can't do it.'

The big attraction for Tom was game hunting. He'd hunted small animals with a shotgun in New Zealand but this was different. 'I was in and about Johannesburg, in the Transvaal, for about three months, and I never saw a country I liked better,' he later said. 'In the bar of the hotel was a collection of heads and animals shot by the proprietor, and it was a great sight. Africa has almost every kind of game there is and half the country is wild as when it was first discovered. It is the greatest game country in the world. And there is more than game there, too, with all the metals and everything.'

South Africa was rich in gold, platinum, silver and diamonds — so game hunting could wait while Tom and a friend went in search of some sparkling souvenirs. They were assigned a group of black diggers, as white men didn't toil under the burning sun. After an hour or so Tom got bored so he and his friend started digging. All they acquired was a bad case of sunburn. A swim might be just the thing to soothe their burning skin, they thought, and they found a pool used for washing diamond workers' clothes. Tom jumped in and was attacked by tiny fish in the water. He said nothing to his friend who dived in, came to the surface, started yelling and jumped out. Burned, bitten and angry, the friend swore revenge on the fish. He and Tom took some explosives and blew up the pool. 'Such a roar! A series of terrific explosions shook the whole diamond fields, bowling us over like feathers and shaking the suits in the village like kitchen rocking chairs,' Tom wrote.

The adventure ruined his preparation for a match with Nic Morace. Rubdowns were out of the question and he had to fight with a painful, blistered back. It didn't seem to matter, as he won 'by the short route' in four rounds. It was still enough time for the man handling the gate to run off with the cash and Tom only got about half his pay. It came, so the story goes, in the form of 39 uncut diamonds donated by the spectators who'd heard of Tom's plight. 'I wanted to make a necklace for my mother, but every time I showed them to Tom, Dick and Harry there was one short, until all went the same way,' Tom recalled.

His last two fights on South African soil were farcical. During a brawl at the Johannesburg Town Hall in October, the former Australian champion George 'Blackie' Miller hit Tom low in the seventh round. Tom appealed to the referee and the pair 'battered one another as hard as they could with their four hands'. Tom beat Miller to the canvas, blood pouring from his face, but he leapt up and the pair went at it again. Miller hit low again and Tom slipped to the boards, protesting to the referee. A doctor was summoned at the end of the round and pronounced Tom unhurt. The fight went on and the men 'punched with absolute abandon'. Miller hit low again and was disqualified. He strode across the ring to shake hands with Tom but was waved away. Most of the audience claimed Miller had been robbed of the bout. For half an hour they demonstrated and refused to leave the hall until the police arrived. Miller lingered in the ring and was cheered when he said he'd meet Tom again for £200 a side. The referee said he'd found a slight dent in Tom's shield. He was criticised for consulting a doctor instead of having the courage to be the sole judge of whether a punch landed below the belt. He later ruled Miller hadn't hit low intentionally. The Australian received his end of the purse two days after the fight.

The return with Miller the following month at Durban was another fiasco — but this time it was Tom who was disqualified. Miller slipped to the boards in the fifth and as he sat on the floor Tom threw a blow at his head and narrowly missed. When the referee stepped forward to force Tom back he swung again at Miller who was trying to stand up. Tom's second jumped into the ring with his hand in the air and the referee stopped the fight. The spectators had now seen three aborted fights. The two preliminaries ended with disqualifications, in one case for holding and in the other for the use of a kidney punch. The crowd yelled for the fight to go on, but the referee's decision was final. 'Heeney's defeat,' wrote the *Cape Times*, 'means his end as an attraction in South African boxing circles.'

Tom appeared before the Durban Boxing Control Board. There were rumours around town that the fight had been fixed. The referee said the rumours started because there was so much betting. The only thing that made him suspicious was the way Tom stood over Miller after he'd slipped. He was satisfied, however, that there was no collusion, as Tom kept boxing his opponent.

Tom's second Walter Baker said he got overexcited. 'Durban's the only place in the world that would give that as a foul,' he said of the referee's decision. He'd lost £12 on Tom. A Board member said it was rumoured Baker had backed Miller, and the second countered with an allegation against a Board member. He was aggressive and unrepentant and infuriated the Board, which suspended him from seconding for a year in Durban. Another of Tom's seconds denied that a taxi driver had put £20 on Miller on his advice. Miller said he had money on himself and was more surprised than anyone at the decision. Tom told the Board he thought Baker must have lost his head. He said he hadn't backed himself and was therefore unlikely to put any money on Miller. He thought the referee's decision was correct. 'He's a sportsman,' remarked a Board member. Tom had said just what the officials wanted to hear.

Tom had been attacked and nearly killed, severely sunburned, hit below the belt, and had to leave in disgrace. But he'd developed an enduring love for South Africa. 'There is the country for a man to settle in,' he later said, 'and if I do not go back to New Zealand, which I sometimes think I will do when my time comes to retire and take life easy, I will head for South Africa.'

Tom returned to Britain having made some money and having done enough in the ring to keep alive his ambition of meeting Scott again. In early 1926, however, lots of fighters were chasing Scott. And he was choosing his opponents carefully. He was planning a move to the United States and wanted to build up a reputation. He'd agreed to fight George Cook, and Tom made it known he was prepared to take on the winner. Scott defeated Cook and continued to ignore Tom.

Former British heavyweight champion Joe Beckett announced he was returning to the game and there was talk he might meet Scott. In his last fight Beckett had been knocked out in one minute and 15 seconds by Georges Carpentier. And there could hardly have been a British fighter more lampooned by the great New York sports columnists of the twenties. Damon Runyon described him as 'the greatest resin-sniffer that England ever produced'. Bill McGeehan told the story of how Beckett humiliated Bernard Mortimer's brother John one day:

> It was after one of his early fights, which was witnessed by the Prince of Wales. The Prince expressed a desire to have Beckett presented to him. Mr Mortimer found the champion stretched in his characteristic attitude on a canvas-covered couch and dragged him out.
>
> The Prince of Wales was just complimenting Beckett on his showing when Big Ben struck 1. Immediately Beckett toppled over backward and closed his eyes. After ten seconds he arose and said rather sheepishly, 'Ger bli' me, your 'ighness, but I thought that was the gong in the ring.'

In March Tom appeared in the same place on the same night as Scott, but not in the same fight. He was matched with southpaw Charlie Smith of Deptford in a minor bout on the night Scott challenged Frank Goddard for the British heavyweight title. Scott knocked out Goddard in the third, even though, according to *The Times*, Goddard 'was not much more dangerous than a punchball'. Afterwards Tom beat Smith so severely, especially about the body, that his opponent kept holding on to 'avoid getting broken in half'. After repeated cautions Smith was disqualified in the fifth round.

Tom now had his own pursuers: Jack Stanley, Harry Persson, Blackie Miller and others. But the opponent he really wanted, Scott, still couldn't find a promoter to offer the necessary 'inducements'. In April it was announced that Scott was to meet Boy McCormick, and a sympathetic scribe wrote, 'this suggested side-tracking of Heeney comes as a sorry surprise'. Tom wrote of his intense frustration to family in Gisborne: 'Some of the fights I have been offered to fill in time would not earn enough to buy fish and chips for a week . . . Scott is side-stepping me . . . My backer has challenged him for any purse, winner to take the lot and a £200 side bet . . . I am beginning to feel like Paddy with the barrow — plenty of places to go but nothing to go for. One day I am going for home; the next to America; and the next back to South Africa.' Tom had friends in Britain who put him up when he was down on his luck. A group of Gisborne businessmen were prepared to advance him money if he wanted it, but he was too proud to ask for their help.

In May 1926, the month of the General Strike when most of the British workforce came out in support of the coal miners, when there were power stoppages, buses and trains stopped running and many newspapers ceased printing, Tom hunted for opponents in Paris. He chased French fighter Franccis Charles and Spanish heavyweight Paulino Uzcudun. Meanwhile, Harry Jacobs offered a purse of £1000 for a match between Scott and Tom, which Mortimer accepted. In July Tom outpointed Tom Berry, the British light heavyweight champion, in a 15-round contest at The Ring. Trevor Wignall of the *Daily Mail* said this was Tom's best fight in Britain and now that he had found his form he should be matched with some of the recognised heavyweights. And then came a chance to meet Phil Scott.

Scott didn't plan on fighting Tom. He was due to meet Joe Beckett, who was notoriously accident-prone. There was the time he injured his back taking a bath. Another time he complained of a chill or it could have been chilblains, no one was quite sure. There was an injury to his right hand. Now he'd managed to tear a tendon in his leg — while shadow-boxing. Doctors said he needed to rest for at least a fortnight and ordered him to bed. Scott sent him a bunch of flowers.

Normally the fight would have been postponed, but promoter Henry Wakefield asked the Mortimer brothers whether Tom would substitute. Tom agreed without asking how much he'd get. When Wakefield called Tom, wrote one commentator, he acted like Marshal Saxe at Fontenoy, who remembered that 'the Irish Brigade remained'. 'Heeney hails from New Zealand, but one has only to take one look at him to realize that he is Irish to the core, a man who is ever spoiling for a fight and as determined to take full revenge on his "Saxon foes" as was ever Lord Clare, when the French and British Guards exchanged their historical courtesies.' Tom had spent a couple of days relaxing after the Berry fight and only had two days to get back into condition for what was billed as the Championship of the British Empire. Because he was a New Zealander, Tom wasn't eligible to fight for the British title.

Around 6000 spectators turned up to see the 20-round fight with Scott on a Saturday afternoon. There would've been twice as many if Beckett hadn't cancelled. The event was held in an open-air ring at The Dell, the ground of the Southampton Football Club constructed from what had been a lake surrounded by woodland. Those in the open fled for cover when it rained but the ring, which was so cramped the fighters barely had enough room to move around each other or to sidestep rushes, had a roof of sorts. Scott began with a series of left leads to Tom's face and did better in the opening rounds. But in the infighting Scott 'looked quite distressed' reported one ringside observer. Tom often rested his head on Scott's chest while he thumped at his opponent's ribs with his free hand. 'Scott doesn't like those and cannot stand them,' John Mortimer yelled.

'Do to him what you did at the National, Tom,' Mortimer continued.

'Oh! Oh! Is that the Mayor of Southampton?' Scott's trainer Jack Goodwin retorted.

'Keep moving, Tom,' someone in the New Zealander's corner urged.

'It's cheaper than paying rent,' Goodwin shot back.

Mortimer shouted incessantly at the fighters during the rounds and at Goodwin during the breaks. At one point brother Bernard had to come over and tell another of Tom's noisy seconds to quieten down or leave.

Scott fought back. Tom was tired and had to be refreshed with champagne baths between rounds. But it looked as if either man might score a knockout. Scott was hit off balance by a left swing in the eighteenth and Tom almost fell in the nineteenth, but the New Zealander was still fighting hard at the end, leaving Scott's victory less than impressive for a champion. Some observers thought there was very little in it. But the champion got the big pay packet. Of a £1500 purse, Tom got just £300.

Tom lost because he lacked speed. Even though he was punished badly at times, he seemed untroubled by a bad cut inside his lower lip and damage to his left ear and his right eye. He was proclaimed the next-best heavyweight in Britain after Scott. After the fight Scott said: 'I found Heeney harder to beat than when I met him some time ago, but form has worked out correctly, although Tom has improved since then. I understand that Joe Beckett is still willing to try conclusions with me, and for my part there is nothing I would like better.' On Monday Tom called into the *Sporting Life* office, showing few signs of Saturday's fight. The next day the newspaper reported that Tom was going to America and was anxious to meet Scott again.

Tom's photograph appeared on the cover of *Boxing* alongside an advertisement that 'the great New Zealander' had recently been added to a collection of postcards of boxers for sale. He got a match in Ireland that could help raise his profile in America, and he had Scott to thank. Belfast promoter Jim Rice had hoped to match Bartley Madden, a 35-year-old veteran New York fighter, with Scott, but Scott's manager held out 'for what may be described as impossible terms'. Scott wasn't that keen anyway, as he wanted to rest and go on holiday. So Tom agreed to meet Madden for 20 rounds, side stakes of £100 and a purse of £750.

Madden was known as a tough 'trial horse' for title-seekers. His most impressive fight had been against Harry Wills, who he managed to hold off for 15 rounds at a disadvantage of 28 lb. Wills had been trying to fight Jack Dempsey for years but was denied a title shot because he was black. Madden had only been knocked out once, in his previous fight with Gene Tunney, the man about to fight Dempsey for the world title.

And so an Irishman by birth and an Irishman by descent were to fight in Dublin. It was only three years since the end of the Irish Civil War and Dublin was still visibly battle-scarred. On O'Connell Street the General

Post Office was slowly rising again and shop owners and businessmen worked amongst ruined buildings and the dust of construction.

'Faith now and if it's a foight ye want at all, at all, it's the broth of a wan that you'll say whin Tom and Bartley trow their hats into the ring, mind ye,' wrote *Boxing*. 'Glory be, there'll be wigs on the grave for shure when these two broths of bhoys hand one to the oder a shmack on the gob. 'N, who'll win? Begorra now, ask me something aisy. Begob, neider of dim kin win, ain't dey both Oirish begob. Shtill, I tink Heeney sounds more Oirish than Madden. Ut sounds so, at anny rate, wherefore my nimble tanner goes on him.'

'This visit of mine to Dublin', Tom said shortly after his arrival in the city, 'has long been looked forward to. The last time I wanted to come here was on occasion of the All Blacks' visit, when they met Ireland at Lansdowne Road.' He talked of his rugby background and of his friends in the New Zealand team such as George Nepia, Jock Richardson, and the Brownlies. 'So you see, I started life in the proper way, which enables me to take a lot of knocking about without feeling any effects.' Tom had been tracked by a reporter to Barry's Hotel, an elegant four-storey establishment created from two terraced Georgian houses on Great Denmark Street off Parnell Square. It was from a first-floor window of Barry's that Michael Collins fired at British soldiers shortly after the Easter Rising. 'I am going to win all right, and I am going to come back here again and bring Phil Scott with me. I am very dissatisfied with the result of my fight with the English champion, and the next time we meet you can tip me to win.' Scott's manager had promised his man would meet the winner of the Dublin fight — provided terms were favourable, of course.

Close to 12,000 people crowded into Croke Park on the night of 9 August 1926. Some had stayed on in the city after attending the hugely popular Dublin Horse Show the previous week. More than a thousand travelled south from Belfast on a special train. Into the stadium filed sportsmen, men from the army and the Garda, politicians, doctors, lawyers, and a 'fair sprinkling' of women. The ring was overlooked by reminders of the city's violent recent history: a grassy mound of earth built with rubble from O'Connell Street after the Easter Rising on the eastern side; and opposite, the Hogan Stand, named after the Tipperary Gaelic footballer who was killed on the pitch on Bloody Sunday.

About an hour before sunset Tom entered the ring to a rousing reception, but Madden got the loudest cheer. Against the Irishman's pale complexion Tom looked dark and weathered and once the robes were shed it was clear that Madden was out of condition. Strict training bored Madden, Gene Tunney once wrote. 'He went into many fights completely untrained, but on getting in fought until he fell.' Puffs of smoke escaped skyward from a sea of heads level with the floor of the ring. At the bell the men rushed into a clinch but it wasn't long before Tom was landing hard rights. In the second Madden did his best to keep Tom off but was pummelled by a succession of jabs. Then the rain fell. Heavily. And it didn't stop falling until the fight was almost over. Ringside spectators leapt from their chairs and the glamorously dressed referee Moss Deyong donned a hat and coat. In a clinch Tom looked over to see rain pouring off John Mortimer. 'Hey, John,' Tom recalled yelling, 'grab yourself my dressing gown for a mackintosh.' 'Don't mind me,' Mortimer replied. 'Win the fight.' It was too late to put up the tarpaulin and the ring was greasy.

Tom was the better man in the early rounds. But the constant jabbing and jolting at close range seemed to spur Madden on. 'The massive, symmetrically built Heeney expended all his powers in scientifically hooking, swinging and driving the big Irishman, but Madden, like Oliver Twist, was always asking for more,' wrote a ringside scribe. In the twelfth a third hard left to Tom's stomach caused him to slip on the wet surface, but he quickly rose and had Madden on the ropes. Madden withstood blows that 'seemed powerful enough to put out nine out of ten boxers'. The intensity endured until the last round and the men didn't seem to hear the final gong and continued going for a few extra seconds. 'If we describe the first round as having been a series of left and right jolts and swings by Heeney to Madden's jaw,' commented one scribe, 'we have simply to add, "rounds 2 to 20, inclusive, ditto."'

Tom was declared the winner on points and no one disputed the referee's decision. 'Does Madden ever madden?' *Sport* pondered. How he managed not only to survive the battering but to emerge from the fight unscathed was seen as something of a miracle. The prizefighters returned to their dressing rooms as darkness closed in and the electric lights flickered to life for the last bout of the tournament. 'I shall cable fifty pounds to the mother tomorrow,' Tom remarked. 'Tom's a good boy, and so are all our boys — and the girls too. He always sends home money to us after a fight, but we don't need it,' his mother wrote. 'We've got plenty to keep us going, unless we live too long, or the rates get too high.'

Madden urged Tom to go to America, returning there himself to continue a career well past its peak. In February 1930, a few weeks after his wife died, he watched Jack Sharkey knock out Phil Scott in Miami. The following week in Washington he fell 20 feet from the west steps of the Treasury Building. During moments of consciousness he said he was almost penniless and wanted to get back to New York to look after his motherless son. He died in hospital that night.

The chase for Scott was on again. The champion had promised to fight Tom if the New Zealander beat Madden. More than one offer was on the table but none seemed good enough for Scott, so Tom agreed to fight the former London policeman Jack Stanley at the National Sporting Club for £50 a side and the club purse over 15 rounds. During training Tom went into hospital for an operation to remove a tapeworm. He didn't mention health problems to his parents when he wrote to them before the fight: 'The old horse is still alive and in the pink. I am fighting Jack Stanley at the National Sporting Club on October 28th. There is not much money in it, and, as I cannot get Scott to sign up for a match with me, a chap has to be doing something. If I don't beat Stanley, it will be the same old song, "Show me the way to go home".'

Some notable New Zealanders in London came to see Tom fight. Prime Minister Gordon Coates was in the city for the Imperial Conference and had been invited by the Mortimer brothers. Half a dozen rugby players from the Maori team touring Britain were also there. 'The presence of these native New Zealand Maoris [*sic*], as loyal supporters, brought back memories of my own Rugby football days, when the Maoris [*sic*] would put on their native dances after the games,' Tom said. His countrymen didn't see Tom at his best. The longer the fight went on, the worse he got. He found it difficult to avoid Stanley's left and the fight wasn't as easy as he thought it would be. He got so annoyed at times that 'he quite frankly went wild', which only increased Stanley's lead, reported one scribe. Tom won narrowly on points. But he punched with an open glove rather than the knuckle, 'slapping' his way to victory, which wasn't considered sporting. Stanley and his supporters weren't happy and announced they would stake £100 on a return match. But Tom's fight with Stanley proved to be his last in Britain.

A final, shambolic effort was made to match Tom with Scott. Bickering over side stakes meant neither side seemed to want to trust the other. The Mortimer brothers and Tom finally gave up chasing Scott. Bernard arranged with American promoter Charlie Harvey to jointly manage Tom in the United States. One report claimed the Mortimers cut Harvey in for 15 per cent; another that the Mortimers and Harvey would each take a third of Tom's earnings. Harvey was a gentlemanly, fatherly figure who was universally liked and had a reputation for honesty in a notoriously corrupt business. He was an 'old school' manager, wore gold spectacles, had a short, flat nose, small dancing eyes, a smiley face, and a stiff leg from a terrible automobile accident in 1923. He was in his early sixties but had the enthusiasm of someone a quarter his age. He had made good money but spent liberally. He didn't use profanities or tell crude stories. Where others swore and cursed he would blurt out, 'By Jiminy Christmas!' or maybe even 'By Jiminy Crickets!'.

Charlie Harvey had a gentle disposition for someone with such a tough background. Born to Irish-American parents in the gas house district of lower New York, Harvey used to go to Long Island to play basketball and take part in running meets and it was there he got into the fight business. At 15 he became an announcer, and at 16 began promoting matches. Back then, bare-knuckle fights to a finish were held at least once a week. The crowds were rough and arguments over betting would sometimes end in a gunfight. Professional boxing wasn't legal so Harvey worked with the amateurs, putting on tournaments that drew packed houses. He took over the Star Athletic Club in Long Island City, a crude old club where a boxer was given a shower bath — whatever the weather — by climbing out a ground-floor window into the alley while four men poured a tub of water over him.

Harvey instigated semi-professional baseball and marathon racing in New York; he managed a lightweight wrestling champion and an Olympic marathon runner. At the turn of the century he amassed a fortune peddling tickets from the sidewalk for hit shows such as 'Florodora'. Known as 'Handlebars' Harvey because of his ostentatious, flowing moustache, he switched to management and specialised in bringing British fighters to the States. Owen Moran and Jim Driscoll were two of his famous imports, although he passed on Jimmy Wilde, which he admitted was his biggest mistake. 'Mr Harvey has been behind all of the British fighters who have come to the United States,' wrote New York scribe Bill McGeehan. 'This alone makes a hero of Mr Harvey. There is no danger in being in front of a British fighter, but a man who habitually is behind one, despite his agility, is bound sooner or later to have the British fighter knocked on top of him.' Tom was heading to the United States 'at the fag-end of a none too brilliant career', and Harvey must have had doubts about the New Zealander who'd been beaten by 'such British rug-bumpers as George Cook and Phil Scott', wrote one American reporter. But Harvey had no great fighters at the time and decided to gamble on Tom.

John Mortimer had a parting shot for Phil Scott. He wrote a letter to the editor of the *Sporting Life*.

> Sir, — I should like through your columns to lay before your many readers the true reason why Heeney and Scott have not met for their return fight. It will be remembered that Heeney met Scott at The Ring some two years ago, and while not wishing to take anything from Scott for his victory, it is but just to say that Heeney had only recently arrived in this country, and was certainly not acclimatised. Briefly, Scott won on points, and his party promised us a return fight.
>
> In the meantime, Heeney, like the good sportsman he is, assisted Scott in his preparation for a contest with Stanley, and one afternoon in the National Sporting Club gymnasium — I have for this statement the word of Mr Gene Corrie, who was present — Heeney, in a mix-up, had Scott beaten. This is the reason why the Scott party did not want the return, I presume.
>
> Last July Heeney fought Tom Berry on the Monday of the week in which Scott was matched to box Beckett on the Saturday in Southampton. Beckett could not box, so on the Thursday Heeney was asked to take his place, which he did, having only two days' notice. There was a purse of £1500, and all Heeney got of this was £300; but what we wanted most of all was to get Scott in the ring. In this contest Heeney, under all disadvantages, went the 20 rounds, and 75 per cent of the press and people present said that at least it should have been a draw.
>
> Since then Heeney has had £200 deposited for a return match, which was never covered by Scott, and only last week, at Premierland, the MC announced, just prior to Scott taking the ring

with a Frenchman that few people had heard of, that as Heeney could not get any response to his challenge and money, he was going to America.

This nonsense of Scott boxing two men in the same ring does no good to the game, and is all wrong, especially as here in Heeney is a worthy opponent with good money. A substantial purse has been offered for the contest but Scott wanted all — at least, the promoter in question said he could give Heeney only £250 after meeting the demands of the champion.

I should like, in conclusion, to say that Heeney and myself are leaving for America soon after Christmas, and I trust that we shall be able to meet Scott in the ring on the other side. Tom Heeney wishes to take this opportunity of thanking all friends for their kindness during his stay here, and of hoping they will welcome him on his return from his American tour.

John E. Mortimer
Southampton, Dec. 13

The following day it was announced that an offer had come in to stage the Scott–Heeney match in Johannesburg and a letter to the editor from Scott's manager was published.

Sir, — In reply to Mr John Mortimer's lengthy letter in your issue of today Scott and I plead not guilty to the various misdemeanours with which that voluble gentleman has charged us.

For the information of the public I wish to state that Scott is not afraid of any boxer, and certainly not of Heeney. The only stumbling-block in the path of a third match between the two is that Mr Mortimer refuses to consider it on a level basis.

Mr Wilfred Ward, who used to back Scott, repeatedly offered to put up a level side-stake of £500, which Mr Mortimer just as often refused to cover on the ground that he could get 2 to 1 to his money.

Apparently, therefore, Mr Mortimer agrees that the match is an unequal one.

With regard to Heeney beating Scott in the Club's gymnasium,

> I would respectfully point out that he was unable to repeat that performance at Southampton.
>
> As to the offer of the purse to which Mr Mortimer refers, I would like to ask him why Scott should not be entitled to the big end of any purse offered, seeing that he has already twice beaten Heeney. How many times is Scott required to win over any boxer to establish superiority?
>
> Mr Mortimer may rest assured that his wish that Scott and Heeney may meet in America will not be gratified, as American promoters never pit two Britishers together.
>
> If Mr Mortimer really desires a third match, he can have one by going to South Africa, where Tom may get anything from £1000 to £1500 for his end.
>
> C. Rose

John Mortimer scurried back to his typewriter.

> Sir, — In answer to Mr Rose, I would like to freshen his memory as to what he said if Heeney beat Bartley Madden in Dublin — a match previously offered to Scott by Mr Rice, the promoter. Well, Heeney beat Madden in Ireland, but the promise of a return fight was not kept.
>
> I may inform Mr Rose that I also have had a letter from South Africa regarding a Scott and Heeney contest. It is estimated they would take between £3000 and £5000. Well, Mr Rose is hereby assured that the only terms on which Heeney will meet Scott again are a 60 and 40 per cent division of any purse offered.
>
> John E. Mortimer

The spat ended when Mortimer announced that he and Tom were sailing to the United States on the *Berengaria* from Southampton on 29 December.

Tom was nervous about an American campaign. He was overawed by the reports of the heavyweights being produced there, imagining them to be almost superhuman. But he intended to go back to New Zealand through America anyway, so this was a chance to compare himself with American fighters and perhaps to earn enough money to return home at least as well off as when he left. He was living in London on a few pounds a week, he would later admit, and it was a 'long time between drinks'. Maybe he could also restore some pride. Even his father thought he was 'practically a failure' in England.

It wasn't luck that sent Tom to America, his mother said. 'He wrote and said people would laugh at him if he came home a failure, and he made up his mind to show people what he could do.' She wrote back and told him to ignore what people said and that if he wanted to come home his home was waiting for him. 'If he wanted money, that was waiting for him, too. He didn't send for money, and he didn't come home.'

Looking for Another Dempsey

It was a night of rain, records, and memorable one-liners. On 23 September 1926 James Joseph Tunney challenged Jack Dempsey for the world's heavyweight title in Philadelphia. The fight drew more than a hundred thousand people and close to $1,900,000. The pair had been 'ballyhooed' as the handsome, refined marine — who'd never seen combat — and the rough war slacker with a draft deferment. The largest crowd ever to attend a boxing match saw Gene Tunney become the first New Yorker to win the world's heavyweight championship. Dempsey suffered a terrible beating and later, bloodied and battered, he answered his wife's question about what had happened with, 'Honey, I forgot to duck.'

Dempsey was a 'swarming, snorting, snarling roughhouse fighter' wrote his biographer Roger Kahn. He was popular with men for his fighting and with women for his sex appeal. He shook the hands of children in the street. Tunney was very different. He lacked a knockout punch, was a cool, methodical boxer, showed pretentions to gentility and was alleged to have a 'yellow streak'. Tunney managed his own affairs, mixed with society, appeared snobbish and aloof. He was ridiculed for 'training' on literature and for spending hours reading Shakespeare. He became friends with George Bernard Shaw after making some apparently disparaging remarks about Shaw's *Cashel Byron's Profession*, the story of a fictional Irish boxer who became world champion. Tunney was seen as an accidental champion and Dempsey became more popular in defeat than he had been as titleholder. A rematch seemed likely.

'Do you want to fight Tunney?' a reporter asked Tom not long after he arrived in New York in early January 1927.

'No.'

'Dammit, you're honest. Most of the heavyweights want to fight Tunney the moment they land here.'

Tom said he hadn't come to America for the title but that he was ready to meet any of the contenders. He trained in the stuffy, low-ceilinged, two-storey Saint Nicholas Arena at West 66th Street and Columbus Avenue. He wasn't used to working without a fight booked, but it was what boxers did in America. An unknown boxer couldn't afford his own sparring partners — a top one might even be paid *by* them — so at a place like St Nick's a new arrival trying to get into condition had to box anyone who was willing. If he was lucky he might be allowed to work with a big-name boxer who happened to be training there.

Tom boxed two rounds with future world light heavyweight champion Tommy Loughran, who battered him in the first round. Tom retreated to his corner and asked Charlie Harvey to take off his gloves. Loughran came over and asked him what the trouble was. 'No trouble at all,' Tom said, 'I'm all befuddled,' and promptly walked out of the ring. Tom had already gone four rounds with a 'couple of hams' and was about to head for the dressing rooms when Harvey had come over and said Loughran was ready. It was only later that Tom's trainer Jimmy Hennessey found out Harvey thought it was Tom's first boxing workout for the day.

Tex Rickard, the promoter, president and director of Madison Square Garden, was the person Tom needed to impress if he was to get fights in New York. The man who once herded cattle in Texas, and still had the manner of a gambler from the West, had turned boxing into a multi-million-dollar industry, several champions into millionaires and Dempsey into a public idol. He'd given boxing an air of respectability. He'd filled the ringside seats with society men and women, elegantly dressed and bejewelled, and he knew how to use money to make more money. He had come to prominence promoting the 1906 lightweight fight between Joe Gans and 'Battling' Nelson at Goldfield, Nevada. He'd raised a $100,000 purse for the Jim Jeffries–Jack Johnson contest in 1910 and later promoted million-dollar fights for Dempsey with Frenchman Georges Carpentier and Argentine Luis Ángel Firpo. Now Rickard had a virtual monopoly on the best heavyweights in New York, offering promising fighters 'exclusive services' contracts that effectively tied their futures to him.

Rickard also had newspapermen working for him. A boxer looking for fights needed good publicity, so payoffs to writers were common. Boxers looking for more flattering and expansive coverage would offer payoffs too. Damon Runyon, who'd later become famous for writing *Guys and Dolls*, was one of the writers Tunney paid off on his way up. In the twenties New York boasted some of the best sports writers ever produced: Runyon, Paul Gallico, Bill McGeehan, Grantland Rice and Westbrook Pegler. Not only did they help to make the boxers they wrote about more captivating and more famous, they were celebrities themselves.

John Mortimer carried letters of introduction from his friend and well-known *Daily Mail* cartoonist Tom Webster, who was well connected with New York scribes. 'This chap Heeney that my friend Mortimer is taking to America may not be the greatest fighter in the world, but he is a satisfactory performer and can beat a lot of the heavyweights I saw in your country,' was how Damon Runyon remembered the tenor of Webster's letter to him. 'I have seen him fight and I am sure that his style will please the American fans. It is more American than it is English. I am sure that Heeney will give a good account of himself.' Runyon remembered meeting Tom for the first time and thinking he had never seen 'a more unprepossessing pugilistic aspect'.

> Thomas Heeney handed me a rugged paw, all knotted and gnarled as if from hard labour, and went on devastating a huge mutton chop, saying very little as Mr Mortimer chattered his praise.
>
> 'If you say anything nice in the paper about Tawm, 'e won't let you down,' said Mr Mortimer, earnestly. 'No, Tawm won't let you down, will you Tawm?'
>
> 'No,' said Thomas, shortly.
>
> I gathered from this statement that Mr Mortimer meant that Thomas wouldn't make any praise of him give forth a hollow sound.

> ''E can fight a bit,' confided Mr Mortimer. ''E will be better when 'e learns something your Hamerican ways of fighting. A strong fellow. And 'e won't let you down. Not Tawm. Will you Tawm?'
> 'No,' said Thomas Heeney.

And from Bill McGeehan's meeting with Mortimer at the Friars Club sprang a tale of woe entitled 'The Blight of Beckett'.

> Upon being introduced, Mr John Mortimer immediately announces, 'I am the man who discovered Joe Beckett, the heavyweight champion of England.' If the person to whom he is introduced does not turn with a gesture of repugnance or look upon him with an air of pity and tolerance, Mr Mortimer will recount the story of his tragic life.
> 'Wherever I go they seem to know me,' sighed Mr Mortimer. 'I have attended fights three times in this country and each time they put me in one of the corners. Each time the fighters used me as a cuspidor. Oh no, it was not mere chance. They must have been informed that I discovered Joe Beckett.
> 'Southampton, where I live, is one of the great ports of the world. Each day, as Mr Kipling has it, there go great steamers, white and gold, from that port to sail strange seas and to make strange discoveries. Would that I had sailed on any of them! But no, I had to stay home and discover Joe Beckett. Oh, yes, I know that a rolling stone gathers no moss, but what did I get by being a stationary stone, as it were? I got Joe Beckett.'

McGeehan wrote that while Mortimer was trying to redeem himself he came across someone in a pub in Auckland who just might be able to help him do it.

> He noticed at the end of the bar a young man standing firmly on his feet, but fast asleep and snoring gently. He made inquiries of the barmaid.
> 'Oh, that's Tom Heeney,' she replied. 'He always sleeps standing up. It is one of his idiosyncrasies. He cannot sleep in a bed, so he sleeps here in the taproom. He never was known to lie down at any

time in his life. Men have tried to knock him down, but they cannot get him off his feet. His case has puzzled the greatest medical authorities of New Zealand. Once he did go to sleep in a folding bed, by way of an experiment, but the bed was closed and he did his sleeping in a vertical position.'

A ray of hope came into the life of Mr Mortimer, of Southampton. Here was the opposite of Joe Beckett, whose natural inclinations consistently were horizontal. The dream of his life had come true: A British fighter who would not leave the vertical position, even to sleep.

Mortimer signed Tom immediately and now he was looking for fights with anyone. 'But, so far, no promoters will listen to the story of Mr John Mortimer. It does sound incredible, at that,' wrote McGeehan.

British heavyweights weren't highly regarded and Harvey had long been associated with poor fighters. Tom's record in Britain was unimpressive. He had no scrapbook, no fights, he didn't look good in the gym and he wasn't attracting the fight fans. One night he was ringside at Madison Square Garden while champions, ex-champions, contenders and would-be contenders were introduced from the ring.

'Come on, Tom, up you go,' someone said.

'I'll stay here.'

'No, it's your chance to get introduced to the public.'

'I'll be fighting up there when I'm introduced.'

'You'll get exported back to Ireland,' someone else said.

'New Zealand,' Tom said.

'They won't let you fight if you're not introduced.' This made Tom reconsider. 'It's one of the queer American laws.'

Tom finally made his way into the ring and squirmed as Joe Humphreys yelled, 'And the champion of New Zealand — Tom-m-m Hee-ee-ney.'

'Where is it?' came a voice from the balcony.

Tom hurried back to his seat.

These were the roaring twenties, the era of the post-war boom, when women bobbed their hair and New Yorkers seemed drunk on money, glamour and celebrity. 'New York is the concentrate of art and commerce and sport and religion and entertainment and finance, bringing to a single compact arena, the gladiator, the evangelist, the promoter, the actor, the trader and the merchant,' wrote E.B. White in his famous essay. The writer warned that no one should come to the city to live unless 'he is willing to be lucky'. And now there was a new gambler in town.

Tom had little money: he landed with $400 and one report claimed he was penniless. He denied being broke but admitted needing money to get home. So he spent his days tucked away from the bitter winter under electric lights in the sweaty St Nick's. The steam heating was strange, as were the people riding horses in Central Park. In New Zealand he rode a horse 20 miles to a rugby field and 20 miles home again, but that was merely to get there and back — the rugby game was the exercise. He thought American football was rougher than rugby but that rugby was harder. 'You seem to knock off every few minutes and have a conference, and if we did that the rest of the team would keep on playing without us.' He 'could see no head or tail of the game' when he watched his first baseball match. He loved swimming but he couldn't see the point of taking a hot crowded subway train from New York to Coney Island for a swim only to ride the stuffy train back.

It wasn't until he got to America that he found out his mother's maiden name. 'Sure, Tom, you might look up my two sisters in the States,' she wrote. 'They left Ireland the same time I went off to New Zealand. I don't know where they live, but you can find them by the name of Coughlan.' Tom realised that his mother had no more idea of the size of the States than Americans had of New Zealand. New Yorkers seemed to think New Zealand was a town in Ireland, perhaps partly because Tom's managers played up his Irish roots. They claimed the championship of Ireland for him on the basis of his win over Madden and his Irish parentage. To New Yorkers, Tom had a peculiar, unsophisticated-sounding accent likened to cockney, British-Canadian, and West Indian. He was scruffy. His coat was always bunched up around his wide shoulders and his trousers bagged at the knees. The contrast with his manager could have been striking, except that Harvey wasn't much into clothes either.

Tom missed his family and friends. Moe Fleischer talked of training him for some of his early New York fights. 'You couldn't find a nicer guy than Tom . . . You never got any lip from Tom. No sir, anything I told him to do he did with a smile. Harvey told me to watch him real good because he was lonesome in this country so I never left him alone. There was this time I was getting married and I worried about what Tom would do that night by himself so I took him to my wedding. He felt at home there with the rest of the fight mob like "Three-Fingered" Jack Dougherty and Charley Goldman, who later trained Rocky Marciano.'

But then Marion Estelle Dunn came along. 'We met at a party, just a small affair, and I liked him very much,' Marion remembered. Her parents died when she was young and an aunt in Port Washington on Long Island brought her up. She was close in age to Tom and was divorced from her first husband, William Hyde, a post-office employee in Port Washington. After her divorce she left the Port and found work in New York. She was described as a model and saleswoman and worked as a mannequin in a large fashionable New York store. Marion became Tom's friend and much more. But that was all in the future. Right now, life looked pretty bleak.

'There was not much doing in New York,' Tom said, 'and I hung about a long while waiting for a fight. I didn't have the money to pay my fare back to England when they threw me in with this Charley Anderson, a pretty smart boy, and told me I'd get enough to cover my return fare.' Harvey finally got Garden matchmaker and old friend Jess McMahon to sign Tom for a match on 25 February with Anderson, a Senegambian from the Chicago Stockyards. McMahon recalled meeting Tom for the first time. 'I thought the poor fellow was on the bum. He was so poor that he didn't have an overcoat, and it was a bitter cold day, too. His clothes looked like the kind they give away at the Rescue Missions, and his shoes had seen their best days. He was a seedy-looking individual.'

Once again, Tom stepped in at short notice and replaced the injured Arthur DeKuh. 'I had an awful time getting a break, and I will always be rooting for this fellow DeKuh,' Tom said later, 'for if he hadn't got hurt when he did, Lord love me, I would have chucked it. I was trainin', trainin' and trainin', and believe me, it gets mighty tiresome, trainin' for a fight when one has no fight in view. And after I had given it up as a bad job, Charlie Harvey told me that I would fight in four days, and I hopped to it again.'

The fight was at Madison Square Garden, the home of boxing in New York even though it wasn't a garden and it wasn't on Madison Square. It was Madison Square Garden III, completed in 1925 at 49th and 50th Streets and 8th Avenue and made of steel and concrete. It had a terrazzo floor, modern gadgets, ice-making machinery, wires of all sorts, a ventilator under every seat and great fans in the roof to circulate warm air in winter and cool in summer. Tex Rickard writers called its backers the 'Six Hundred Millionaires'. Tough, intimidating ticket-takers were stationed at the doors. The hordes in the darkness that surrounded the bright white light of the ring were a varied bunch. Close to the ring were celebrities, bootleggers, gangsters, politicians and newspapermen. Elsewhere there were pickpockets, narcotics peddlers, nightclub runners, ex-convicts, gamblers, gunmen, bankers, hookers and actors. Rickard rarely sat in his private box, preferring to stand in the lobby.

In the early rounds they were given the 'Harlem hoot' every time the bell ended a round. But in the eighth the 'jeers turned to cheers' when Tom unleashed such a rally no one could understand how his opponent remained standing. A groggy Anderson kept holding and the referee stopped the fight one minute and 45 seconds into the ninth round. McGeehan wrote that Mortimer had been redeemed. He wouldn't show Tom, 'the Vertical Kangaroo', in Britain for a while though, as 'the patrons of British pugilism are so accustomed to seeing their heavyweights in the horizontal position that their heads have a peculiar slant and the spectators at the National Sporting Club have taken to watching heavyweight bouts while reclining on divans in order that they may get the illusion that the fighters are on their feet'. *The Ring* wrote that Tom was the type of heavyweight American boxing fans liked to see.

On the top of the bill, Paulino Uzcudun from Spain got the decision from Knute Hansen and the next day Rickard said he might match Tom with Paulino as part of his elimination tournament. Rickard liked Paulino, 'The Basque Woodchopper' who claimed the heavyweight title of Europe, because he was colourful and played to the crowds. If he missed a swing he laughed, showing a mouthful of gold teeth. After the Hansen fight he flipped to the back of his neck and jumped upright again. He was a prankster and liked trying out new tricks and games on his friends. And like Tom, he was tough — he was said to have been a bullfighter as well as a woodchopper.

The four big names fighting to meet Tunney were Paulino, Jack Sharkey, Mike McTigue and Jimmy Maloney. Harvey went to see Rickard and got Tom a match with Paulino, promising to sign for any figure Rickard saw fit. He reportedly got $2000 for the fight. But Paulino, who had so many managers they were called his 'board of directors', wasn't cheap.

One report said he wanted $35,000. Rickard gave the Spaniard an ultimatum, he lowered his demands, and Tom and Paulino were matched in a 10-round bout on 23 March. The fight was later postponed until 1 April after the New York State Athletic Commission suspended activities at the Garden because Rickard had paid a fighter a bigger percentage of the gate receipts than was allowed.

Jack Dempsey had announced his return to the ring and Rickard wanted his first fight to be in June, possibly against Paulino as long as he got past Tom. Could it be that the outcome was already known? Paulino seemed so sure of winning he was already dictating terms under which he'd fight some of the other contenders. If he won he wanted Dempsey. After Dempsey he hoped to get Jack Delaney and then a title shot.

Tom surprised a sports writer who dropped in to St Nick's when he admitted he hadn't done any boxing that day because he thought he'd done enough. He might give boxing a miss the next day, too. 'After seeing Thomas in action against Charley Anderson a few weeks back we thought that even Tom's best friend would tell him that there was at least SOME room for improvement in his boxing,' admonished the scribe. 'However, if a fellow elects to put away the mitts five days before a fight of such major importance — to Tom — that's his business.' Harvey later revealed Tom had injured his ribs and had to stop boxing a week before the match. On the eve of the bout Paulino was the favourite at odds of 2½ to 1, although there had been a swing towards Tom in the previous few days, put down to compliments from his sparring partners. After a mild workout on the eve of the fight Tom had his usual afternoon tea, a regular item in his training diet.

A crowd of about 15,000 saw Tom dumped on the canvas in the first. 'Paulino got a long start toward the eventual verdict when he scored his clean knockdown in the first round,' wrote one observer. But Tom was up before a count could be started. Later he joked that his brief spell on the floor might have been due to 'too close association with British heavies'. In the second he unleashed a 'dreadful right hander' that gave Paulino a 'stationary convulsion'. The crowd got excited when either boxer did anything well. Bursts of booing, cheering and clapping in the gallery of the Garden near the roof would often erupt and fade so perfectly in unison during a fight it were as if the vast crowd responded on cue.

Paulino smiled at his opponent's punches, except when Tom landed a heavy right to the head that brought up a lump under his eye. Tom's eye was cut in the fourth, and by the fifth both faces looked battered. Paulino was said to have had a great start and a great finish but that from the third to the eighth Tom racked up a points lead 'that seemed insurmountable'. Despite Rickard's bias towards Paulino he went up to the press during the eighth and said: 'You fellers didn't give Heeney the credit he deserves. He's a mighty good fighter. He'll make a lot of money here.' Tom had gone into the fight with an injured rib, and Paulino, who did a lot of blocking with his ribs, emerged from it with a similar complaint. Eight years later Paulino admitted this had been his hardest fight.

One judge and the referee voted for Paulino while the other judge favoured Tom. It was an atrocious decision, lambasted in the newspapers as an April Fool's joke. John Mortimer went over to the press row and complained about a lack of fair play in the judging. He claimed to have been told the fight was in the bag by a journalist three days before. *The Ring* insisted no fight at the Garden could be in the bag because the referee and judges weren't picked until just before the fighters entered the ring, but that Tom won by a round. Grantland Rice thought the worst Tom should've had was a draw.

'That Heeney-ous Decision' was the title of McGeehan's column on the 3rd. It was clear Rickard was letting nothing stand in the way of 'building up' Paulino. If Tom had won he'd have been in line for bouts with Maloney and Sharkey. But Rickard wanted to keep them for lucrative later elimination bouts. He certainly didn't want Tom to make them look bad or eliminate them prematurely. 'He has made this quite plain when he has frightened or bought off all possible opponents,' wrote McGeehan.

Tom didn't complain, and he certainly won the moral victory. He was written up as the best heavyweight from England or its territories since Bob Fitzsimmons. Suddenly, he was interesting. Rickard said he was prepared to use Tom in a semi-final in one of his Yankee Stadium shows in a campaign to develop him as a headliner. Mortimer told Rickard that Tom wanted a return in five weeks, but Paulino saw his victory as a closed issue. He was after bigger names and bigger purses.

The New Zealander's next opponent was Jack DeMave, the 'Hoboken blonde'. He was Dutch by birth but had spent several years fighting around New York. On a late June evening at the Coney Island Stadium in Brooklyn Tom won comprehensively on points, and it seemed the only reason he couldn't score a knockout was because he lacked a decisive punch. 'Heeney hit DeMave with everything but the water bucket and the ring posts,' was one summary. Harvey said the lights nearly blinded Tom and it took him three rounds for his eyes to properly adjust. Tom had improved a lot and the Garden took notice.

Tom was enough of a name to be introduced from the ring at the Dempsey–Sharkey bout in July. Eighty thousand spectators who paid an estimated $1,100,000 saw Sharkey knocked out by Dempsey amid a flurry of what many believed were low punches. Tom's next fight would be marred by fouls as well. He took on Bud Gorman at the Garden with an understanding that if he performed well he'd be in line for a return with Paulino. He didn't get much of chance to perform at all. He won after one minute and 17 seconds of the third round following Gorman's third offence.

Gorman knocked Tom down with a foul blow in the first, after an earlier warning. Explaining how he got knocked down for the second time in his career, Tom said he was punched low so he instinctively dropped his hands but before the referee could do anything Gorman landed a right. He had no chance to get away or duck so he hit the deck. He got up mad and chased Gorman around the ring. But McGeehan suggested Tom had revealed a 'paper temple' and didn't think he would go that far after all. There was no fouling in the second, but in the third Gorman threw a very low punch to the groin that made Tom wince and the referee called a halt. Harvey said doctors confirmed Tom had been hurt by the blow that ended the fight. 'That should settle the matter, as Mr Harvey's word is just as reliable as a Government bond,' wrote one scribe. There were rumours of a set-up; Gorman was 'punished' with a 30-day suspension, which had no effect at all as he was about to sail for Stockholm for his next fight.

Offers started to come in from better-known managers than Harvey. Some suggested that under Harvey Tom would never meet the real champions; that Harvey was out of date. The implication was that he needed to take on a manager who was 'connected'. But Tom was too loyal to abandon Harvey.

Jess McMahon signed Paulino to meet the best heavyweight available in the Garden and said the opponent would be either Sharkey or Tom. Paulino had recently fought Harry Wills and Jack Delaney, while Tom had been sidelined by the top heavyweights. Rickard seemed to be building up the Spaniard at Tom's expense. Paulino only agreed to the return bout with Tom over 15 rounds, as he was the type of fighter to get stronger as the fight went on. Damon Runyon was in McMahon's office while the number of rounds was being thrashed out. When McMahon suggested 10, Paulino's managers 'went into executive session in accents wild, employing the French, Spanish, Italian and English languages, and mixing in many gesticulations. Mr Harvey continued to stand by, saying nothing, but thinking heavily in pure West Side Americanese.' Paulino's board insisted on 15; Harvey wasn't happy. McMahon suggested splitting the difference. Harvey seemed amenable but Paulino's board went into another session before making a telephone call, presumably to the 'old Beezark of the Basque himself'. Fifteen was the final word.

Despite the belief that Tom had won their previous encounter, Paulino was the favourite because of the 15 rounds. Paulino attracted supporters as colourful and enthusiastic as he was, and residents of Little Madrid in uptown New York collected $15,000 with contributions of $25 to $200. Harvey was told he could have any part of the pool if he felt 'sporty'.

There was a crowd of around 13,500, a gate of around $40,000, another tough, action-filled fight and another questionable decision. Paulino swung the first punch, a wild left at Tom's stomach. But Tom landed more blows, cleaner blows, and won the rounds — the kind of things that generally won a match. The crowd was with him from the seventh round to the end. So much for the prediction Paulino would last the best. In the eleventh Tom 'backed across the ring . . . in little jumps. Paulino, of course, followed in order to lay his head on Heeney's chest, and each time he took a step forward Heeney measured him with a left and ripped an uppercut to his lowered head, jolting Paulino's head with each blow. As a result of these blows Paulino's progress was a bobbing advance.' As the gong sounded for the fifteenth they faced each other with a smile and at the end they were still pounding away at one another, Paulino's head on Tom's chest. The crowd's roar was so deafening the bell could hardly be heard. Tom's eye and the bridge of his nose were cut and his 'left side was a raw, red stretch of flesh, practically the only place where Paulino could land a punch'. Paulino's face was very swollen and he seemed unable to control the movement in his lips because of his battered face and mouth.

The fight was declared a draw. Several hats were chucked into the ring as jeering fans showed their dismay. Newspapermen who tried to find out how the votes had been cast were told the Commission had introduced a new rule banning the announcer from making that information public. It was later revealed that one judge favoured Tom, another thought the bout was even, and the referee gave it to the Spaniard. 'It seems that Tom Heeney of New Zealand cannot get a decision over Paulino Uzcudun of Spain, no matter what he does,' wrote one scribe. 'Paulino received a draw after taking one of the most terrific beatings the writer has seen.' Another pointed out it could be April Fool's Day even on 8 September. The eversportsmanlike Tom told his parents the decision was correct and Paulino was 'a hard nut to crack'. 'When I fought Uzcudun, I found another fellow just the same as me,' Tom later said, 'and the two of us walked forward and punched at each other all night . . . All the papers said I was robbed both times and they played this up, which got me far more publicity than if I'd beaten Paulino.'

Rickard didn't see the fight as he was in Chicago but was impressed by the reports. He matched Tom and Jimmy Maloney in a fight that would become part of a new elimination tournament to find a title challenger for Tunney, who had successfully defended his title against Dempsey in the infamous 'long count' fight in Chicago's Soldier Field. He was contracted to promote at least one more fight for Tunney in 1928, for which the champion would be guaranteed at least half a million dollars.

Tom's New York training routine changed with the seasons. In winter he got up around 7.30 a.m., but in summer he rose at four to beat the heat of the sun. Before breakfast he ran and walked through Central Park, past the zoo where the animals lived under dilapidated corrugated-tin roofs and the bars of the wolves' cages looked so rusty they might break apart and where there were lots of discarded candy wrappers from the nickel-candy stands. His route also took him around the reservoir across which could be seen the city's famous skyline. A shower bath and a rubdown followed. Breakfast was a grapefruit or other fruit, followed by chops, eggs and bacon or something similar. At 5.30 p.m. he had dinner with plenty of salad and fruit. 'Two meals a day is enough for anybody, and the three meals is simply habit,' he said. Tom summed up his thoughts on diet as 'I eat everything that I like, and I like everything to eat'. He had smoked in the army but realised he had to give it up to become a good fighter. He liked a good glass of beer when he could get it, too. After breakfast he spent the morning quietly, perhaps taking a stroll. At one o'clock he started two hours' work at St Nick's that included skipping, punchball, ground exercises, shadow-boxing and sparring. Sparring partners weren't cheap at $25 for two, three-minute rounds. Tom had developed more punches and learnt the tricks of the American fight trade. He had his own masseur and ended the afternoon's training with a rubdown and massage. After dinner he liked to go to the cinema or the first part of a show. In summer the theatres were the coolest places to be and in winter they were comfortably heated. He was always in bed at ten every night.

Six months previously Jimmy Maloney was a leading contender for the title but then was knocked out twice. This was the Boston Irishman's last chance to get back in the running. Tom was a 2 to 1 favourite. If he won he could be in line for a winter fight with Dempsey, who was already hinting he might like to tackle Tunney again after some lead-up bouts. Dempsey arrived in the Garden just as Tom and Maloney were clambering up to the platform. He said he could be facing one of them in the winter. The reception he received was one of the greatest ever heard in the arena, filled with some 12,500 boxing fans. Tom said he'd never heard anything like it. Announcer Joe Humphreys began to refer to Dempsey as a fallen idol before being shouted down by the gallery. 'No, no!' they cried. 'He's still a champion to us!' James J. Jeffries climbed through the ropes to greet Dempsey and the noise from the crowd became deafening as they admired the sight of two former heavyweight champions. The uproar lasted for almost five minutes; the fight lasted one minute and 17 seconds.

Tom smashed a right into Maloney's jaw during an exchange near a neutral corner that sent his opponent face-first to the canvas. Maloney was counted out on his knees. The crowd was just settling back to enjoy the fight. At ringside Dempsey turned to friends and pointed to Tom. 'They'll have to come pretty good to lick that guy,' he said. Maloney was helped to his corner. 'It was just luck — he was coming in and I caught him cold,' Tom said. Maloney said he hadn't warmed up. 'I had just broken away from a clinch and was dancing away with both hands down to my sides,' he explained. 'I stumbled as he stepped back and "Pow" Heeney slammed two right-hand punches. The first was enough and I went down to defeat in a bout which I felt confident that I would win.'

Maloney was finished and Tom was a serious contender. His prize was Jack Sharkey with the winner to meet Tunney. Sharkey, a former sailor in the United States Navy from Boston, hadn't fought since losing to Dempsey in the summer. Until then he'd been seen as a leading contender and he had a much more impressive record than Tom, with victories over Harry Wills, George Godfrey, Maloney and McTigue. A couple of days after the bout was confirmed Sharkey's car overturned. His front wheels hit a stone, throwing the vehicle into a nearby fence and tearing out several posts. But he was only slightly injured and there were still six weeks before the fight.

Tom had written home saying he wasn't taken with America and its high cost of living and that he expected to be home for Christmas. He thought he had to earn about three times as much money in the States compared to New Zealand to have the same standard of living — although it was easier to get regular fights. But his fight with Sharkey now meant he'd probably stay put. He wanted to 'put New Zealand on the map', to get enough money to set up his parents and then have plenty left over to go to South Africa and live comfortably.

There were now three boxers who could give Rickard a title fight with an 'international flavour': Tom, Paulino, and Tom's old adversary Phil Scott, who was now plying his trade in America. Rickard said if Scott or Heeney won the right to challenge Tunney he had every intention of holding the title fight in London or Manchester. But the promoter would have to convince the fans that one of the three posed a real threat to Tunney to bring in a big gate like the $1,600,000 he got for Dempsey–Carpentier or the million or so for the Dempsey–Firpo bout. And that didn't seem very likely. The Americans hadn't warmed to Tunney and were looking for another Dempsey. Tom's Irish parentage, his service with the Anzacs, and his boyish looks and manner appealed. He was humble but not too humble. He was friendly and jokey. And he earned respect for the way he took on anyone and didn't grumble about decisions. He'd also acquired a nickname that would stay with him for the rest of his life. In an article in September about the current crop of heavyweights Damon Runyon wrote about 'Paulino, the Beezark of the Basque' and 'Thomas Heeney, Rock of the New Zealand'.

Tom had already signed to fight Johnny Risko in Detroit. The former baker boy nicknamed 'The Cleveland Rubber Man' was a crude, slashing, tearing type of boxer. He was short for a heavyweight and slightly pudgy. He'd given Tunney a hard fight and others had avoided him. Rickard thought of Risko as a 'spoiler' because whenever he was put in with men the promoter was trying to 'build up' he managed to extract whatever glory there was in the fights.

The Risko fight marked the opening of the $125,000 Olympia Stadium at the corner of Grand River Avenue and McGraw Street in Detroit. The most palatial boxing arena to open since the Garden was draped with huge Allied flags, and the 17,000-strong crowd filled the seats, jostled for standing room in the exit and entrance runways and hung from the rafters. They paid a dollar for space among the rafters and a top price of seven dollars for a polished chair close to the ring. A big contingent of New Yorkers motored up for the opening. It was 'a test of strength and enduring powers', wrote Tom's father. Tom 'slugged, slammed and socked his way to a decision', wrote one observer. 'It was a bitterly contested encounter, jammed with slashing action and exciting moments as the pair fought one of the fastest heavyweight battles of recent years,' wrote another. 'Heeney kept marching into Risko from bill to bill, taking all of John's wild fire in the earlier rounds,' Runyon wrote, 'then out-boxing and out-slamming Risko towards the finish. Heeney is a staunch and durable type of fighter and uses his head for something beside a hatrack — a surprising trait in these pugilistic times.'

After winning the opening round, Tom lost the second and third. He struggled through the next few rounds before picking up the lead as Risko weakened. He launched an unrelenting attack with both hands as his opponent sought cover and 'hugged him like a long-lost brother'. In Detroit the referee decided the winner and a mix of cheers and boos erupted when he held up Tom's hairy right arm. Tom said Risko's left hook, 'that curls around your right hand, no matter how you defend', was the most powerful weapon he'd faced. Away from the ring the two men liked each other and Tom found Risko to be 'a nice fellow', a 'friendly sort'.

After the fight a group from a theatrical company invited Tom back to their hotel. 'It was about the funniest experience I've had,' Tom recalled. 'In the American hotels, each bedroom has a bathroom attached.

Practically every male member of the company invited me to his room and then made a bee-line for the bath! Gee, I wondered what I had struck. There was good reason for the invitation, however, for in each bath were numerous bottles of beer surrounded with ice, the weather being extremely hot. It was highly amusing. As soon as I got into one bathroom another member of the company would come and drag me out to see his bathroom, where he had a different brand. All laughed at the Prohibition stunt, for, as they proved to me, it did not mean that liquor could not be obtained.'

It had been illegal to buy a drink in the United States since 1919. The movement to ban alcohol had gathered pace until it triumphed during the Great War and Prohibition followed. Its roots were puritanical but it was later seen as a way of tackling alcohol abuse. Tom soon realised that 'dry' America was actually rather wet. He was now meeting all sorts of people, many of them sportsmen, and travelling to many towns. Wherever he was there was always someone inviting him for a drink. He believed anyone could get as much alcohol as they wanted. There were a huge number of speakeasies — what New Zealanders would've called 'sly grog shops' — in New York and one on the corner of a street in the heart of Manhattan had wide swing doors. Tom was in a speakeasy one time when some policemen walked in, nodded to friends at the counter, enjoyed a drink and left. 'In some exceptional cases,' Tom wrote, 'when one knocks at the door of a "speak-easy" a little wicket is opened, and, unless the visitor is accompanied by someone known to the proprietor, it is hard to gain admission. In the great majority of cases, however, and I speak from actual experience, there is not the slightest trouble in getting into a "speak-easy" and liquor can be procured practically during the whole of the twenty-four hours.'

When Tom was visiting an American at home he was often offered a whisky and then told it had just come off a boat. 'I heard that yarn so many times, that I really began to get a bit suspicious. Still there is no doubt in my mind that a great deal does come off the boats, but what boats they are I cannot say,' he explained. 'My own opinion is that much of the whisky used is made in America. I personally am acquainted with a man who makes whisky every morning and does his selling in the afternoon.' The favourite drink in America at the time was the 'highball', ginger ale and whisky. Tom preferred beer but that was harder to come by so he settled for a highball instead. That was one side effect of Prohibition — it encouraged people to drink stronger alcohol. But Tom also saw the very dark side of Prohibition, where the cheaper alcohol sold to workers was a dangerous and vile mixture. Different 'brands' were priced differently even if they'd all come from the same still. Liqueurs, too, could carry the most expensive continental labels and turn out to be fake.

Tom earned around $27,000 from the Risko fight and through careful selection of opponents Harvey had manoeuvred him into increasingly lucrative matches. There was much jockeying for position as the next title fight loomed. Delaney was signed to meet the winner of the Sharkey–Heeney fight in early December. Paulino signed for a bout at the Garden against Risko, and one report had it that if he won *he* would be matched with the winner of the Sharkey–Heeney fight and the survivor of that match would probably meet Dempsey battling for the chance to meet Tunney.

Going ahead with the Risko fight was well, risky, for Tom. If he'd lost, his match with Sharkey might well have been cancelled. And it was the fights at the Garden for Rickard that really mattered in the race to the challenger's corner. A less scrupulous pugilist might have 'taken the run-out powder' as the boys would say. Tom had remained true to the promise he made in New Zealand that he'd 'play the game' and always put up a straight fight wherever he was. Unfortunately for Tom, not all the top heavyweights in New York held such lofty ideals.

A Ring of Gold in Filth and Slime

Tom's next opponent boasted: 'If I don't knock that guy's block off, my name ain't Sharkey.' It wasn't. It was Joseph Paul Zukauskas. Born to Lithuanian parents, his ring name was a combination of those of his boxing idols Jack Dempsey and Tom Sharkey. Sharkey usually had a lot to say and most of the talk involved him punching someone's head into someone's lap in the gallery. 'Dempsey? Why, that's the bum I'm going to fight. I'll knock him flatter than a Victrola record. He's just a big, overrated paluka,' he said before meeting the former champion. 'I'll probably jab that Dempsey's head off.' That's why he was known as the 'The Talkative Tar', 'The Garrulous Gob', 'The Lisping Lith', the 'I man'. But James J. Johnston had recently been taken on to handle Sharkey's publicity for 10 per cent of his ring earnings — and Johnston told Sharkey that he'd do the talking from now on. 'Jack is through with the blood and thunder stuff,' Sharkey's manager Johnny Buckley explained. 'They ragged him so much in New York before and after the Maloney and Dempsey fights that he now is through with the wordy noises. From now on he is Silent Jack Sharkey.'

Paul Gallico asked Jimmy Johnston to remove the muzzle from his fighter as it made better copy. 'I like to hear Sharkey gab because he has humour and is alert and alive, and not like nine-tenths of our rising young pugilists who are too thick to say more than "Pleestameetcha," and "Howarya." Let the boy talk, Jimmy because if you don't he will develop a psychosis or a phobia or something and will have to be psychoanalysed or something even worse.'

Sharkey was matched with Tom but something wasn't right. In December 1927 a cartoon appeared in a New York newspaper that featured three men. On the left was Tom in his boxing gloves and boots, wrapped up in a large robe. 'The floors are too bloomin' 'ard — I'll have none of it!' he was saying. Next to him stood Harvey, clutching a towel and saying, 'Beastly dangerous y'know Thomas ole dear!'. On the right was a man in a suit and hat behind a stand marked 'The Well Known Business' with bags of money on top of it. 'Have at it gents — do have at it!!' he was calling to Tom and Harvey. His arm pointed to a poster. Under the title 'Golden Swan' was a picture of a man diving. The story was that Sharkey was trying to get Tom to throw the fight.

On Monday 14 November Sharkey called off the fight, blaming an incomplete transverse fracture of the small finger of his left hand suffered during sparring. But it was suspected the real reason for the postponement was pitiful advance sales. Rickard was usually concerned when a fighter postponed a bout, but didn't seem too worried this time. Harvey was bitterly disappointed. McMahon suggested Tom fight former light heavyweight champion Jack Delaney or Knute Hansen. 'We'll fight nobody until we fight Sharkey,' insisted Harvey.

The Massachusetts State Boxing Commission had Sharkey examined and informed its New York counterpart it couldn't substantiate the fighter's claim of a fractured bone in his left hand. There was a very slight swelling and Sharkey complained of pain, that was all. The New York commission ordered Sharkey to appear before it. After an examination it approved Sharkey's injured finger. 'We find clear evidence of a recent injury to the region of the proximal end of the fifth metacarpal bone,' the Commission's doctors said. 'This condition renders him physically unfit to engage in a contest at this time.' It would be three or four weeks before Sharkey could put on the gloves. A new date of 13 January was set for the Sharkey–Heeney fight.

It was rumoured that Rickard wanted to keep Sharkey back while the eliminations ran their course and then bring him out as an opponent for Tunney now that it looked like Dempsey was definitely retired. Rickard strenuously denied that the bout with Tom would be cancelled but a source in Boston close to Sharkey's manager claimed the boxer still had problems with his hands, especially the left, and that he would probably ask for another postponement due to his weak hands. But after another examination of his finger in New York the troublesome digit was pronounced to be in such good condition he was 'almost certain' to be able to meet Tom on the 13th. He was to start training straight away using a specially constructed finger guard.

Still the rumour mill churned. Maybe Sharkey *was* really injured but it wasn't his finger that was the problem. Perhaps he was still troubled by Dempsey's smashing low blows. He hadn't fought since being knocked out by Dempsey the previous summer, after which he was said to have suffered internal injuries. Gallico wasn't convinced. He thought it was just a story fuelled by awful tales of Sharkey's supposed injuries and pictures of him — albeit looking rather dapper — in a hospital wheelchair. 'I saw Jack Dempsey dig both his gloves into Tunney's tum as violently as he ever laid into Sharkey's midriff and I don't see Tunney being wheeled around. No, there's something else in the wind.' Gallico thought Sharkey's team was trying to pay Tom to take a dive.

> If I were inclined to be cynical, which I am not, having implicit faith in the boxing game and all those who operate it today, I would suggest that the honesty of Messrs Heeney and Harvey might be one of the major stumbling blocks in the path of this bout. Heeney and Harvey simply won't do business and this makes it very difficult to arrange the contest so that it will be conducted properly. You might think the two honest fellows refuse to negotiate, but that is relatively unimportant. The mere fact that a fighter will not do business is enough to make him most unpopular in these parts.
>
> You see, the fighters who do business so vastly outnumber those who merely fight that if you do not belong to the fraternity your chances of getting any worthwhile shots are pretty slim. Thus, doing business is a particularly apt phrase. I hope that Tommy and Charlie never get drawn into it, but I also wonder how they are going to eat when the dough gives out.

'Honest Tom', lauded for his modesty and 'good ring manners', had paired up with a man regularly praised for his fairness and good character. 'I don't think Charlie Harvey ever phenagled with a fight in his life,' wrote Gallico. Harvey was 'one of the few members of the profession known to be completely honest', wrote Westbrook Pegler. 'A man who is even partially honest is a rarity in the profession so Mr Harvey being absolutely honest is a sort of fetish. Gentlemen who wish to defend the prizefight industry against sweeping denunciations, invariably say, "Well, anyway, Charlie Harvey is honest."' Unfortunately, wrote Pegler, 'being honest has made a marked man of Mr Harvey and for several years he has been doing rather poorly in business'.

Big fights were usually shrouded in conspiracy theory. Reliable and not so reliable sources often tipped off reporters that a match was sewn up. Far more fights were rumoured to be faked than was actually the case. It did happen but the problem was proving it. Any number of things might have been arranged, from a sympathetic referee to an agreement that one fighter would take a dive, also known as 'the Barney' or 'going into the tank'. In a heavyweight championship match a fighter could 'protect' himself in the ring with a secret contract guaranteeing him part of the new champion's future earnings or an agreement could be reached that one fighter would take a dive this time and the other the next. Racketeers could be found among prizefighters, managers and boxing commissioners.

In 1920s New York, prizefighting was legal and respectable. Long gone were the days of fights in grubby back rooms of saloons amid shootouts and crowds of brawling thugs. But never before had prizefighting been surrounded by so much money. The cash-rich era of prizefighting coincided with the era of Prohibition and the liquor racketeer and the prizefight racketeer were natural bedfellows. 'So vast was this felonious network, consecrated to procuring us a snort, that it became a government within a government with its own territories, rulers of same, kangaroo courts, laws, and executioners,' wrote Gallico. 'These lords of the underworld had the power of purchase and the power of terrorism. Prizefighting and prohibition gangsters gravitated toward one another like "H_2" to "O".' Charles J. McGuirk wrote in *New McClure's*: 'The fight game is like a great, rich, ring of gold embedded in a morass of filth and slime; or like a brave gallant ship whose bottom is so cluttered with barnacles that she fails to obey her helm and finds herself on the reefs of oblivion.'

Stories reached Manhattan from Boston that Sharkey had only been doing very light training. He was supposed to be sparring, after which he would be examined again, and if he was fit he would fight Tom as planned. The medical was Rickard's suggestion as he was fretting about ticket sales. Fans were losing interest in the heavyweights and since the second Dempsey–Tunney fight several high-profile heavyweight bouts had brought in lower gate receipts than Rickard hoped. A year previously even second-rate heavyweights were drawing in the region of $75,000. But now fights in lighter divisions were proving more successful.

Sharkey was ordered by the New York State Athletic Commission to attend the medical examination. But he failed to show. The Commission received a telegram from Buckley saying his fighter had been summoned as a witness in a civil suit concerning an automobile accident and that he would leave for New York as soon as his testimony was completed. The Commission accepted the excuse and told Sharkey he would be examined as soon as he arrived. Sharkey was being indulged, presumably because of the influence of James J. Johnston, who was seen as an invisible member of the Commission.

Throughout all the uncertainty Tom had been training hard in New York, perhaps too hard, and was getting stale. Harvey suggested the conflicting reports were a ploy to discourage Tom from taking his training seriously, so he'd been making his fighter train hard every day. Bernard Mortimer was back on the scene: he'd arrived from Southampton before the postponement and decided to stay on. He made it known that he had the last word on Tom, telling Rickard that if Tom beat Sharkey and didn't get either Dempsey or Tunney he might take his man away for a while to England or New Zealand until conditions were more favourable for a big 'shot' in America. Tom was keen to go home to see his mother. Mortimer also talked of a possible Heeney–Dempsey battle in London and assured Rickard he could get a million-dollar gate at Wembley. Phil Scott, too, was now eager to fight Tom for £1000 a side in London or New York. Annoyed by what he saw as disparaging remarks Tom made about British heavyweights, he said he'd put up half the money himself. But Tom had loftier aspirations. 'If we win,' Bernard Mortimer said, 'we shall make a bid for Tunney, if we lose we shall start all over again.'

Unbeknown to Mortimer or any of the contenders, Gene Tunney asked Rickard for two fights in 1928, one against Dempsey, the other

Tom entertains French Senegalese soldiers.

On holiday in England before the Tunney fight.

Tom Heeney cables as follows~

"It is a privilege to inform you that I am very much pleased with the Whippet Sedan which I purchased from you and which was recently delivered to me in Fairhaven. Of course I am taking the Whippet back to New Zealand with me and I am sure that I will get a lot of pleasure out of driving this remarkable car."

POWER, SPEED, AGILITY, AND ENDURANCE

THE Whippet offers you all the qualities of Sportsmanship. POWER...it runs like a "four" but pulls like a "Six." SPEED...tuned to 55 miles per hour consistently and continuously. AGILITY...from 5 to 35 miles acceleration in 13 seconds. ENDURANCE...no hill is too stern a test, no country too hard a trial for the WHIPPET. It is built to last and perform lasting achievements.

If YOU want a car with POWER, SPEED, AGILITY, AND ENDURANCE choose a Whippet

On behalf of all Whippet Owners in New Zealand the Canadian Knight & Whippet Motor Co., offer their best wishes to Tom Heeney in his forthcoming fight with Gene Tunney.

THE CANADIAN KNIGHT AND WHIPPET MOTOR CO., Corner WAKEFIELD AND TARANAKI STREETS, WELLINGTON. And COOK STREET, AUCKLAND.

Advertisement in the *Poverty Bay Herald*, July 1928.

The training camp, Fair Haven, 23 July 1928. Behind Tom's left shoulder are sparring partners Jimmy Lawless and Jimmy Braddock. Second from right is sparing partner Ed Crozier, who stands between Phil Mercurio and Charlie Harvey. Charlie's brother Eddie is third from the left, between Jim Hennessey and John Mortmer.

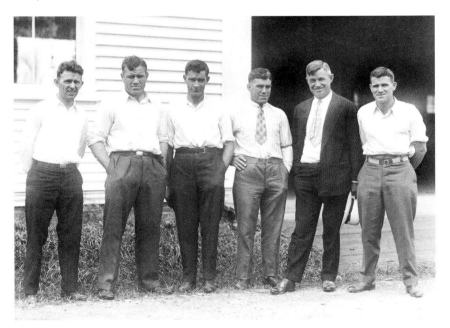

The Heeney brothers at Fair Haven. Left to right: trainer Jim Hennessey, Tom, Pat, Jack, American humourist Will Rogers, Arthur.

Taking a break from the training grind.

The 'bleacherites' queue for $3 tickets outside the Yankee Stadium, 26 July 1928.

An 'exceptionally nervous' Tom weighs in for the Tunney fight, 26 July 1928.

The neutral corner before the fight.

Tom lands a left to Tunney's jaw in Round Two.

Saved by the bell in Round Ten.

Tom and Marior. Inset: The newlyweds at Luna Park, Coney Island, August 1928.

Gisborne welcomes Tom, September 1928.

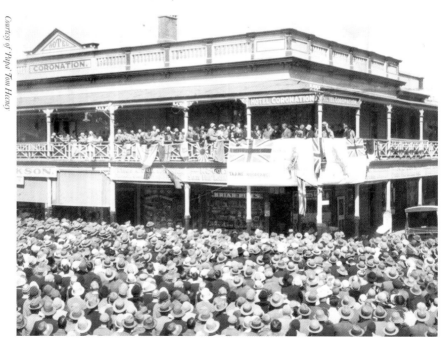

The balcony of the Coronation Hotel, Gisborne, September 1928.

against the winner of the elimination tournament, the favourite being Sharkey. However, Rickard wanted Tunney to fight only once in 1928. He desperately hoped Dempsey would come back, but if not he would pick a title challenger from Sharkey, Tom, Delaney and Risko. It was clear Sharkey was the one being readied for a shot at the title.

Sharkey finally arrived in New York late on 11 January. He went to the Bretton Hall hotel on Broadway, where he assured boxing writers he wasn't going to run out on Tom. He'd seen Tom in his first fight in New York and didn't think he was good enough to cause talk of a run-out. He walked 45 blocks from his hotel to his examination the next day. Two Commission physicians, Dr William H. Walker and Dr Joseph S. Baldwin, stripped him to the waist and drummed on his body and put his left hand through a series of tests. 'Jack Sharkey is in very excellent condition, the best of his career,' they pronounced. 'There is no functional defect in the fingers, wrist or elbow of his left arm. There is absolutely no outward evidence remaining to indicate that he suffered lasting harm in his fight with Jack Dempsey.'

So Sharkey would have full use of his best weapon, his left hand, and he shouldn't be unduly troubled by Tom's midsection jolts. But there were stories that he'd trained badly. He loved New York and he loved to show off in front of a crowd, so why had he flouted the wishes of Rickard and the Commission by staying in Boston? 'I never will train in New York again,' was Sharkey's explanation. 'Too many persons have quoted me wrongly in the past. I don't say that was done wilfully, but it was an injustice to me. I have been made out by some misquotations to be an ignorant lout, with no knowledge of grammar. Such words as "ain't" and "mug" I never use. I trust I know enough to talk like a gentleman. As long as I refuse to talk, though, there is not much chance of my being misquoted, though I notice in one morning newspaper that I have been made to use a lot of rough language.'

Sharkey hated not being quoted like a gentleman and Tom hated dressing up like one. Hearing there was a plan to photograph him in evening dress and a monocle, he hid for two days. 'I couldn't stand for anything like that,' he said. 'If such a picture ever got back home I never would be able to face the gang.' But the day before the fight a photo appeared of Tom in the *New York American* in his 'Londonese regalia'. He was pictured in evening dress with parted and slicked hair, doffing his high hat with one hand and holding a cane and gloves in the other. The headline over a remark about Tom being more at home in fighting trunks ran "Ow Do You Like Me an' Me 'Igh 'At".

Sharkey was a 3 to 1 favourite. Gallico assessed Tom as 'a strong, willing fellow with a short, stocky body and very short arms. He has a fairly strong chin and when slammed on the button acts the way nine-tenths of our heavyweights do. He falls to the floor and squirms, but arises whenever possible.' But he picked Sharkey to win. He thought he'd improved since his fight with Dempsey when he 'disported himself like a royal ninny' and 'boxed as though he had checked his brains in Boston'. Grantland Rice wrote that Sharkey 'will have to be near his best to rumple up the cool and game Australian, who is no picnic for any one'.

Close to 17,000 people paid $160,000 to see the fight. The ringside was adorned with women in fashionable evening gowns and men in dinner jackets. There were leading political figures, as well as light heavyweight champion Tommy Loughran and Benny Leonard who retired undefeated as the world's lightweight champion. Sharkey came in shortly before ten o'clock wearing a flowing blue silk robe with the yellow insignia of the Navy embroidered on the back. His black hair was neatly slicked down and his face wore its usual scowl. Tom followed seconds later looking nervous. He had a dark blue silk robe and tousled brown hair. Sharkey was 194 lb, Tom 193. When they were introduced Sharkey was cheered and booed, but Tom, the underdog, got an 'unadulterated roar'. Tom once said he never went into the ring with a plan. 'You never know what the other fellow is going to do, so why bother worrying about it in advance?'

The first few rounds were tough but uninspiring. Tom provided the only glimpses of 'spectacular thudding', wrote Gallico, when he 'crashed a couple of right handers onto Sharkey's bland countenance early in the fracas, sending the sailor skittering into the ropes'. Looking stale, Sharkey only got home a couple of swinging rights in the early rounds on the back of Tom's neck and on the side of his face. 'Did Sharkey hurt you with that uppercut in the second round?' Tom was later asked. 'What uppercut?' he replied. Sharkey changed tactics and went for Tom's body at close quarters. He hit Tom with body blows that made him grunt. Tom drove the action in the third and fourth rounds, winning points and pleasing the crowd. The referee failed to penalise Sharkey for holding.

Tom later claimed his opponent used more holds in the clinches than wrestler 'Strangler' Lewis.

In the fifth 'Thomas provided the lone thrill of the fight when he balled Sharkey with a long right hander to the whiskers that would have been good for three bases in any regulation park,' wrote Gallico. 'However, the short right field ropes kept Sharkey from falling down and his head cleared quickly. He went on to win that round by stabbing Heeney's seamed and hemstitched pan with sharp lefts.' From the sixth onwards the fight was 'just a weird spectacle which offered proof positive that neither man is anything approximating a formidable opponent for Tunney, and that Tex Rickard's plans to fight Gene twice this summer are all shot to pieces,' wrote Jack Farrell of the New York *Daily News*. Sharkey failed to show championship skills and Tom just proved he could take a lot of hard hits.

Sharkey misjudged a powerful right swing in the tenth that missed Tom's jaw and propelled him onto the floor. Tom laughed, the crowd joined in, and Sharkey leapt back onto his feet in embarrassment before leaning over Tom's shoulder and winking at his handlers. 'During one round he peered up at the standing of the teams in the hockey league. He spent another round reading the sign that bore the program for this week's fights at the Garden. He looked up to see that all the lights over the ring were in perfect working order. It would have astonished nobody if he had run downstairs to bank the furnace or start the electric washing machine,' wrote one observer. Sharkey already had a lot of money and seemed as if he was so tired of boxing not even the idea of becoming champion was enough to make him perform. The society types also looked bored, while the crowd in general failed to warm to Sharkey's attempts to show off and the boys from the East and West Sides raucously encouraged Tom to 'knock the nonchalant bored expression' from Sharkey's face.

As the fight drew to a close Tom moved in with rights and lefts to the head and body. 'Heeney was like a stone wall,' Sharkey later recalled. 'You hit one of these guys flush on the lug and he keeps coming at you and you say to yourself, "How do I get out of this ring, where's the exit, the hell with trying to knock him out, I'm just busting my hands." Heeney could take a punch.'

The fight was declared a draw. One judge voted for Sharkey, one for a draw, and the referee gave Tom the verdict. The crowd was split. Those in the upper tiers generally thought Tom won and the ringside observers favoured Sharkey. But it was a disappointing fight and the crowd's jeers were quickly drowned out by jazz music from the amplifiers suspended from the ceiling. Gallico thought Sharkey won but didn't get the decision because the judges and the referee were determined to show Jimmy Johnston wasn't influencing them. McGeehan wondered 'whether or not Mr Johnston's 10 per cent did not accomplish more during the fight than the 90 per cent which was controlled by other interests. Perhaps if Mr Johnston had been a majority stockholder Sharkey, or Cukoschay, might have won by a k.o.' Jack Kofoed thought Sharkey would have won if he hadn't acted like a stubborn schoolboy, refusing to listen to his corner, boxing in spurts and missing badly in his attempts to land a knockout.

After the fight Tom said: 'I thought I won, but I guess I didn't. I was very much disappointed in my showing, and I can do much better. I guess the boys were right when they said I was stale from too much gym work. I was away below form and did not show my best.' Sharkey broke his vow of silence to give a brief comment in his dressing room: 'I thought I won the fight but the judges thought different. Heeney never hurt me once, and I was never in trouble.' He blamed his performance on his injured hand. Before leaving for Boston he said, 'I was away off. I looked like a bum.'

It was the outcome Rickard feared. Tom and Sharkey had effectively eliminated each other. He was 'terribly disappointed' at the lacklustre fight and more convinced than ever that Dempsey was the only drawing card against Tunney. 'After all the trouble I have taken to build Sharkey up, his bout with Heeney last night merely reduced his standing to that of Heeney, Uzcudun, Delaney and Risko. You can toss them all into one group of about the same rating. I must do something drastic with them if a title contender is to rise from that bunch. Fifteen-round, "do-or-die" matches are the only solution.'

Tunney was determined to have two fights. Had Sharkey knocked out Tom, he'd be a credible challenger and Dempsey could take the second bout. Rickard now needed to persuade Tunney to take just one fight. 'Of course, Mr Rickard is anxious to have another elimination or two, which will leave Dempsey the one and only logical contender, but the heavyweight champion has his own ideas about these proceedings. He has figured that he might as well do a little eliminating himself, for one bout at least, and gather in the elimination purse,' Bill McGeehan wrote. It was later confirmed Rickard had signed Tunney to defend his title against either Dempsey or the winner of the elimination tournament in June.

Rickard's eliminations — or 'e-lemon-ations' — were farcical. Most of the contenders had been eliminated more than once. Dempsey lost twice to Tunney. Sharkey was eliminated by Dempsey and eliminated himself against Tom. Tom lost to Paulino and eliminated himself against Sharkey. Delaney was eliminated by Maloney and Risko. Risko was eliminated several times. Paulino was eliminated by Delaney and Tom and he would soon eliminate himself when he agreed to a match in Mexico City. 'Many of these challengers seem to think the public is lucky just to look at them clinch and jab for a mere $100,000,' wrote Grantland Rice.

Brooklyn promoter Humbert Fugazy condemned the heavyweight elimination contests. 'I have come to the conclusion that true fans and friends of boxing share my disgust with the present practice of handpicking contenders for the heavyweight championship through a series of elimination tournaments that are arranged with one eye on the box office and the other peeled for the possibility of the wrong entrant slipping into the challenging position,' he wrote. He labelled the previous year's tourney a 'fistic farce' and the present elimination matches a 'burlesque on boxing' that would probably end with Tunney meeting Dempsey again even though Dempsey would have no part in the elimination bouts. He proposed to 'break the monopolistic hold on the heavyweight situation, a grip which permits an individual to dictate to the champion and to name the contenders whether or not these named deserve the distinction on past performances or promise for the future'. He was organising his own heavyweight matches and claimed Dempsey was finished and was only being used for his crowd-pulling power.

The only challenger not to have lost ground was Tom, but the fight crowds weren't really interested. He was still being given fights to build up his opponents rather than to groom him for a title shot. Even so, he was now earning huge sums of money. Against Sharkey he'd earned just over $25,000. Tom wrote home that he had put his earnings into government bonds. He was a valuable commodity and his numerous managers began arguing over money. At one point Bernard Mortimer announced a split with Harvey and threatened to take Tom back to England.

There would now be a final 'tournament of five' consisting of Tom, Sharkey, Delaney, Risko and Dempsey — if he came back. Negotiations started for a match between Tom and Delaney for 1 March and between Sharkey and Risko for 12 March. The winners would fight and the victor would meet Dempsey or Tunney. French-Canadian Delaney, whose real name was Ovila Chapdelaine, had had a glittering career as a light heavyweight with an open, classic style of boxing. When the gong sounded to end a round he had a habit of walking at once to his corner with his right arm raised. Delaney was the type of boxer that drew crowds. He was a 'killer' like Dempsey. But when he relinquished his light heavyweight crown to try for the heavyweight title things didn't go so well. He promptly lost a decision to Maloney and won on a foul from Paulino.

'These heavyweight prima donnas give me a headache,' fumed Rickard as he grabbed his amber-topped walking stick and green fedora and left the Garden to travel to Miami. 'I've talked and talked until I talked my head off, but it was of no use. There will be no Heeney–Delaney match unless Heeney's managers and assistant managers decide to take something less than the roof off the building.' He said he'd name Tunney's opponent from Miami and if Tom didn't want to fight his way into a title match he would name Sharkey.

Tom's stock had shot up after the Sharkey match and Bernard Mortimer thought Tom was entitled to the lion's share of the purse. There seemed to be no way of resolving the financial aspects of this fight. But Tom's real problem wasn't the money. What could he gain from this fight? He had beaten Maloney who had beaten Delaney. He also didn't seem happy about having to fight 15 rounds. On one of his frequent trips from the conference chamber to get iced water Harvey admitted to a reporter he didn't want the fight. 'But we may have to take it if we cannot get anything else and they will give us enough money.' Delaney's manager Joe Jacobs said, 'We will take it if we get what we want.' It was a stalemate, so an exasperated Rickard left for Miami where he would spend several weeks, socialising and doing business with Tunney. While Rickard was still on the train, newly appointed vice-president and assistant general manager of the Madison Square Garden Corporation, John McAfee Chapman, somehow managed to persuade Tom to take the Delaney fight. The terms were not divulged.

As the other contenders fought with each other inside and outside the ring, the 'will he/won't he' saga of Dempsey's return raged on. Rumours circulated that the former champion had retired from the ring for good due to eye trouble. Rickard asked Dempsey whether he'd be ready to fight in June in case all the others eliminated themselves, and Dempsey said not to count on him. There was a suspicion that Dempsey's apparent retirement was announced merely to fuel publicity for a Dempsey–Tunney match in September. If he came back Dempsey would fight a preliminary bout in which he would get the biggest share; together with a match with Tunney he would earn close to a million. 'You probably will be reading that Dempsey's eyesight has been restored to normal or at least that it is keen enough for him to see the chance of a million dollars more,' wrote McGeehan. Runyon looked ahead to the latest instalment in 'the longest elimination contest the world has ever known . . . Of course it is all by way of killing time while Jack Dempsey is back in his dressing room making important changes, such as changing his mind, and it is a harmless pastime, with no danger of anyone being permanently injured.'

Delaney finished training for his fight with Tom in private at Bridgeport, flouting, like Sharkey, the rule that main eventers had to train for at least seven days in the city of the fight. Tom trained for a while in Atlantic City and then returned to St Nick's. To relax he went to the movies every night, and if he liked the picture he'd watch it twice. He was cut over his left eye sparring but wasn't worried. He was asked whether he would carry the fight to Delaney. 'Well I guess I can't expect Delaney to carry it to me,' he smiled. 'He has never been the aggressor.'

'Take a little swig, Jack. Best cure in the world for fatigue,' Tom told reporter Jack Farrell as he passed over a bottle. Tom was sure he'd become stale through overtraining for the Sharkey fight and because he refused Harvey's advice to drink his regular portion of ale. He was so anxious to perform well he took his training too seriously. Now he was back drinking his half-pint, which he thought would stop him losing his edge. After his final workout Tom lay on the rubbing board grunting and talking. He said he saw in the papers that his sparring partners were finding his chin an easy target for right-hand shots.

'Well, Tom, isn't it a fact that Phil Mercurio put over some good rights on you this afternoon?' asked a reporter.

Mercurio was sitting in a corner waiting for his turn on the rubbing board.

'Sure, he hit me with some rights. And I want to tell you that Phil is quite some boy. I think his right hand is as fast as Delaney's. I don't count it anything disgraceful to have been hit by a right hand thrown up by my young friend.'

Mercurio stood up and bowed.

'You no doubt noticed that when Mercurio nailed me with his right he was stepping in. When he was stepping back, if you watched closely, you saw that he did not reach me with his right. Now, unless I have Delaney figured all wrong he is not going to come to me as Mercurio does. Delaney likes to lay back and counter, from what I have seen of him, so you can leave out of your calculations the way my young friend Mercurio finds my chin with his right hand. And what if Delaney does nail me with his right? I have been hit on the chin before by good fighters who are bigger than Delaney and I have managed to survive.'

It was the longest speech Tom had given.

The usual rumours of the fight being 'in the bag' surfaced. Rickard clearly hoped Delaney would win and Paul Gallico wrote: 'What I figure is this: Charles and Tom are a couple of square, honest guys, OK, on the level and on the up and up. That makes the chances a thousand to one that they ever get up to a shot at the heavyweight title.'

The fight was a sellout. People queued all day at the box-office windows of the Garden with tickets priced from $5.50 to $22. Delaney had been a consistent 7 to 5 favourite, but support for Tom increased and just before the bell it was about even. The preliminaries all ended in knockouts and were over by 9.20 p.m. Delaney arrived late. Tom was ready when he was told to go to the ring, but after Harvey found out Delaney wasn't he told Tom to stay put. The fans were restless and half a dozen brawls broke out. Finally, Tom came down the aisle in a faded blue silk robe. Behind him were the Harvey brothers. Charlie had been laid up for three weeks after falling and breaking his collarbone so he left the corner work to brother Eddie and trainer Jimmy Hennessey. Delaney followed. Tom sat gloomily in his corner while Delaney smiled and waved at people he recognised. Observers noticed the contrast between the handsome, smiling Delaney and the hirsute, grim Tom.

Announcer Joe Humphreys jokingly introduced 'the Adonis of the Ring' while pointing at Tom. Tom weighed 198 lb, Delaney 178¼ lb. The boxers took off their robes and Tom revealed purple and blue shorts while Delaney wore red and black. The referee wiped some grease off Tom's face. At the bell Tom rushed out of his corner and Delaney was forced to sidestep and dance around. And that was pretty much how the fight continued. Tom kept boring in, preventing Delaney from attacking. He was plodding and slow. Delaney shot out a powerful left hook — his once famous 'haymaker' — several times but Tom just laughed, shook off the blows and bored right back in. Delaney clinched to foil Tom's attacks. The fight seemed to consist of a repeated sequence: Tom attacking with heavy blows to the body and head that were partially countered by Delaney with left and right hooks to the chin, and then a clinch. Delaney's objective seemed to be to keep away from Tom — or when he couldn't, to hug him. 'Stop holding, Delaney. Come on and fight,' shouted the mob.

Delaney held so much that after the fight the Commission introduced a rule that fighters who held too much and ignored referee's orders to break would have points deducted. Fighters had been getting too much money for too little fighting. 'One of the worst exhibitions of this unwelcome condition I ever witnessed was the recent Heeney–Delaney bout,' Commissioner William Muldoon said, 'in which the holding of Delaney was shameful. Twice in that battle Heeney sought to shake himself free from clinches, and even went so far as to lift Delaney clear of the ring floor on two occasions, yet he was unsuccessful.'

In the tenth Delaney complained he'd been hit low but it seemed like an act. Delaney's seconds tried to stir up their man, who unleashed a few resounding left hooks to Tom's face. His followers whooped. But it didn't last. In the fourteenth he came out with his mouthpiece askew and Tom punched him hard around the stomach. They wrestled, the crowd booed, they exchanged more blows and clinched. Tom got the decision. It was greeted by a mingling of boos and cheers. Most thought Tom won because he overwhelmed Delaney. Few ring critics disagreed. But did either deserve the purse? Officially both fighters got $41,244.20, 25 per cent of a net gate of $164,925.80. But it was thought Tom really got 32½ per cent and Delaney 27½ per cent. If that was true, Tom got well over $53,000 and Delaney earned close to $45,000. Tom shook hands with Delaney, smiled and padded quietly to his corner. The police roughly cleared a passage for him, water dripping off his chest, through the crowd.

Both fighters believed they'd won but Tom admitted it 'must have been a lousy fight to watch. Delaney is overrated. I would rather fight him a million times than Paulino once. The fight was not near so hard for me as the Sharkey fight. I was much stronger tonight at 198 pounds. I was too fine for Sharkey.' Gallico thought they both lost. 'Both men eliminated themselves as thoroughly as any two of Tex Rickard's trained elephants ever did.' Tom 'throws himself into the pugilistic breeching like a staunch old horse pulling through sand, and he hauled himself home to victory last night largely by a steady grind', wrote Runyon. Another writer, perhaps annoyed that Tom upset his prediction Delaney would win, described the New Zealander as a 'squat, corrugated-ribbed granite-jawed, super-courageous slugger, who could not hit a barn door if it happened to be swinging'.

Tom and Delaney were really bad. How could either one of this pair trouble Tunney? Even worse, the fight had killed off interest in the Risko–Sharkey match. Another Heeney–Sharkey fight wouldn't make sense. Rickard described all the contenders as 'terrible'. If Sharkey and Risko fared no better it was thought a June title fight would be abandoned and Dempsey would fight in September.

Rickard thought he might use Tom in a fight in England because the Delaney bout was the first New York fight in years that had attracted huge interest in Europe. Tom still hadn't convinced the New York State Athletic Commission that he deserved a shot, however. Muldoon and fellow commissioner James J. Farley thought Sharkey had beaten Tom and the worst Delaney should have received was a draw. Their opinion was at odds with the overwhelming majority of scribes and spectators. Commentators cried foul: Tom should be the leading contender and it seemed there was a bias towards Sharkey.

Meanwhile, Dempsey announced he was definitely through with the ring. 'This time I mean what I say,' he declared. It looked as if he really was serious. The great box-office attraction wasn't coming back. 'It is quite apparent now that the peak of the cauliflower industry has been passed and that you never again will see anything even remotely approaching the customers and the gate receipts mustered for the Battle of the Slightly Less Than Three Millions at Chicago,' wrote McGeehan, who thought it would be at least five years before there'd be a marked upturn in gates.

Tom had a ringside seat as Risko beat Sharkey on a split decision. As Rickard feared, the fight turned out to be a 'dull and dreary affair' and he walked out before it had finished. Sharkey had entered the ring a 16 to 5 favourite. After the fight Risko said: 'He said to me, "get 'em up you bum"; and I said, "you're the bum, you bum."' Broadway agreed with both of them: they were a pair of bums. The gate and attendance were about half what they had been for the Heeney–Delaney fight. The fans had made clear their displeasure. Rickard was eliminating his customers as well as his fighters. Just one million-dollar gate in 1928 was now optimistic.

The Commission broke a promise to Harvey that Tom would become the number one contender if Risko beat Sharkey, presumably because of Jimmy Johnston's influence. Rickard and Muldoon decided a Heeney–Risko match was the best way forward. But Tom had already beaten Risko. 'So Rickard and Muldoon want Risko and Heeney do they?' Harvey said. 'Well, Heeney wants Tunney.' Harvey was adamant that if there was anyone left between Tom and Tunney who hadn't been eliminated it was only Dempsey. But Garden matchmaker Jess McMahon was indignant. 'Heeney only drew with Sharkey, and Risko defeated Sharkey. Risko has beaten Jack Delaney, Paulino Uzcudun and Jack Sharkey, three men who are listed among the best in the division. If Harvey wants to compare records, Risko has a better one than Heeney. The records show that Heeney lost and drew with Paulino. Risko beat the Basque decisively. Harvey is changing his tune. He wouldn't fight Jack Delaney until I signed an agreement to match the winner with the winner of the Sharkey–Risko fight. Now, he's trying to back out of it.'

The title shot continued to elude Tom and neither Rickard nor the Commission wanted him in the ring with Tunney. But there was one very influential person on Tom's side: the champion himself. Tunney considered Tom to be his next logical opponent and the winner of the tournament. He'd done everything Rickard had asked of him. Tunney probably didn't want to fight the boorish, rough Risko again. But he had other concerns. The contenders might keep eliminating each other until there was no one left to fight.

Rickard travelled to Florida to talk to Tunney. It was thought he'd tell the champion there'd be no defence on 14 June as originally planned; that he wouldn't get his $500,000 guarantee if he insisted on fighting Tom; that a Tunney–Heeney fight wouldn't be popular; that he should wait until a better challenger turned up — at least until September when there was still an outside chance Dempsey would change his mind. It would go against the Commission's edict that a champion must defend his title every six months, but as punishment the Commission might 'revoke his licence to carry a cane for a period of sixty days' wrote McGeehan.

'Mortification Has Set In' ran the title of McGeehan's column in the *New York Herald Tribune* on 14 March. 'At the current writing it looks as though the plodding Thomas Heeney is about the best of a very bad lot of contenders. Even that is going a little strong. It might be more expressive to say that Thomas is the least fromagenous, with Johnny Risko, the Bouncing Bohemian Baker's Boy, the runner-up.' The gloom at the Garden was thick and Rickard wallowed alone in his sorrow in his private office. 'Somehow it seems to me that if Heeney did not happen to be one of those "foreigners" the ballyhoo might be on for him. But the cauliflower ears, being at least 100 per cent American, never wiggle with enthusiasm for an invader.'

The Path to Logical Contendership

'Pick me! Pick me! I deserve it!' cried the contenders. Each had a manager pleading his case to Rickard. Tom won the elimination tournament. Risko had a better record than Tom. Sharkey would draw the biggest gate and was the best boxer. Delaney could be another Dempsey. The prize was — at the very least — as much money in one night as the boxing greats of the previous generation had made in a lifetime. The scramble to find a challenger for the world's heavyweight crown was nearing its climax. Yet Tom went back to Britain for a month-long holiday, largely because of a yearning for some decent beer. Damon Runyon wrote that *Daily Mail* cartoonist Tom Webster had invited Tom to join him as a drinking buddy. Runyon imagined a scene with Tom looking at the message from Webster and persuading Charlie Harvey to let him go.

> 'Hi must go,' 'e said. 'Mr Webster is one of the greatest men to drink hale with that Hi know, so excuse me to Mr Tunney, and tell 'im Hi'll return.'
> 'It's real old musty ale he speak of, I suppose?' inquired Mr Harvey.
> 'Hit h s,' replied Thomas Heeney.
> 'Well, by Jiminy Jupiter Christmas, Thomas, my boy, for two pins I'd go with you myself!' said Mr Harvey.

On Friday 23 March 1928 the White Star liner *Olympic* landed at Southampton with Tom on board. A rather romantic portrayal of the scene was that he'd left the same port less than a year and a half earlier without a penny or an overcoat and returned with £15,000 cash in his pocket. The thought of her boy shivering in a northern hemisphere winter upset his mother. 'Tom never went without an overcoat in his life,' she said. 'If he needed one, or wanted money for anything, he knew just where to get it.' Paul Gallico later asked Tom about the story. '. . . 'ow did that story git around,' was how he recalled Tom's reply. 'I 'ad me 'ole bloomin' trunk full o' coats.' Overcoat or not, Tom left England as a little-known boxer unable to make a decent living out of the sport. He returned a rich and pampered celebrity and the man likely to challenge Tunney for the world's heavyweight championship. Awaiting him were newspapermen, photographers, crowds of fans and piles of telegrams. The questions began even before he'd disembarked. Was he likely to meet Tunney and might the fight take place in England?

'In spite of all the talk about Sharkey and Risko, you can take it from me', Tom said, 'that I will be Tunney's next opponent. I am not in a position to divulge details yet, but it is practically settled that I am to fight him in June or July. Where? Either in New York or at Wembley. My manager, Mr Bernard Mortimer, is in close touch with the Wembley authorities, and the results of his enquiries as to finance, taxation, etc., will be cabled to Rickard.'

John Mortimer intervened. 'There is only one bar to the Wembley project. Can the British public be induced to pay sufficient money to make the match a paying proposition? Tunney's price is $800,000 and Heeney, of course, would want some sort of guarantee.'

And what did Tom think about his chances against Tunney?

'Well, everybody laughed when they matched me with Maloney, but I knocked him out in 77 seconds. People said it was a shame when they sent me against Delaney, but I licked him, too. So why shouldn't I whip Tunney? I can say this. Nothing would please me better than to represent the Old Country in a world's title fight, and, fit and well, I guarantee I'd not disgrace myself. Naturally, I would prefer to fight in London — it was there that I first began making a name for myself. But I would have no fear about boxing on the other side, because I know I'd get a square deal.'

'But did you not get badly treated when they only gave you a draw with Paulino?' interrupted a reporter.

'Well, yes, I suppose the decision was a bit questionable, but the crowd showed what they thought about it in no uncertain fashion. I must say that American crowds, as I've found them, are most fair.'

What did he think about Phil Scott's manager protesting his man had beaten Tom twice and couldn't be ignored? He'd met Scott in New York, Tom said, and admired his grit in trying to get back into Rickard's favour after a disastrous start. But he didn't see Scott getting ahead of him. And if he ever fought Scott again it would be on *his* terms. He talked of his small share of the purse last time they fought. 'I'm afraid it will be a long time before we fight again.'

The Tom on the deck of the *Olympic* seemed different to the old Tom. To New Yorkers he was a novelty alongside the suave Dempseys and Tunneys and the boastful Sharkeys. But to the English he had been 'bitten by the bug of loquacity', possibly in an attempt to outboast Phil Scott. 'Now, with every possible sentiment of affection for Tom Heeney, we are sadly unable to distinguish between these sentiments of joyful association with London and the stereotyped effusions of other visitors, such as cinema stars, concert artists, actresses, acrobats, jockeys, and other public performers,' wrote one scribe.

When he fought in Britain Tom was a New Zealander, but now he was in line for a title bout he was British, someone to pull the country out of a decade-long pugilistic rut. Tom's success had regenerated interest in the sport throughout the Empire, and for the first time in 30 years — since Fitzsimmons beat Corbett — a Briton was said to be fighting for the biggest prize in boxing. 'Seven wealthy towns contend for Homer dead, Through which the living Homer begged his bread,' Thomas Seward once wrote. It was the same with Tom, wrote John Kieran of the *New York Times* who thought there was far too much switching of nationality and local allegiance in victory and defeat. 'Two years ago [Tom] was practically a man without a country, the Lieutenant Philip Nolan [protagonist of E.E. Hales' short story *The Man Without a Country*] of the prize ring. Born in Ireland and raised in New Zealand, he sank so low that he was fighting for "bread-and-butter stakes" against mediocre heavyweights in England, and not too brilliantly, either. Irish fight fans referred to him as "that New Zealander". New Zealand sent the blame back to Ireland, collect.' Now that had all changed. 'Tom is riding the crest of popularity. He's a British hope, an Irish warrior, a New Zealand product and an Australian representative. The British Colonial Empire may break up in the bitter battle over the claiming of the credit for bringing Tom Heeney up to fame.'

Meanwhile, Rickard talked to Tunney in Miami. A title defence was planned for July and Rickard would pick the opponent. 'Every contender so far has had his chance and it seems to me that any further talk of elimination is idle,' Tunney said. Both Rickard and Tunney now accepted that Dempsey really had retired and that without him the plan of one fight in June and one later on had to be abandoned.

The 'Solons of Swatland', otherwise known as the New York State Athletic Commission, ordered Tunney to select an opponent from Sharkey, Risko and Tom. If he refused he faced indefinite suspension. The Commission and Tunney had a frosty relationship as the result of previous disputes. Tunney's licence had expired in August and the only way the Commission could punish him was to place him on the ineligible list. McGeehan said that by harassing Tunney the 'KKK' ('Komical Kauliflower Kommission') had 'unconsciously' ('One says unconsciously advisedly, because the normal condition of the three members of the KKK is unconscious or semi-conscious, at best') drummed up some ballyhoo for Rickard. Tunney told the Commission Rickard was choosing his opponent.

When Tunney failed to give the Commission a name Harvey made for Humbert Fugazy's office. He was sure Rickard intended to ignore Tom so he courted the rival promoter. 'Rickard is not the only promoter in the world,' Harvey said. 'He claims I am obliged to match Heeney with Johnny Risko. What for? Heeney has defeated Risko. Rickard talks about our agreement . . . Suppose Sharkey had knocked out Risko? Would Rickard have given Heeney another thought? No, you bet he wouldn't. Well, I'm in the golden chair now, and I intend to sit tight. I may hear some big news from England any day now. Bernard Mortimer, my partner, is negotiating with an English syndicate, and we may have a world's championship fight in London before the summer is over. Rickard doesn't control the whole world, he'll find.'

Nevertheless, Rickard insisted Tom fight Risko again. Fight Risko or

Risko would meet Tunney. But Harvey was adamant. 'As long as there is a Chinaman's chance for Heeney to get a direct shot at Tunney I will work for that goal,' he vowed. Harvey planned to go to Miami to meet with Rickard and Tunney. McGeehan wrote that the depression in the cauliflower industry was now a 'near-panic'. 'With a few more of these eliminations, Mr Rickard himself would be eliminated and with him the few remaining customers.' Grantland Rice ran a letter in his column suggesting a strange conspiracy:

> Dear Sir: This heavyweight scramble has been written in a strange k-ey. Pipe the following:
>
> Tunn-EY.
> Shark-EY.
> Delan-EY.
> Heen-EY.
> Godfr-EY.
> Demps-EY.
> What's the idea?

The Commission thought Tunney was spending too much time with the 'idle rich'. He must pick one or all of Sharkey, Tom or Risko. If he didn't fancy one of the 'big three' he could pick one or all of the 'little four': Paulino, Delaney, Scott or George Godfrey. He could even name his own challenger; they just wanted him to fight. McGeehan noted that at the meeting of the 'KKK', when it was decided Tunney should agree on one of the 'seven illogical contenders', it was also decided Dempsey would not be allowed to fight Tunney, even though Dempsey had knocked out the man on top of the Commission's list, Sharkey. Risko had beaten Sharkey and Tom had beaten Risko. 'On the face of it Heeney ought to be No. 1 in anybody's list of contenders, but the Comical Cauliflower Commissioners cut their paper dolls from right to left instead of from left to right.'

Grantland Rice analysed the records of the contenders and uncovered 'the most complete tangle in ring history'.

> You will find Paulino with a knockout against Scott.
> You will find Scott with a twenty-round decision over Heeney.
> You will find Heeney with a decision over Risko.

You will find Paulino with a decision and a draw against Heeney.
You will find Risko with a decision over Paulino, Heeney [sic] and Sharkey.
You will find Sharkey with a decision over Godfrey, Godfrey with a decision over Paulino and Risko with a decision over Sharkey.

Tom had fought a total of 62 rounds with the leading contenders and he'd barely been hurt. He didn't hurt his opponents much either, but he'd remained unbeaten. He was ranked on a par with Risko, who he had beaten by a shade but who had beaten Delaney, Paulino and Sharkey more decisively. Rickard wasn't rushing to pick Risko, however, because he still saw him as a spoiler.

Harvey went to Miami Beach to try to talk Tunney and Rickard into naming Tom as the challenger. Tunney repeatedly said he favoured Tom's style of fighting as it provided the best artistic contrast to his own. 'It is rather flattering to Thomas to call his style a style at all,' wrote Westbrook Pegler. 'It is like speaking of the trotting style of a brewery steed or the literary style of a "Post no bills" sign. Thomas is a thick-built blacksmith with the equivalent of a full beard of sorrel whiskers on the calves of his solid legs and a chin like the corner stone of a State prison.'

On 31 March, a day after Tunney and Rickard denied seeing Harvey, Rickard announced Tom would fight the champion in July. But it was Tunney who picked Tom, with Rickard's reluctant approval. 'Heeney, in my opinion, is the winner of the tournament to pick the contender for the heavyweight crown,' Tunney said. 'Heeney has done everything Tex Rickard asked. He has displaced every opponent, including Risko, Sharkey, and Delaney.' Harvey and Rickard were photographed in Miami signing papers for the battle.

'I am rather pleased that Thomas Heeney, the old Rock of Down Under, gets the championship bout with Mr Gene Tunney,' wrote Damon Runyon, 'though I will never be able to understand how Mr Tunney reconciled himself to the difference in their social positions.' Tom liked to drink with the boys in the back room, swore, and had little regard for how he dressed or for conventionality.

'At last the walrus mustache gets a break,' wrote Gallico, who thought Tom was the best of a bad lot and the most deserving. It was true that Rickard's eliminations didn't include men like Godfrey, Hansen and Roberto Roberti, but Tom was the best of the fighters who showed in the

Garden. 'The Australian has never made a bad fight in this country, has never let up upon his endeavours to please, and has never once stalled or faked, or behaved in the traditional manner of the American pugilist.' He picked Tunney to win the decision in 15 rounds.

'Through this march into the challenger's corner the Anzac was the triumph of mediocrity, hooked to deep earnestness, rare courage and iron-shod durability . . . He kept coming on, wave after wave, and this wading in was the factor that finally left him the survivor named to take Jack Dempsey's old nook,' wrote Grantland Rice. He thought Tom had an advantage over Tunney because he'd fought nine times in the last year, while the champion had only fought twice in the last two and a half years; but he'd have to develop a wallop.

McGeehan believed Tom had 'plodded his way to the logical contendership in a convincing fashion'. Paulino's victory and the draw with Sharkey were 'Madison Square Garden' decisions, the appetite for a third Dempsey–Tunney fight overstated. 'Patience and earnest endeavour never availed much in the cauliflower industry until the arrival of Tom Heeney on our shores. The customers have become convinced that at least Thomas has been trying, which is more than the Cukoschays [Sharkeys] and Chapdelaines [Delaneys] have done.' McGeehan predicted Tunney would win decisively.

'It ought to be a real fight,' said Dempsey. 'A combination boxer and hitter like Sharkey probably would be better — the Sharkey who fought me, I mean — but Heeney will make the champ step. Rickard didn't make any mistake in naming him.'

Sharkey claimed Tunney picked the softest opponent. Johnny Risko's manager turned up at the Garden saying Rickard had given him a verbal contract for Risko to fight Tom. Stories wafted along 'the street where there's a broken heart for every electric bulb'; one rumour was that Tom only got the shot because he underbid Risko, offering to take 10 per cent of the gross receipts.

'GREAT NEWS' blazoned the *Gisborne Times* headline. Tom had accumulated $125,000 and expected to make at least $300,000 more from the Tunney fight. He was now earning as much as a great lawyer or film star. The late Sir James Carroll's wife, Heni, wrote that Tom was battling for the glory of New Zealand. 'To Sir James Carroll, as all New Zealand knows, New Zealand was before all things. And so with Tom. That I know. For do not his letters home, do not his interviews with people in England and South Africa and the United States, all show that he is proud to be a New Zealander born and bred?' She wrote that Tom had not forgotten Sir James' words when he left Gisborne. 'His courage, his strength, his determination, have brought honour to us and to our land.'

'All I have to say is that Tunney'll know he's been in a fight,' said Tom in a Paris restaurant. He'd travelled to France with Bernard Mortimer after receiving an invitation the previous day to attend a charity event. But it hadn't been a very relaxing holiday. 'They talk about the rush and bustle of America,' he remarked, 'but since I have been in London it has been nothing but rush and bustle.'

Mortimer thought his fighter far too modest. 'Why, my man will knock Tunney's block off.'

Tom squirmed.

'How do you feel about being chosen ahead of all the other contenders?' the reporter asked Tom.

'Why, I'd fight the whole lot of American heavyweights over again if I had to to get a fight with Tunney.'

Tom didn't take to Paris. In a characteristically short letter he wrote: 'Dear Mother, — I am spending a few days in Paris. Can't say I think much of the place, and will be glad to get back to London. Well there's no more news, so cheerio. — Tom.' There was a story that an American friend hankered after some bananas and cream in a Paris café but didn't know how to ask for it in French, so Tom suggested *he* try. He placed the order with the waiter who said, 'Oui, oui' and disappeared smiling. Ten minutes later a pair of boiled eggs were brought to the table. One night Tom had trouble dressing for dinner. He put on the first hard-boiled shirt (a dress shirt with a stiff front) he'd ever worn. It was several sizes too small and tore halfway down the back. 'This is worse than fighting Tunney,' Tom joked. 'Give me back the old buttoned up front.'

Tom's only exercise was walking and swimming. 'I like this better than road work in the Bois de Bologne,' he said as he stepped out of the perfumed waters of the fashionable Lido swimming pool on the Champs Elysées and headed for the lockers.

'Superb, magnifique, quelle physique!' shouted a group of admiring Parisian girls.

'Swimming is my favourite,' Tom went on. 'I believe it is the best preparation for intensive training. I weigh 208 now and can easily get down to 196 whenever I want to.'

When the cameras were on he pretended to work hard. He was photographed working with a medicine ball with two French Senegalese soldiers at the Joinville military camp. In a film clip Tom, 'whose rise to fistic fame is a real romance of the ring', was captured in a vest and trousers skipping rope and throwing a ball in a yard.

Rickard had 'officially' promised Tunney 37½ per cent and Tom 12½ per cent of the gate. But he'd actually guaranteed Tunney $525,000 and Tom $100,000, something approaching US$1,000,000 dollars in today's money or NZ$1,300,000. Under Commission rules guarantees weren't allowed, but after the fight the Commission claimed it had given Rickard permission when he explained the match couldn't be made otherwise.

The bookmakers of Broadway made Tom a 3 to 1 underdog. Johnny Firrone, 'the big bet and book man of West 47th Street', had $30,000 to wager against $10,000 that Tunney would win. He picked the odds to be 5 to 1 in Tunney's favour by fight night, so he would be able to bet $7000 against $35,000 on Tom and make money whichever way the verdict went.

Rickard had yet to pick a venue. A syndicate of London men headed by Bernard Mortimer was bidding for the fight and Rickard acted as if he was taking the prospect of a fight at Wembley seriously: 'I am now waiting for final word from London and if their terms are agreeable I shall take the fight over there.' Harvey cabled John Mortimer at Southampton and said Rickard was keen to stage the fight in London; it was a question of money. Rickard liked to go to new territory every time he staged a big fight. But no one on either side of the Atlantic really took the idea seriously. High taxes would eat into the profits and the weather was unpredictable. The talk was that the bout would probably be held on 26 July at the Yankee Stadium.

'By ginger goodness,' Harvey said, 'I feel sure the Tunney–Heeney fight in New York in July will draw at least $1,500,000 and that Tom has an even chance to defeat the champion.' Tom also said he had a 50–50 chance. Signing of final articles for the fight would be postponed until Tom returned. Bernard Mortimer had cabled Eddie Harvey to say his fighter would be back in New York on 18 April. But Tom stayed on in England to give an exhibition bout at Harry Preston's annual tournament at The Dome. For several years the councillor, sportsman and philanthropist had promoted a boxing tournament in aid of the Royal Sussex and other hospitals. Carpentier and Dempsey had both appeared at The Dome, the concert hall in Brighton that used to be stables attached to the palace of George IV. Tom sparred with the tall, ex-amateur world heavyweight champion Captain Ernest Chandler. The general talk was that he was a better and faster fighter than when he last appeared in England, but Bernard Mortimer said Americans didn't realise what rugby had done for his speed.

Harvey cabled Tom ordering him to return on the first available liner; Rickard wanted him back immediately. Tom was booked to sail on the *Leviathan* on 24 April. 'Heeney has come to be the mystery man to British fight fans during his short vacation here,' wrote one correspondent. 'He spends much of his time walking in the outskirts of the city, sightseeing. Tom is leading a simple life and is seldom seen in the cafés and other haunts of boxing followers.' Tom didn't like the bitter and damp April weather in London and always having to carry a greatcoat. Worst of all, there was no sun. It was cold in New York, but it was a kind of cold he could cope with.

Tom met New Zealand High Commissioner Sir James Parr and the two were photographed shaking hands on the roof of New Zealand House in the Strand. He'd been invited to a reception at the Waldorf-Astoria in New York, which Tunney and Dempsey were to attend. As he couldn't make it back in time he cabled: 'Sorry the next heavyweight champion will be unable to be present at Gene's party. Tell him for me he's a great champion and a credit to the game.'

There was one last function in England, a farewell luncheon on board the *Leviathan* in his honour. The commander of the 'floating palace' chaired the event, at which there were almost a hundred guests. Tom made a short speech in which he expressed thanks for the kindness and encouragement he'd received in England even when he was an unknown. He hoped to return as champion and could be counted upon to do his very best. The Mortimer brothers said Tom was the greatest British heavyweight since Fitzsimmons.

On the deck of the giant liner Tom played around with a medicine ball

THE PATH TO LOGICAL CONTENDERSHIP

and a shuffleboard disc for the cameras. Trevor Wignall asked him what he'd do if he won the title. 'That's not easy to answer, but if I have a chance I'll go to Africa for a few months for some big game shooting. That's the sport that appeals to me.' Finally, after plenty of back-slapping and shouts of 'good luck', Tom was on his way back to New York. Bernard Mortimer wrote a letter to his parents:

Dear Mr and Mrs Heeney,

You will no doubt be surprised to get a letter from me, but I thought that, as Tom is leaving today on his great adventure to meet Tunney for the World's Championship, possibly a few lines would be acceptable. In the first place, my dear Mrs Heeney, I can assure you that in not one of Tom's fights has he had any injury to speak of, and I am confident that Tunney will not be able to hurt him. Tom is made of wrought iron. His want of real success in England was due to the fact that he had an enormous tape worm, and we did not discover it until he was about to leave for America twelve months ago last Christmas. After receiving attention he was entirely different, and I date his rise from then.

I know he is very backward in writing, as during his stay in America and while I was at home he never wrote to me, and I am always on to him to write home, but his thoughts are often with you, and, win or lose this match he is coming home to New Zealand with either my brother John or me. Perhaps, in the event of his winning, you both would like to visit America, and Tom could meet you at San Francisco. You would have a good, comfortable time on the ship, and I know Tom will send all the necessary funds for you both to travel in the greatest comfort.

I am sending you some photos which were taken on the ship today, and even as his photos show you can take it that Tom is still a great big schoolboy, and all the success that has come his way has not altered him in the slightest, as he is just the same as he was when he came from New Zealand to join me.

I hope I shall see you along with Tom, and that he will then be Champion of the World.

The send-off yesterday from England was the greatest

demonstration that has ever been accorded an athlete, and Tom knows that he has behind him the whole support and sympathy of the British Empire.

With kindest regards to you all,

I am,
Yours very sincerely,
Bernard Mortimer

P.S. — My younger brother John has gone back to America with Tom to be with him during his training for this contest, and I leave England at the end of June to join them, and we have every confidence in Tom winning.

Tom kept to his cabin during the trip. John Mortimer talked to the famous American actress Peggy Joyce on board who told him: 'Tell your man I want him to whip that Tunney because of the terrible things he said about actresses.' Mortimer replied 'if Tunney said anything about actresses his education had been indeed neglected'. Tom dressed for dinner in a tuxedo, but when he turned up on deck for a golf tournament he wore an old training sweater, crumpled old trousers and shoes with worn heels. A 'big blonde' in the barber's shop tried to persuade him to have a manicure but he didn't think he could face the boys in New York with polished fingernails.

Tom arrived in the United States after a 'jolly good holiday' and Harvey was there to meet him. Wearing a 'nobby pearly-grey fedora and trim blue suit' Tom emerged self-consciously from the ship. Atlantic City was his preferred location for training, he said. Rickard knew that fighters attracted more publicity if they moved out of New York to a seaside or country resort. 'Makes no difference to me where I train,' Tom said, 'but I prefer to work indoors. You see, I'm inclined to be a little muscle bound around the shoulders, and I'm not going to take any chances working outdoors for so important a fight. The slightest chill may make all the difference in the world in my showing against Tunney.' What did he think of Tunney lecturing on Shakespeare at Yale while he was away? Tom said he had no interest in Shakespeare and that a fighter should fight instead of taking up literature. The only thing he knew about the Bard was that he was dead.

Tom arrived back just in time to see Sharkey knock out Delaney in

73 seconds. Rumours abounded that the fight was fixed. The word was that Sharkey's team hoped to make a last desperate attempt to replace Tom with their man. Racketeers in New York, Chicago, Detroit, Philadelphia and other towns bet on Sharkey to win by a knockout. Sure enough, 'Delaney took a poke on the teeth and went to the floor grovelling and growling like a young father playing bear with a cooing child,' Pegler wrote. 'Sharkey raved and wept along the ropes, lurching like a stock actress doing Camille.' One racketeer moaned he couldn't even trust people in the racket any more. He said he'd been given a tip that Delaney was going to take Sharkey and then they were going to sidetrack Tom and put Delaney in with Tunney. He bet heavily on the wrong man. He later heard Delaney didn't even train for the fight.

Mortimer worried Rickard might yet replace Tom as the challenger, as articles for the fight hadn't been signed. 'The contract signed by Rickard and Harvey at Miami Beach isn't worth the paper it is written on if Rickard suddenly discovers he made a mistake in selecting Heeney to fight Tunney and decides to run in Sharkey in his place,' he said. 'You see if Harvey had posted a forfeit at the time of signing we would be protected; but he didn't. Rickard had to post a substantial amount of money to protect Tunney against unforeseen events and Tunney had to do likewise to protect Rickard. Everybody is protected but us. I'll feel more secure when some forfeits are up.'

'Calm, Sir Mortimer, Calm,' Paul Gallico called his column on 9 May. 'Certainly it is the weirdest binder that any challenger ever had, because it doesn't seem to mean anything,' he wrote. 'According to Sir Gorblimey Mortimer, all Rickard has to do is stroll into the gymnasium while Heeney is working, place his thumb and forefingers to his nostrils and say, "O, O, you're just terrible!" and the contract may be abrogated, and Takesus may substitute some one he considers more fitting — let us say One Round Sharkey.' But Gallico thought the Commission knew 'plenty about the Sharkey–Delaney affair' and wouldn't approve. Suspicion that a Sharkey–Tunney fight might be fixed would also keep the fans away and Rickard would make less money.

Mortimer needn't have worried. Sharkey's team decided not to draw attention to the suspicious win over Delaney. Sharkey stopped trying to displace Tom. The Commission investigated the affair. Delaney quietly took a sabbatical from the ring. As for Tom, he had little to say about the farcical fight. 'It was too short for me to have an opinion.'

Heeneyville, Formerly Gisborne

In a small movie theatre in a village nestled in the southern range of the Adirondacks sat Gene Tunney. The flickering black-and-white images showed Tom in the ring with Sharkey and Delaney. 'He certainly is strong and he has plenty of power in those shoulders,' Tunney said to Bill McGeehan afterwards. 'It seems strange that he is not a knocker out or what you call a killer. I am satisfied now that he is the best heavyweight of the contenders. I would have preferred Dempsey, of course, first for the money part of it, naturally, and second for the personal satisfaction I would have received in that third meeting, which would have been for fifteen rounds. I tried to make it Dempsey. But I was convinced that there was no chance. Heeney is good, very good, but I do not think that either Sharkey or Delaney fought him intelligently. This may sound bombastic, but it is my opinion for what it is worth.' He noticed Tom often hit just under his opponent's heart and he would work out a defence against those punches.

At the village of Speculator, where his war buddy Bill Osborne ran a mountain training resort, the champion could roam the banks of Lake Pleasant on the Sacandaga Trail amid picturesque nooks and dells and the occasional deer or other wild animal. It was cool and dry and the coming of summer drew mosquitoes, black flies and bumblebees, and bullfrogs that sang in the evening. He jogged over the hilly Adirondack trails until he got up to 12 miles. He hit the bag, wrestled, skipped and shadow-boxed. While training for his first fight with Dempsey he'd read Samuel Butler's *The Way of All Flesh*. For the second Dempsey fight he trained on Somerset Maugham's *Of Human Bondage*. For this bout he would train on Thoreau. He'd had to suspend his training for several days after he 'was attacked in the left heel by a malignant pebble' wrote McGeehan. While his stone bruise healed, Tunney studied his opponent on screen.

Tunney looked better than when he trained for the Dempsey rematch and had no bulging waistline to hone. 'I do not hold Heeney lightly,' he said. 'Every champion who refused to take his opponents seriously from the time of Sullivan down was disagreeably surprised at some time or other. I have no intention whatever of letting the title slip to Great Britain.' It seemed the champion was taking his preparation more seriously than the challenger. Tom had returned from England podgy, weighing 211 pounds and hoping to get down to about 195 or 196. And he hadn't even arrived at his training camp.

While he waited for Harvey to organise a training camp Tom ran around the reservoir in Central Park. He worked out at St Nick's, where he was happiest and would have willingly stayed. 'It was good enough for me when I started and it's good enough now.' Tom was a man about town. He attended amateur boxing bouts and dinners and was the star attraction in a restaurant famed for its illustrious customers and the best-cooked food in New York. He sat with Harvey at a front table at Billy La Hiff's Tavern in the roaring forties a couple of blocks from the Garden. It was a good place to eat before going to prizefights or hockey matches and attracted boxers and their managers and hangers-on, actors, artists, politicians, chorus girls, radio announcers, agents, lawyers and writers. Everyone stopped to observe the bashful New Zealander. Tom ate his corned beef and cabbage between the steady flow of obligatory handshakes. He sipped the iced water he'd got so used to in restaurants he missed it back in England. When Damon Runyon saw Tom in Billy La Hiff's 'performing his daily callisthenics with a huge English mutton chop' he thought the New Zealander had assumed a continental air. He looked more spruced up and wore a newfangled English tab collar.

New York teemed with famous people, but Tom wasn't a typical celebrity.

He had a strange accent, was uncultured and unsophisticated. He liked city life, parties and socialising, but he didn't enjoy fame. 'None of that show business for me,' he told one writer. 'Just between ourselves I'm afraid of all the pretty girls.' He wouldn't spend his time at country clubs either. What would he do if he won the title then? 'That will be the easiest job I ever had,' Tom answered. 'I've got a lot of friends and I know where I can get some good ale — none of that ale you buy around here, but good ale.'

'But will you be doing right by the title?'

'Haw, haw, haw.'

The *New Yorker* described how it annoyed Tom that he couldn't find good tea in New York and had to drink coffee; how he came from a place he pronounced 'Gisbin', which he claimed was superior to New York and even had better tailors; how he was proud that at 80 his mother could still do a full day's milking; how he preferred to talk about his family than Tunney; how one of his sisters had 'possibly twenty children'. He sat for a portrait intending to send it to his mother if it turned out well. 'It did,' reported the magazine. 'It depicts him as an amiable, ungainly fellow with blond and slightly curly hair and — perhaps his most salient feature — deep-set and brightly blue eyes.' Tom never wore shoes, preferring high boots whatever the weather. He liked to shop, especially for shirts — 'in which he has a nice taste,' reported the *New Yorker* — and usually chose light solid colours. But Tom's clothes quickly became rumpled 'because of the play of his muscular bulk within them'. There was a story that after a dinner party 'he loitered with the gentlemen, sitting quietly in a chair but somehow or other managing to get his clothes to looking the way they do. When, after half an hour, the gentlemen joined the ladies, his hostess, who had never been clear in her mind anyway as to just what Mr Heeney did, cried, "Why, Mr Heeney, you've been wrestling again!"'

Much was made about the contrast between the Shakespeare-loving Tunney and the New Zealander who professed to only having read six books in his life. His favourite was the life of Ned Kelly, the notorious Australian bushranger. Tunney had given his talk at Yale, while Tom got a chance to address a highbrow audience when he was invited to a function by the Phi Sigma Kappa fraternity and urged to give a speech.

'I'm not much of a talker,' he said, 'and whatever I have to say I shall leave to Mortimer.'

John Mortimer got up.

'If Tom has anything to say, consider it said,' he replied.

A few days later at the Manhattan College gymnasium it was Tom's turn to speak after Mortimer and Harvey. He got up, said there was nothing more for him to say, and sat down.

Tom played golf at the Crestmont Country Club in West Orange where he attracted quite a crowd. He'd only recently got into the sport, but he'd picked it up easily and was hooked. When Tom played golf he wore street clothes not plus fours. 'I play in whatever pants I happen to have on,' he said. 'I spot the other fellows in their plus fours and beat them.' Tom and Mortimer were guests of club member Samuel A. Archibald of Upper Montclair. They planned to search for training sites in the afternoon but it got too late. After the golf Tom spotted two boys shooting marbles and joined in. Tom and a 'Mrs Heeney', according to the *Newark Evening News*, spent the weekend with Archibald and his wife, old friends of Tom's. On Sunday morning Tom got lost after church. He decided to hike home even though he didn't know the area very well but he made it back.

Harvey and Mortimer eventually found Tom a training camp at the Rumson Farm Kennels in Fair Haven. Tom and his group had been given several cottages on the estate. The New Zealander was to start intensive training on or about 1 June. This was pushed on to 7 June and that deadline passed too. When Tom was introduced from the ring at the McTigue–Emanuel fight Grantland Rice thought he 'looked almost as round as two barrels'.

Tom had spent much of his time since his return to New York sitting, wrote Bill McGeehan. 'This, they tell me, is one of Mr Heeney's favourite exercises.' He thought Tom must either be very confident of his ability or he didn't care what happened to him on 26 July. Then the columnist found out Tom's chief trade was plumbing not blacksmithing as widely reported. 'It may be that Thomas acquired this habit of sitting while he was a plumber. They say that plumbers, on reporting to the job, immediately place themselves in a chair and sit with infinite patience waiting for the arrival of their tools.'

> When Mr Heeney does depart for Fair Haven, the problem will be to keep him out of the various chairs in that resort. At first Mr Rickard proposed that all the chairs in the camp be removed. But

the Mortimer Brothers, Limited, of Portsmouth, England, who know Tom's peculiarities, said: 'It would do no blooming good. It would only make the beggar sit on the stoop, where everybody could see that 'e was sitting.'

Mr Charles Harvey, the American representative, who has an inventive turn of mind, was seen in a hardware store the other day purchasing a quantity of tacks. 'It is an old idea, of course,' said Mr Harvey, 'but it might work.' As you may have surmised, Mr Harvey had planned to place tacks with the points upward in all the chairs at Fair Haven.

But I understand that this was given up for fear that some innocent bysitter might be injured during the training period. A large phonograph is being installed in the training camp with only one record, 'God Save the King.' The managers were making an appeal to patriotism. But they were dubious as to its efficiency. One of the Mortimer brothers was heard to remark: 'Tom will stand just so long, then 'e will sit, no matter what you play.' As Mr Heeney instinctively is a polite person, it was suggested that ladies be encouraged to visit the camp during the day and occupy all the available chairs. ''E never would go so far as to take a chair from under a lady,' said one of the Mortimer brothers. 'But I do not think that 'e would get up to give his seat to a lady — at any rate, not while 'e was in training.'

But the English and American representatives of Mr Heeney declare that they are not worried. There is only one danger — that Tom may over-sit during the training period, and get himself into such a sedentary state that he might forget to get off the stool when the bell rings. But that is unlikely.

It was because of this peculiarity of Mr Heeney's that the managers flouted the suggestion that Thomas train at Atlantic City. They feared that once he got into one of those wheelchairs on the Boardwalk there would be great difficulty in extricating him from it. In fact, they would not even let Tom visit that resort for fear that he would elect to spend the rest of his life being wheeled back and forth. This, they figured, would be Mr Heeney's idea of heaven.

On Monday 11 June Tom and Harvey motored to Raymond Hoagland Jr's estate on the Jersey coast. A ring had been erected in an old barn that once accommodated the country's finest coach and driving horses. Opposite the barn an outdoor ring had been put up in a two-acre clover field. Tom could work inside during the week and outside at the weekends when the crowds got too big. Admission would be 50 cents during the week and $1 on Saturdays and Sundays. Behind the barn lived 140 yapping prize hunting dogs. Hoagland raised English setters and pointers, pigeons and chickens, and his prize-winning white-and-lemon pointer Dapple Joe became 'the almost constant companion of the Australian boxer' wrote Frank E. Davies in the *American Kennel Club Gazette*. Tom lived in a house about 200 yards from the barn, and his entourage of trainers and sparring partners stayed in a cottage adjoining the barn, which also housed a press room with telephones and telegraph wires.

Fair Haven resembled an English village transplanted into a sizzling New Jersey summer. Roses twisted around whitewashed cottages in front of wide green lawns and people played croquet. The training camp smelled of horses and leather. Tom fitted the picture of an old English boxer and 'would need only a pair of long pants with a sash at the waist and sideburns to make him look like a woodcut of some of the old London bruisers', wrote Gallico. Sparring partners were introduced from the ring. Men in dishevelled clothes drifted around. 'The first impression I got in the training stable was of a man who thought he was a boy again, stepping around in ludicrous poses,' wrote Frank Wallace. Tom wore a bathing shirt and regulation boxing tights with ruffle effects on the sides. 'You think it is all so silly; then you remember the million dollar gate.'

Tom had brought his chief sparring partner with him, New Rochelle heavyweight Phil Mercurio, and planned to bring in more. He boxed a little for the cameras. But then he eased off and said he was doing too much. Tom had never trained for long periods and even at St Nick's he could be stubborn enough to resist Harvey's attempts to get a few more rounds out of him. But he was now harbouring a secret that would've disrupted any boxer's training. He'd fractured a bone at the base of his right thumb. 'I broke my thumb about two weeks ago,' he wrote home, 'and I have to keep it dark from the papers, but it's a hell of a job. They are all against my not working, but I tell them that is the way we train in England. If it leaked out they might get someone else to fight Tunney,' he explained. 'So that is how my luck is at present. Still I think I'll get through, but how things will go when I start work God only knows. It would be a great joke if the boys came all the way for nothing.' Tom's three brothers were on their way to Fair Haven. In another letter home he said a doctor told him he'd broken the thumb before and the bone wasn't set properly. Years later Tom said he had never been shown the right way to throw a hook and that he was hitting people with thumbs not knuckles.

Tom couldn't fight for several days and had trouble with his hand throughout training. But he had to act as if nothing was wrong, so he told journalists he was worried about overtraining. His team pointed out he'd kept fit through fighting so often. One reporter, however, did mention just before the fight that 'a slight accident' had forced a short respite from Tom's glove work.

Bill McGeehan had his own explanation about the further delay to Tom's training:

> The reason, as we heard it, was that there were not enough chairs in the camp for Mr Heeney to do himself justice, and that he would not start his preliminary sitting until this defect was corrected.
>
> This seems a bit strange, because the Fair Haven site was selected by Mr Mike Jacobs, the ticket broker. Mike can let you have seats for anything at a premium. His service is so efficient that the legend is that Michael would sell you the Presidential chair on the opening night for the right price.
>
> It does not seem possible that Michael, with seats for everything, could be caught short-seated at Fair Haven. My own theory is that Michael had plenty of chairs of all descriptions at the camp, but that he demanded that Mr Heeney pay a 10 per cent minimum every time he took a chair. As Mr Heeney does much sitting while in training, it could easily be seen that, with the arrangements, Mr Heeney would sit up all the profits which might accrue to him from the Battle of the Century long before that event took place.
>
> And so the matter seems to rest. Mr Jacobs has cornered all the chairs in that section of New Jersey, and if Mr Heeney wants to train there he will have to see Mike about the sedentary arrangements. If he does not start sitting soon experts predict that he will not be able to enter the ring at the top of his sitting form.

Rickard took a group of boxing writers and photographers on his yacht

Maxine to the official opening of Tom's training camp on Thursday 14 June. From the pier at East 26th Street they sailed to a clambake hosted by Rickard's friend Mike Jacobs at Connor's Cedar Grove Hotel in Atlantic Highlands before travelling along the Shrewsbury River to Tom's camp. John Mortimer, the Mayor, Harvey and Rickard posed for the cameramen as several hundred visitors milled around. Tom worked eight rounds but failed to impress. He grumbled that the ring was 'slow as a blinking sand bank' because there was too much deadening padding under the canvas. The scribes looked around the kennels, collected wild flowers and returned in good spirits to New York.

Tickets for the fight at the Yankee Stadium ranged from $5 to $40 for a ringside seat. The Commission thought $40 was too much but it was powerless to intervene. Rickard refused to lower the cheapest seats to $3, arguing that he'd tried it at the Dempsey–Firpo fight and it had created such a stampede for the cheap seats he couldn't sell enough of the pricier ones. He had to create a demand for the expensive $40 ringside seats to avoid a loss. If the stadium were full, with some 97,000 fans, the gross receipts would be around $2,400,000. In his previous four heavyweight championship matches Rickard had made well over a million including around $2,500,000 for the second Dempsey–Tunney fight. But for the gate to reach a million for this fight the fans would have to believe Tom had a good chance of victory. Neither boxer had the punch or popular appeal of Dempsey. It was expected Rickard would play up the international angle to encourage a patriotic fervour among American boxing fans, as he successfully did with the Dempsey–Firpo and Dempsey–Carpentier fights. Rickard believed it took up to six months to 'steam up' a big heavyweight fight and he was short on time.

Both fighters were given public relations advisers. Tunney's counsel, Steve Hannagan, a 'live wire press agent' from Miami and the Indianapolis Speedway, tried to dispel the champion's aloof image. Tom got Garden publicist Francis Albertanti. But boxing writers were tired of the annual 'steam up'. 'Is a fight a big one just because Mr Rickard says it is?' asked Gallico. 'Does the mere fact that he is running it warrant the printing of page after page of pure hooey, or should there be something about which to write before the wild typewriters are loosed?' Dempsey would have been accompanied to camp by reporters recording his activities at length daily, yet there was only belated interest in Tom and Tunney. 'The machinery which ordinarily operates the Rickard prizefight ballyhoo, silently and efficiently, creaked so alarmingly,' Gallico wrote, 'that even the dullest of the sports reporters assigned to cover the training camps were able to distinguish the noises and label their stories as moonshine from time to time.'

> The first bid for space came when the chunky Australian took his spar mate out canoeing with him on the Shrewsbury, rolled over, seized said spar mate by the scruff of the neck, and received official credit for a save. The sparring partner later turned out to be a reasonably good swimmer, but as the story didn't get more than three paragraphs on an inside page, it didn't matter much . . . With admirable promptness, Tunney did the same thing on Lake Pleasant, only his companion was at least three streamers more eminent, it being none other than Mr Thornton Wilder, author of *The Bridge of San Luis Rey*, and a friend of the champion . . . The next dispatches from Fair Haven had to do with the discovery by Heeney of a human cadaver floating about somewhere or other, but unfortunately this prime find was too far gone to permit identification, and another swell story blew . . . This was followed almost immediately by a touching yarn of a little gold-locked fifteen-year-old maiden with elfin ways who lived on a barge and who was to be adopted as Heeney's protégée. The gal never made page one, but she did last for two days, my own paper going for her because things were dead, and then she, too, passed out of sight to be followed immediately by the lost boy gag — the pathetic youngster who hitch-hiked, staggered, walked, and crawled for hundreds of miles to wish Tom well. Four days later, his prototype bobbed up in Speculator.

Even Rickard seemed to lose interest in the fight and lavished more attention on his new boat. Tom's mind was on golf. He was visiting a nearby links before breakfast and Mike Jacobs had set up a five-hole putting green on his private lawn for Tom's exclusive use. 'I'll never be happy', Tom said as he was pounded by trainer Jimmy Hennessey after an energetic workout, 'until I am able to handle those golf clubs like, lemme see, Johnny Farrell, Walter Hagan and Gene Sarazen. I'd give a million dollars to shoot a game like either one of those bounders.' Harvey tried to steer the conversation towards the fight. 'O, to 'ell with the fight,' interjected Tom. 'There's a lot of guys around this town who thinks they are good golfers because they wear those bloomers, but I'll show 'em,' the New York *Daily News* reported. Tom then moaned about his inability to get distance out of his drives and his poor timing of putts. 'Yes, sir,' he said as he got off the table, 'I'm going to break 90 around these here links before I fight for the world's heavyweight title.'

Tom was more accessible than Tunney. McGeehan found none of the 'bootleggers, racketeers, gamblers and guerrillas' he'd encountered at Dempsey's camps in Chicago and Atlantic City and he wondered if that was one reason why few people appeared to care about the fight. Neither boxer seemed worried the other's manager might try something underhanded.

'Gentlemen, be seated!' was Tom's greeting wrote McGeehan.

> Under the supervision of Mr 'Eeney, Mr 'Ennessey, his trainer, and Squire John Mortimer (Mr 'Arvey being absent at the time), Negro boys were at the gate with wheel chairs to carry the visitors the remaining distance of a hundred yards. It must be explained at this point that all h's in proper names are dropped or are silent in deference to Mr John Mortimer, who has yet to pronounce his first h.
>
> The wheel chair assigned to your correspondent was somewhat dusty and the Negro boy in charge looked somewhat fatigued. It was explained to your correspondent that Mr 'Eeney had conferred upon him the signal honor of offering his own personal wheel chair, the one in which he does his road work. Judging from the appearance of the chair, Mr 'Eeney has been doing enough road work to satisfy the most nsistent critic among the experts.

Once inside, Tom sat in a Morris chair and 'apologized for the shortage of chairs, though there seemed to be plenty in the establishment'. He also gave an exhibition in the barn.

> Your correspondent was warned in advance that Mr Heeney was awful in the gymnasium. But the awfulness of the logical contender is highly exaggerated, it seems. The footwork of Mr Heeney is not to be compared with that of the gazelle nor yet that of the antelope

of the prairies. It is a cross between that of the elephant and the kangaroo, if you get what I mean. Mr Heeney frequently leaps into the air after the fashion of the marsupials of the antipodes, as the boys call them, and always he is pushing in after the fashion of an elephant pushing a teak log with his forehead.

McGeehan suggested Tom's affability might be a problem for the champion. When Tunney fought Dempsey the first time he could approach his opponent coldly because if he won he would become a millionaire and because he faced a 'killer' who would take any advantage he could. In the second Dempsey fight he drew on the bitterness he felt after the first, in which he claimed to have been hit with illegal blows. He also wanted to prove himself to the fans who still believed Dempsey had let him win. There would be no personal scores to settle with Tom.

'I'd be a sucker to stand up and try to outbox Tunney,' Tom told Jack Farrell of the *Daily News* on the lawn outside his cottage under the trees on the banks of the Shrewsbury. 'I figure I can wear him down with a body attack in ten rounds and then chase him all around the ring for the last five.' He continued: 'They tell me that Tunney has not boxed over ten rounds in four years. Those five extra rounds will take a lot more out of him than people imagine. Don't think I am boasting when I say that I don't think he can hit hard enough to knock me out. Sharkey, if you recall, planted three corking rights on my chin in the first round of our fight and yet I did not know I had been hit until I came back to my corner and my seconds gave me hell for leaving my chin exposed. I don't imagine Tunney can hit harder than Sharkey; if he could it would not have taken him fourteen rounds to dispose of Georges Carpentier.' Tom had been teased a lot for his rocking-chair style of training apparently designed to conserve energy for fighting. But he just grinned at the jibes and said he thought his problem was rest as he'd been fighting hard and often.

A Newark reporter arrived on Tom's day off. It was raining, there were few people around and the New Zealander was relaxing. What would he do if he got the winner's purse? 'I have not given it much thought. I have a few thousands now and I have put them into bonds. I get lots of letters from people who want to tell me how to make money, but I throw them all in the waste basket. If I get a lot of money I will not go into any such schemes. I know what being poor means.'

Jack Kofoed of the *Evening Post* found a tranquil, near-deserted camp when he visited towards the end of June. Charlie Harvey and John Mortimer were attending to business matters and Charlie's brother Eddie was the only member of Tom's team who was always around. He collected the gate money and did other odd jobs. The telegraph wire chief had yet to be besieged with work from visiting scribes. Tom seemed like 'a big English squire loafing about under the trees with his dogs'. He claimed he wasn't worried about the fight. 'This racket is just a state of mind,' he said. 'Most guys go in to fight a champion and they're licked before they start. I'm goin' in to fight another man who ain't got any more hands than I have: just two of them.' He seemed to have come round to the idea of outdoor training in the summer. 'This place is the top of the tree. I've never done any trainin' in a place like this. It's all been in gymnasiums before. At first I didn't think I'd like it, but it really is great.'

Tom was looking forward to seeing his brothers. In fact, the camp had an unusual number of male siblings. There were Charlie and Eddie Harvey, and John Mortimer would soon be joined by Bernard. Phil Mercurio had his brother Joseph in camp, while Mercurio's manager Joe Welling had his brother Johnny. Raymond Hoagland was often seen with brothers Joseph and John. The telegraph wire chief had his younger brother to help him to get the journalists' pieces out on time via Morse code. South African Johnny Squires and his boxer brother Tom popped into the camp too. And then there was the sad story of William J. Hennessey, the 36-year-old brother of Jimmy Hennessey. On 19 June he was found dead on the floor of his room in the camp. A blood clot on the brain as a result of an earlier accident was suspected. A brick had fallen eight storeys while he was working as a contractor of electric elevators and fractured his skull. He'd undergone several operations.

When Pat, Art and Jack Heeney arrived at New York's Grand Central Station on 29 June photographers picked them from the crowd straight away. Art and Pat were builders, and Jack was a blacksmith who had a cauliflower ear and a slightly battered nose. 'I always gave him more than he gave me,' said Jack of his kid brother, 'and maybe I can do it yet.' They had contacted Tom by radio to find out when the fight was to be held. Well-known Gisborne wireless amateur Bob Patty hooked up through a 'ham' in Broadway, Jack Grenan. At 3 a.m. New York time Patty got through. 'He's staying in Broadway, the same as I am,' came the reply.

The radio man phoned Tom who was living about a mile away. 'Will you tell the people of Gisborne that although I have been away for a long time I have never forgotten them, and that I hope before long to be back among them,' was his message. 'Tell them that the big fight takes place on July 26, and I am training hard for it. I am feeling very fit, and Gisborne is not going to be disgraced.' Tom was asked to get Jack a preliminary match and promised to investigate. He requested a photo of his parents, his Royal Humane Society medal and any relevant newspaper clippings, and reports of his New Zealand fights as he was always being asked for them.

Jack denied a rumour aboard ship that he wanted to be matched against his brother. 'Why, man, Tom is big!' he said. 'His arms are as big as my body — no, I don't want to fight that boy.' Jack had long thought Tom had the potential to become successful. 'He was always quick for a heavyweight and exceptionally fast on his feet, but he never put much ginger into his work, and at one stage he was a bit scared to use his strength. There's no doubt that he has learned much in America, but it's not so much what he has been taught as the fact that he has learned to let himself go.' Jack hoped to get some matches but the other two were just planning to see the bout. 'We are going to be at the ringside and maybe if Tom can't lick Tunney, we all might crawl in and help him out,' Artie said.

They were besieged by newspapermen and cameramen. 'I have fulfilled my life's ambition to get in front of a moving picture camera,' Jack wrote home. The ship docked in Vancouver where their host Mrs Jack McQuarrie wrote to Jack's wife: 'It's a good job they came round to us because my man Jack had a steady job warding off camera men, reporters, railway officials and the like. Had they gone to an hotel they would have been pestered to death. On Saturday morning the movie man came with his camera and snapped them supposedly arriving at Vancouver, your Jack with what was intended to be a keg of beer under his arm, en route to Tom with it.' She also reported that the brothers were 'greatly amused at the newspaper men here. They have a queer idea that we "pig Islanders" are cockneys, dropping our haitches all over the floor and tripping over them at every step. The boys reckoned they were going to lick the tar off the one who wrote it, but when they tackled him he said it had to be done to distinguish them from Canadians.'

Tom was famous across Australasia. An Australian well-wisher addressed a letter to 'Tom Heeney's Father, Somewhere in New Zealand' and it got to the Heeney house. A Gisborne schoolteacher received a letter addressed to 'Heeneyville'. 'Formerly Gisborne' had been written on the envelope as if an afterthought. In Auckland a comedian performed a song *When Tom Heeney Wins The Big Fight* at Fuller's Theatre. There were also popular jokes about Tom. One involved the inter-island ferry that plied the route between Wellington and Picton:

> YANKEE, on Wellington wharf, to Wharfie: 'Say, guy, how do I get to Picton?'
> WHARFIE: 'Go down and catch that boat over there, the Tamahine.'
> YANKEE: 'Tamahine, eh? Say, guy, is there anything in this gol darn country that you don't call after this Tom Heeney of yours?'

Another went:

> A Scotchman, an Englishman, and an Irishman were engaged in a heated argument on the respective merits of their respective and respected races.
> 'Well,' said the Scotchman, 'look what we've done for the world. We've produced Bruce, and Wallace, and Scott, and Robert Burns, and . . .'
> And then the Englishman chipped in: 'That's nothing. Look what we've given the world — King Alfred, Shakespeare, William Pitt, Dickens, Gladstone . . .'
> 'Nothing at all, indade,' butted in the Irishman. 'We were responsible for St Patrick's Day and Tom Heeney.'

A man described as an Australian boxing promoter talked of Gisborne in an American newspaper as 'one of the great fight towns in the world, where they offer £3000 to boxers to come and fight regularly'. He offered a strange version of Tom's life in which Tom had 30 or 40 fights before he turned professional, only fought in Gisborne once, never fought in Australia but was there in 1925, and worked his passage to South Africa stoking coal on the steamer *Medic* before going back to Australia and fighting George Cook in Wellington. Tom sent home articles that said he was a blacksmith, he played soccer for the All Blacks and his mascot was the kangaroo. Gisborne reporters claimed many stories in the American newspapers were absurd, one asking how it was possible Tom could write pages of reminiscences but only 150 words to his own parents.

Tom's fame hadn't affected his parents. His mother still milked the cows wet or fine. An Auckland reporter found her with her fowls and 'Old Hughie' pottering around the garden, keen to talk about his crop of onions and the size of his apples. Eliza, 'full of life and vigour, bubbling over with humour, and as sharp-witted as a politician', still had a strong Irish accent. She was grey and Hughie fast becoming so. Her son's success was just one happy incident in a full life. 'Sure and he's doing no better than he ought to be,' she said smiling, 'and he's going to do better before he's finished.' Her eyes lit up when she talked about Tom or any of her boys. 'They're all the same to me,' she said and her husband agreed. 'I've never treated any of them differently, and they've all been good boys to me.'

Tom wanted the whole family to go over for the fight but Eliza wouldn't want to leave her cows. He wanted to share his earnings with his parents and wrote home that he didn't think his mother should be milking cows while he had more than he could spend. He suggested building two houses on their property and told them to cable how much they'd need. The cable was never sent. 'No,' Eliza told the reporter. 'I'll work as long as I'm able to. What would I do without the cows and the fowls? I'm better off as I am.' Old Hughie recalled that when the boys built a new home on the old property they had to move the furniture while Eliza was away. She refused to move in immediately and kept cooking in the old cottage. Two of the boys were building another house hoping she might move but she wouldn't even look at the place. 'All the gold in America wouldn't make me give up my cows,' she declared.

Tom had sent his parents more than £500 but they had banked it for his return. 'I don't want his money,' said Eliza. 'If I don't live too long I've got enough to keep myself. I've always been independent, and I won't be beholden to any of them. But it's fine to know that Tom doesn't forget us when he's getting on. That's the part I like,' she said. 'You never know when he might need the money. Why he might get married tomorrow, or have some other bad luck,' she said with a twinkle in her eye and a glance at Hughie. 'Anyhow, I don't need it, and there it is.'

Hugh resented the publicity and riled at some American newspaper articles reprinted in New Zealand. 'We know it's mostly untrue and people in New Zealand should know better than to take it seriously.' In an attempt to balance the coverage Tom's parents told their version of their son's life in a booklet, *Our Tom*. A photographer came to take the couple's picture by the old shed that was used for boxing and wanted the pair to stand arm and arm. 'Why, we haven't done a thing like that for years and years,' wrote Eliza. She also told of a visit from 'two breezy men' who came to the house. 'Hullo, Mrs Heeney! We're representing a motor firm. How are you? Our firm's just given Tom a brand new motor car, over in America. Thought you would like to know all about it,' was how she remembered their introduction. The men talked for around half an hour and took photographs. A few days later a photo and a 'mostly inaccurate' article appeared, 'putting into my mouth a lot of things that I didn't say, and making Mr Heeney say a lot of things that he could never think of'. She wrote that Tom hadn't mentioned getting a car. 'I think the motor car part of the business was just a "try-on". The world's a "shrewder" place than it used to be, but I don't think it's any better for it.' Tom appeared in a number of advertisements endorsing products; in one he was said to have purchased a Whippet car and had it delivered to Fair Haven. Later, Tom's parents and Jack would also be pictured 'in their Whippet Coach'.

The New Zealand government sent a crew to make a 'Publicity Film' of Gisborne and the Heeney home for America. 'I don't know how Tom will take it,' wrote Hugh. 'I know he hates all this boosting business. But I suppose he's getting used to it now.' Tom was certainly used to publicity stunts. He'd even been filmed working as a blacksmith. Some wondered if Tom's ego had got a bit too big. An Auckland newspaper wrote: 'Tom Heeney says that he is going to do his best for himself and the Empire. Nice of him to place the Empire upon the same high pinnacle as himself.' A Gisborne newspaper described how the Hawke's Bay Boxing Association had cabled its best wishes to Tom and that Tom's reply had been framed. 'It is well worth perusing, for the letter shows that Tom has, to a certain extent, become Americanised, at least as far as boost is concerned. The letter is typed on his own letter-heads, which have in big type: "Tom Heeney, contender for the world's heavyweight championship." In both corners of the letter sheet are two large photographs of Tom in his full war kit, and in the centre is a list of his victories during his march up the ladder of world's championship fame.' Notepaper used by John Mortimer also drew attention. It had a picture of Tom in one corner, 'Tom Heeney' emblazoned in vermilion inch-high lettering across the top, 'Champion Heavyweight of New Zealand' in smaller black type and 'Successor to Bob Fitzsimmons' in 1½-inch red letters.

'It was not unknown that a training camp was designed to manufacture one product — a fighter's ego,' Norman Mailer once wrote. The piles of letters, cables, gifts, good luck tokens and other morale boosters from around the world Tom received at Fair Haven must've helped. The president of the American Greyhound Racing Association gave him a brace of racing greyhounds. The New Zealand Prime Minister, the Gisborne MP, the Gisborne Mayor and the Gisborne Boxing Association all cabled best wishes. His British War Medal for his service in the Great War arrived at camp. A carcass of Poverty Bay lamb from the famous Turihau Station was shipped to New York so that he could train 'on the finest possible foundation'. 'Believe me, you have a great chance, and if you have improved in any way, as you should in a lapse of four years, there is no reason why you shouldn't be the next champion and I'm not kidding you,' wrote Tom Gibbons, the boxer who'd advised him in 1924 to go to the States. 'When you make your pile, Tom, don't spend it foolishly, but put it away where you will keep the principal intact,' he advised. 'Don't look for too large an interest yield; don't be what the boys around the corner term a good fellow, because when you are broke they will be the first to turn you down.'

Tom's brothers were swamped with farewells and gifts and messages for Fair Haven. The most significant gift was from Lady Carroll. The historic korowai of flax fibre decorated with feathers of native birds had been presented to Sir James and once belonged to the late Ruahuia Tawhiwhi, one of the leaders of Ngati Porou. It was 80 years old and was only the third such cloak to be given to a Paheka man. With it was a letter from Lady Carroll:

> Greetings to you in your battle for the world's championship.
> Your Maori people are very proud of your prowess.
> Here we live peacefully in our homes, hearing of your uphill struggle to gain recognition.

Our hearts rejoice, for now we hear that you have succeeded in your ambition, and if thou are successful in your fight in July you will become the world's champion.

Far distant from your homeland, it will be well to have an emblem to remind you that the Maori people are with you. So we are sending this korowai, or Maori cloak, that we hope you will wear into the arena.

We hope thou wilt be successful. We are all with you in spirit.

Be strong, be brave, be active.

Heni Carroll

Tom was photographed wearing the cloak over his clothes at Fair Haven. Mortimer said it included at least one feather from every bird in New Zealand, wrote McGeehan. 'Of course, Thomas was pleased with the gift, but not quite as pleased as he might have been if it had been a Maori settee with a cushion stuffed with feathers of all the birds of New Zealand.'

'Books?' Tom said, when asked about his reading. 'Why, I'm doing good to read the letters I get now without bothering about books . . . One fellow said I should win in six rounds because there were six letters in my name,' he said. 'And that's the kind of letters I'm getting — and the handwriting is no bargain, either.'

An Irishman wrote, 'If you don't answer this letter, then I'll know you're not an Irishman.' 'Blimey, I'm an Irishman and a fighter,' was Tom's response.

'I don't want to miss this fight, Tom, and I figured that if you cabled me the money right away I could board a ship that would get me to New York in time,' a Londoner wrote. 'I will have the price of a ringside seat, so that won't cost you a cent, and I'll also be able to pay my own room and board. The passage money I'll pay back to you just as soon as I get a job.'

Tom's willingness to agree to many appeals for financial aid worried his helpers. If he won the title how would he manage the riches that went with it? 'You can't be a bloomin' mug!' Tom reassured his people.

Tom wrote 'Kia Ora' on photographs. He explained it meant 'Good luck to you', and was the prevailing greeting in New Zealand. But he got an indignant response from one girl who said she didn't know what 'Kia Ora' meant and was afraid to ask anyone. A New Zealand girl sent an eight-page letter congratulating Tom on his success. 'I'm not proposing to you,' she wrote, 'but I am seriously thinking of adopting you for my daddy.'

Over breakfast and the morning papers on 13 July Tom read that Tunney was supposed to have said of the fight, 'Heeney won't have but three people there'. The champion had ordered 400 tickets and was annoyed Rickard hadn't given him enough ringside seats. 'Well, blime me if this doesn't take the royal cake for gall,' a normally restrained Tom blurted out, wrote Jack Farrell. 'I shall jolly well tell that blighter where 'e gets off at.' After consulting with his public relations man a reply was drafted. At last there was a bit of antagonism between the two camps for the press agents to exploit.

My Dear Mr Tunney:

Spent my day off reading your brilliant squawk anent allocation of 400 tickets and the fact that they are not in very desirable locations. To add insult to injury you state, or at least you are quoted as saying, that 'Heeney won't have but three people there.'

It may interest you to know that I have already instructed my managers to get me 200 ringside tickets. This order may be doubled in another fortnight. My mail is deluged daily with requests for tickets but none of my friends care where they sit. All they want is a good view of the fight where they can see me hooking you with the left and sending your head back with right hand uppercuts.

All my fights since I landed in America have drawn good crowds. I earned the shot at your title because I was consistent.

The fans like to see a fighter and I can safely state that you are not the only pebble on the beach.

Yours till we meet in the ring on July 26.

Tom Heeney

'For one thing,' Tom told reporters, 'no true American sportsman would make such cheap remarks about a man who came from another part of the world to help him make another million dollars or so. If I were so friendless a fellow why did Tunney accept me as his opponent? Was it because he thought he was picking a sucker or was he egotistical enough to think this will be a one man party? Tunney has gone on record as saying that he and not Dempsey drew the big houses in Philadelphia and Chicago. If that is the case, why is he worrying about how many people come to see me fight? I guess Gene thought that just as soon as the great American fight public heard he was going to fight they would break down the gates to see him, but now it looks as though he has not enough highbrow friends to fill the stadium, he is trying to belittle me. I have been reading where Tunney is supposed to be the Woodrow Wilson of boxing. If that's so, I must be the Theodore Roosevelt, because they say I am rough and I am always ready.'

Tunney 'smiled indulgently' as he read Tom's letter at Speculator, wrote Frank Wallace. 'The use of the words "anent" and "allocate" in the same paragraph caused the impression here that Dommas had found a magic typewriter.'

Taming the Unarmed Killer

Tom emerged from the cottage with Phil Mercurio, his tall, rangy sparring partner and 'the loudest snorer that ever whistled through a nostril', and they climbed into Paul Gallico's car. As usual, Tom had got up before sunrise to do his sprints on the road in the cool of the early morning. There was a heat wave in New Jersey and people had been dying in New York as the mercury soared into the nineties. The trio drove east towards the coast on their way to a picturesque nine-hole golf course just outside Long Branch. As they turned the corner at Sea Bright the ocean appeared and Tom yearned for it. 'That's all I'll do when this thing is over. Get roight in that surf and stay there,' he said. It was an early sign that something was wrong.

Tom, Mercurio and Gallico were joined on the golf course by a young professional and his caddie. But it was too hot for golf. It was so humid it was hard to get a grip on the club. The men sweated. On a short hole Tom's ball ended up in a marsh and Mercurio hit his onto the green.

'Know any more games, Tom? I can beat you at this one,' Mercurio joked.

Tom looked up unsmiling. 'I know one indoor sport I can beat you at any time.'

It was usually a good sign when a fighter was irritable; he was ready to fight. 'In heavy training fighters live in dimensions of boredom others do not begin to contemplate,' Norman Mailer wrote. 'Fighters are supposed to. The boredom creates an impatience with one's life, and a violence to improve it. Boredom creates a detestation for losing.' But to Gallico, Tom was overtrained. Physically he was in good shape but mentally he was suffering. The heat had sapped his energy and even walking around was a sweaty, tiring effort. Perspiration poured off him when he got in the ring and there were mosquitoes and noisy crows. He was bored with interviews although he tried to be polite. Now and again he'd say to his guest, 'Ye know, Paul, I never trained this long in me life before. It's like being in a joil.' Tom was painfully frustrated and the fight was still a week away. Maybe he wasn't stale but he was at least obsessed by a fear of going stale, Gallico thought. The biggest fight of his career was almost upon him and his confidence was shaken.

'Far from me to say anything that would cause me to be frowned upon by the pure, the holy, and the dry, but what our honest Tom needs now is a roaring toot,' wrote Gallico. 'It is still long enough before the fight for him to have it without doing himself an injury.' He didn't know Tom well enough to suggest a detailed plan but 'it ought to start with a plunge in the ocean — only a person who himself has been restricted for a time can realize how Tom is yearning for that ocean — and then move in easy stages. A pretty girl should figure in it here and there, and there should be plenty of ale and things, and sitting around with one's coat off and feet upon the table, and no one to croak "time to go to bed, Tom," and some pals around who wouldn't talk fight, and some more ale. Tom will kill me if he reads this, because it will make his mouth water, and so forth and so on, far into the night.'

After the golf Tom punched the light bag, shadow-boxed, skipped, and sparred with Jimmy Braddock and Jay Lawless. Lawless 'caressed Tom's face with more right hands than Tunney lets go in a week at Speculator, and all of them landed', wrote Gallico. Afterwards Tom threw up his hands in disgust.

Gallico had travelled to Fair Haven from Speculator, where Tunney was relaxed, cool and contented. He was in peak physical condition and his mind was at ease. He was training to knock Tom out to prove he could be a 'killer' like Dempsey. 'During the training period for this fight, I was completely free from annoyance and worry,' Tunney wrote.

His chief second called it the most placid training camp in the history of prizefighting. The champion had changed and now warmed to the reporters he had traditionally shunned.

Tom was more like the old Tunney. He disappeared after workouts and only a few people knew where. He was tired of the constant prying and meeting and greeting and attending events and couldn't see why he couldn't be left alone to train.

'If I were Tunney today fighting Tom Heeney, and I had all the money he is supposed to have, I'd tell them all to go to hell and wouldn't fight any more . . . I don't like this hot weather. I've trained before but never for so long. On July 27 I'll have sugar in the grapefruit and in the tea too. I'll take a swim. I'll do a lot of things.'

'What are you drinking?' someone asked.

'Anything I can get,' Tom replied.

Tom liked his ale. After training he'd go to a private club nearby to drink and talk fishing with Carl the steward. 'In New Jersey I know a place with the sign "Bar" outside, and in it they sell beer as strong as is sold in New Zealand, if not stronger,' he said. He was so hot he needed a 'tonic' to help him enjoy his dinner. Unless an athlete could have a good dinner at the end of the day his training would be of little benefit, was Tom's theory. A boxer must feel strong and enjoy his food and sleep. Without his glass of ale he'd pick at his food. With a glass of beer first he could eat heartily. He would later dispute claims that he might've done better against Tunney if he'd gone on the 'water-waggon'. On Bernard Mortimer's advice he agreed to give it up for the final week of training. 'And it was such good ale,' he sighed. It was later reported, however, that one afternoon in the week before the fight Tom went AWOL and drank three bottles.

For breakfast he had a grapefruit, lamb chops or broiled steak, buttered toast and marmalade and coffee or tea. A typical dinner was roast beef with thin gravy, celery, lettuce and tomato salad with vinegar or oil, buttered beets, buttered string beans, white bread and iced tea. Afterwards he'd have custard pudding with sliced pineapple or sliced peaches or any other fruit. Before he went out on the road Hennessey would break two raw eggs in sherry. Daily five-mile runs had honed and hardened his legs but he was struggling to shift the excess pounds from his waist.

To avoid the afternoon heat Tom tried night training with five 1000-watt arc lights strung around the outdoor ring. This would also get him used to the conditions at the Yankee Stadium. His only other night fight in the open air had been against Jack DeMave when he struggled to see under the lights. What was the point of Tom getting used to the bright lights if Tunney closed one of his eyes? asked McGeehan. 'A scheme to accustom Thomas to any emergency of this character is being evolved. Later in the week Thomas will box under lights with a patch over the right eye. In this manner he will be ready to continue no matter which eye Tunney may render hors du combat for the evening.' There was also a strategy in case both eyes were disabled. 'In the last few nights Thomas will do some considerable boxing with both of his eyes covered by patches in order that he may accustom himself to fighting without seeing his antagonist at all. Some of the severest critics of Thomas say that he swings as though he were in that condition already. But there always are persons who will persist in making cracks of this nature, however unwarranted that might be.'

The lights from the ring could be seen along the seashore. A 500-candlepower globe shone on a stand from which hung a small punching bag Tom slammed for two rounds. Then, under rolling thunder and menacing storm clouds amid fireflies and annoying swarms of other insects, Tom boxed two rounds each with Phil Mercurio and Paul Swiderski. Afterwards he scaled just over 200 lb. 'Greatest workout ever,' chimed John Mortimer and Eddie Harvey. Critics and a large crowd of onlookers agreed. He looked faster and punched harder. 'I never saw a real fight in my life,' said Raymond Hoagland, 'but I'm so certain that Heeney is going to beat Tunney that I have $10,000 laying around that can be covered at the prevailing odds.' Locals, from the Mayor to the assistant dog nurses at the Rumson Farm kennels, had bought $14,000 worth of tickets.

Tom cringed and blushed as a group of young female admirers sang him a song one evening. But he soon abandoned the late sessions. He liked to go to bed early and now he couldn't turn in until close to midnight. Exhaustion kept him awake for another hour or so. He wasn't getting enough sleep and he thought eating later made him sluggish in the ring.

Tom rose at 4.30 a.m. one morning and took a long walk. A few hours later he climbed into an open car with the Harveys and they drove to the ocean looking for cool breezes. While hundreds of fans turned up at the camp, it was reported in the papers that Tom spent the day on the palatial yacht of a millionaire friend, Charles Gaston. Harvey had insisted on a day's rest and Tom apparently retired to a late-model Louis XIV bed in an opulent bedroom in Gaston's mansion. But it was a fanciful story. Gaston turned out to be the owner of a couple of gas stations in Rumson. He was a friend of the millionaire and arranged for Tom to go out on the luxury boat.

'Sad Plight of Tammas' Gallico called his column on 21 July. There didn't seem to be any spot hotter than New Jersey and Tom had 'nearly died of the heat' that was 'baked into his bones'. Tom had been 'sacrificed to personal ambition and a certain amount of small town politics'. Harvey had said Tom's interests would be paramount when it came to picking a training site, but Gallico declared: 'If, by next Thursday night, whatever chance Tom Heeney had has not been cooked, broiled, fried and baked out of him, then you may serve me this typewriter with a little sugar and cream and sit down and watch me while I eat it.'

Pegler wrote of 'Six Weeks in a Blast Furnace'. In selecting Fair Haven everyone's interests except for Tom's seemed to have been satisfied, including those of Mike Jacobs, who had property interests in the area. 'Mr Jacobs is, to state the matter bluntly, a real estate man of the most virulent type, and it was he who prevailed upon Mr Rickard to prevail upon a majority of the stockholders of Thomas Heeney to bring Mr Heeney to Fair Haven to fry in the sun and simmer in the shade for six weeks.' A couple of days before the fight it was reported that 87½ acres at Upper Rocky Point on the North Shrewsbury River had been bought for development by a syndicate involving Rickard, Jacobs and two others. The land was a short distance from Tom's training camp.

Jack Heeney said the heat 'would almost burn you up and take the whole soul case out of you. If I had been Tom I would never have done so much training in the hot weather.' Jack sent updates via radio to Gisborne. In one he said Tom was very pleased to have his brothers with him, 'but of course is completely wrapped up in his work. I asked him what he was going to do after the fight, but he only grinned and said it would be time enough to think about that when the fight was over.' Jack thought the camp was a lovely place and they weren't bothered by the dogs that made a terrible racket at night. 'Everyone except the four Heeneys hears them, and the latter point seems to annoy the others more than the dogs do.' The Heeney brothers didn't talk much but they were close. Tom did get to go out on the water one day with Art, the first time the pair had a proper chance to catch up with Gisborne news. But as Tom was getting out of the boat he slipped on an iron pipe and fell on his back. He was only bruised. 'I won't be sorry when this stunt is all over,' Tom wrote home. 'These paper fellows drive a man crazy and I'm just breaking my neck for a good party. Believe me they have some real parties here; still I can't get mixed up in them yet for a while. The place where I am training is a nice spot, but I will be glad to get back to New Zealand as this place is a bit on the quiet side.'

Tom's brothers were having a great time, mixing with gangsters and celebrities. Pat could out-eat everyone else in the camp and Artie was rather partial to brightly coloured silk shirts. Jack told Gallico the story of 'the finest present I ever got' and showed the writer where a bullet from the gun of a German sniper had entered his chest and exited his side after first passing through the head of a fellow soldier, killing him. Jack had been trying to rescue a man who'd been shot through both legs.

'His brothers, managers, a couple of trainers, and a regiment of self-appointed instructors are there,' wrote the London *Daily Mail*'s Trevor Wignall. 'He admitted to me he was worried about it. He took me by the arm this morning and said, "My goodness, I will be glad when this is all over." He was not referring to his training, but to the bickerings, half-concealed snarls, and the general atmosphere of discontent round the camp. Moreover, this place is too lively and gay to prepare for the championship.' Wignall reported constant bickering between Harvey and the Mortimers over the small issue of Tom's $100,000 guarantee. Tom refused to take sides, but it was rumoured he wasn't happy with the Mortimers and wanted to stick with Harvey. In the end it was reported that the Harveys 'owned' Tom while the Mortimers owned shares in the Harvey brothers. The ever-cynical Gallico described the spat as 'the time-worn Dissension-Among-Managers story'. And then there was McGeehan's interpretation.

> Squire John Mortimer had announced that any place Thomas sat was British territory. Mr Charles J. Harvey, the American representative of the man from the Anzac, hoisted the American and Irish flags

over him immediately after his first bout in this country and took possession of him in the name of the United States of America and the Irish Free State. He justified the claim on the strength of Heeney's Irish parentage and the fact that the chair he first occupied in the United States was made at Grand Rapids, Mich.

At the Heeney camp it was reported that a coldness was developing between Squire Mortimer and Mr Harvey. The chill was intensified when Mr Harvey, walking in the moonlight, fell and sustained some painful injuries when he tripped over the h's that had been dropped carelessly by the Squire in the grounds of the Hoagland estate.

It was intimated that there might be legal proceedings because of the difference of opinion existing between the British and American managers of Heeney. This would be a most intricate business, as it would have to go before the world court in the long run. While the differences were being accentuated Mr Heeney remained seated in a neutral corner.

The managers didn't even agree on how Tom should fight Tunney. Harvey thought he should try to slug American-style and the Mortimers wanted him to box cleverly in the best British tradition. The notion that Tom could outbox Tunney was generally derided and Tom went with Harvey's strategy of 'not a backward step'.

However, Charlie Harvey and John Mortimer put aside their quarrel when romance threatened Tom's training. Marion arrived at the camp on a hydroplane with a friend five days before the fight. As the party prepared to fly back, Marion invited Tom to take to the air for a spin.

'He's mad,' Mortimer said. 'He's doing it out of madness at me.'

Mortimer and Harvey followed Tom down to the boat-club float on the Shrewsbury River, arguing as they walked. 'The women are more trouble than the gladiators,' grumbled Mortimer. Finally, Marion suggested to Tom he stay on dry land.

'Never mind,' she told him. 'We'll come down Thursday morning and fly you up.'

'Okay.'

The immediate crisis averted, the managers hoped they would be able to talk Tom out of flying to the fight on Thursday.

'Do you know Tom well?' Frank Wallace asked Marion at the dock.

'She's his fiancée,' her friend piped up.

'He's a reporter, be careful,' Marion cautioned.

Tom kissed Marion goodbye and watched the flying boat sail into the distance.

'Aren't you afraid to have your girl fly like that?' Wallace asked Tom.

'If it's all right with her why should I worry?'

'I like to go out with the girls,' Tom told one New York reporter, 'but I don't think I'll ever get married.' But Mortimer battled to prevent Tom eloping with Marion before the fight. 'I had the devil's own time to stop him,' he would later admit.

Everyone had an opinion on the fight. Grantland Rice thought Tom was a better boxer and harder to hit than Dempsey, but that without Dempsey's punch he wouldn't become champion. 'Heeney comes of a fighting breed,' wrote McGeehan. 'The New Zealanders in the World War were awed by nothing and by nobody. Mr Heeney will not be awed by the heavyweight championship title any more than he would be by the sight of King George in his coronation robes. They are an irreverent lot, those men of the Anzac.' Both James J. Jeffries and Jack Britton thought Tom had a fair chance against Tunney. James J. Corbett said: 'It is going to be a much better battle than I thought. This fellow is built like Tom Sharkey. He does not hit any harder, but hits oftener and is as rugged as my old pal. His forte is endurance.' Possibly unaware of the Cyril Whitaker fight, Wignall talked of how one of Tom's early opponents had lingered between life and death for days and that even in his British fights the memory of the near-fatality stopped him letting his punches go, but that the new environment in America had banished the memory. That Tom had killed one of his opponents was one of the few stories from his past that barely surfaced in the American papers.

Rickard was desperate for publicity. Gathering together members of his 'Six Hundred Millionaires Club', the stockbrokers and financiers who had bankrolled the building of Madison Square Garden, he put them and several newspapermen on his yacht and sailed down the coast to Fair Haven. The biggest star of the gathering was Dempsey. He greeted admirers in a blue double-breasted serge suit and Panama hat turned down over his eyes. The 2000-strong crowd 'was for all the world like a

Ranfurly Shield match, there being six traffic police regulating the traffic, the traffic parking on the camp ground', Jack Heeney messaged home.

They were ushered to the outdoor training ring where a cooling breeze blew and 'where they sat and gazed at the challenger for the world's heavyweight title go through the most astonishing workout this observer has ever witnessed', wrote Gallico. 'For four rounds, his two sparring partners — a light heavyweight with the imposing title of James Braddock, and a beginner in the heavyweight ranks named Lawless — smacked him about the ring, staggering him with rights and stabbing him with lefts, causing him to miss and flounder, and giving him merry hell until even the spectators gasped as the rights bounced off his chin. Tex Rickard, who sat next to me, chewed convulsively on his cigar and assured me that Heeney wasn't really trying to hit his sparring partners. It was just that terrible.' Despite being hit often by Lawless and Braddock, the New Jersey boxer who'd later beat Max Baer for the heavyweight championship and would become known as 'Cinderella Man', Tom was unmarked. But his bad showing that day wasn't a one-off. The story goes that Tommy Loughran was invited to spar with Tom in the barn, hit him on the chin and 'laid him comatose'. So said Pegler who heard it from Dempsey.

'Well, Jack, how does he look to you?' the scribes asked Dempsey. The former champion, wrote Gallico, 'turned his gaze to the ceiling and, without drawing a breath, recited in a monotone like a little boy getting rid of his piece before he should forget it, "I think that Heeney has more than an even chance to win it will take a superman to beat him he is strong and tough can take a punch and give one I am glad that I came to Fair Haven to see Heeney he is in excellent condition and is a big strong fellow . . ."' Tom was said to be 'downright bewildered' by Dempsey's comments.

'The fight turned up its toes then and there,' wrote Gallico, who wondered 'if stout Tammas weren't going to make possibly the worst showing ever turned in by a challenger for the heavyweight title'. Runyon, who called the fight the 'Battle of the Phonus Bolonus', thought Tom was one of the worst challengers the country had had.

In his dressing room Tom was cheerful. He answered most journalists' questions unless there was one he didn't like and then he pretended not to hear it, turning to shake another hand. He was bent over with his foot on a chair tying his shoe when someone asked, 'How many times a year are you going to defend the title if you win?'.

Tom waited a bit and then raised his head. 'What are you talking about?' He finished tying his shoe, straightened up and grinned.

'Once or twice?'

'Nonce. What do you think I'll do?'

The crowd lingered as the celebrities departed, many going to a clambake hosted by Mike Jacobs. A thief lurked among the throng, as a pickpocket stole Harvey's wallet and five $100 bills. It was the manager's second mishap in two days. The previous night he was out with friends when a car door was slammed on his right hand and he broke three fingers.

As he lay on the rubbing table after his last day of hard training Tom spoke of victory. He was toying with a greenstone tiki that had been sent to him. 'I'm feeling great,' he said. 'I'm looking forward eagerly to this fight. If it rains on Thursday I'm going to burst out crying.' Earlier that day Westbrook Pegler had found Tom relaxing in a big chair in the room next to the telegraph office wearing frayed blue serge trousers 'hitched on with a harness trace' and a shirt loose at the collar and cuffs. It was the trophy room for Hoagland's prize-winning birds and dogs. The mantelpiece was decorated with tarnished silver and gold cups, plaques and ribbons hung on the walls, and medals dangled from the woodwork. Braddock, Lawless and Mercurio were there. Socialising with his sparring partners wasn't something Pegler could imagine Tunney doing. At one point Tom grabbed at a letter Mercurio had begun to read aloud, 'Friend Phil, My Italian Sheik . . .', and between them they shredded it.

Then Tom asked how it was that Mercurio arrived at the camp with one shirt, had sent four to be laundered and still had one in his room and one on his back. 'Bloody burglar,' he said. 'We're going to 'ave bag inspection before we close this camp and everybody that's missing any socks or shoes or a few shirts I want them to stand by while we go through this chap's bag. Charlie 'Arvey 'ad 'is pocket plucked for five 'undred bloody bucks 'ere yesterday, I want 'im to stand by too.'

Then Mercurio asked Tom how to pronounce the Irish or Scottish name of a man who'd given him a card the previous day. He told Tom the name was spelled M-A-C, H-I-N-E-R-Y.

'MacHinery,' answered Tom.

'Ha!' cried Mercurio. 'Listen to him. "MacHinery". It's Machinery.'

Tom disappeared after his last workout on Tuesday 24 July and reporters were told he wouldn't appear again until the weigh-in on Thursday. He would go for a walk with Hennessey on Wednesday morning and a sail on the yacht belonging to wealthy Rumson sportsman Chris Smith in the afternoon. Several reporters drove around in a hired car to find Tom and the yacht, locating him on a beach at Monmouth lying under a large umbrella watching a bathing beauty parade. He was with Hennessey, Eddie Harvey, Mercurio and others from the camp. Apparently Chris Smith was just the name of the man who'd built the tender for the yacht.

Late on the eve of the bout Tom's team didn't even seem to know where the weigh-in was to take place, and there didn't seem to be any plan of attack. 'To tell you the bloody truth, I don't know just what I am going to do against Tunney,' Tom said. 'We have no plan of battle and we won't talk that over until tomorrow. However, I am going to fight my own fight.' He looked up and quickly qualified the remark. 'Of course I am going to listen to advice and heed the little things that are told to me.'

'Heeney will win the decision and if there is any knocking out done, Tom will do it,' Harvey said. 'I figure that Heeney will wear Tunney down and probably knock him out in the latter stages of the fight.' He was rather annoyed about a statement that had come out of the Tunney camp. 'I have just read a statement from Tunney that he will slug with Tom. I dare him to.'

Asked if he had any message for the outside world Tunney simply said, 'Just tell them I'm ready.'

Meanwhile, Rickard was still working. He reduced the price of thousands of seats from five to three dollars. And he picked Tom to win, another attempt to increase ticket sales. The day before the fight, word spread that Dempsey would be Tom's chief second. But Frank Menke of King Features, Dempsey's ghostwriter, worried it would look bad if a boxer accused of being a war slacker helped a foreigner try to take away the title from a former marine. Telephone calls were made, to among others, Paul Gallico.

'Hello, Paul . . . This is Jack . . . Jack Dempsey. The story about my acting as a second to Heeney . . . Ridiculous . . . Nothing to it. Don't know how it got started . . . I wouldn't dream of it. I'm an American first and last . . . get me, kid. You can say I wouldn't go in Heeney's corner if they asked me.'

In his last column before the fight Gallico gave Tom little chance of victory. He wondered if there was a catch somewhere — after all, Rickard made the match so he must have some confidence in Tom. 'I'd better write a piece and say that by catching Tunney's rights to the chin, Heeney hopes to break the champion's hand, and by stirring the breeze as he misses punches, cause Tunney to contract a severe cold which, should it develop into pneumonia, by the eighth round will enable Heeney to come on strongly from then on.' But he believed Tom would be on the floor at least once and that 'as the fight progresses and Heeney looks worse and worse, various figures on hands and knees will be seen trying to crawl inconspicuously toward the exits, and that these figures will be some of the guys that Heeney has licked in this country and who have pretended all along that they were great fighters and entitled to a lot of dough every time they consented to Merry Widow for ten rounds'. Hardly any money was going on the fight, 'probably because it is the first heavyweight battle the integrity of which has not been questioned', wrote Gallico.

McGeehan thought Tunney was flattering Tom, 'the silent sitter of New Zealand and New Jersey', by regarding him as something of an enigma. 'Whatever happens on the night of the 26th of July,' he wrote, 'Mr Heeney will be able to tell all his auditors as he sits behind his own mahogany: "Well, anyhow, I was a blooming enigma once, a blinking, blasted enigma to a heavyweight champion. It was not for long, but I was an enigma once, and you cannot take that away from me."'

Jack Heeney sent a last report home before the fight, describing how he'd sparred with Tom and that he was shocked by his brother's improvement. Tom gave his brother a message to include.

> Jack seemed to send you all sorts of news, just as if he were ringing on the 'phone. I am not much good at saying things, but I want to have a chip in on this wireless business. Tell all old friends in Gisborne that Tom Heeney is not going to disgrace them. I guess I am pretty fit, and after the hard tussle I had to get this far I am not going to be beaten if I can help it. I am right after that title, and if I don't get it it won't be for want of trying. I am more fit than I ever was, and every fight I have had in America has improved me. Tunney is a good boxer, but the old Maori horse isn't so bad himself, and he can stand a lot of knocking about. It's just great the way these stations are working to get the message through, and I

would like to shake hands with all the operators and tell them how good it is to get all this news to the people at home. I hope the next news will be that I am bringing the championship to Gisborne.

'I have never felt better in my life. If I am beaten I shall have no alibis to offer,' said Tom as he arrived in New York. He'd travelled up in a speedboat. Tunney arrived about the same time further up the North River by seaplane. About a thousand people, many of them women, had crowded onto the Columbia Yacht Club pier to greet him. The two boxers' cars drew alongside each other at Riverside Drive and 85th Street; Tunney in a Nile green Rolls-Royce and Tom in a Nash sedan.

The boxers weighed in at two o'clock at the Yankee Stadium at 161st Street and River Avenue. Tom arrived with his brothers and all his managers. Tunney mounted the scales first. He weighed 192 lb, two pounds heavier than he was at Chicago against Dempsey and six pounds heavier than he was in Philadelphia when he won the title. He seemed composed but slightly pale after his plane ride. As he was leaving the room he met Tom about to enter.

'Hello, Gene,' said Tom.

'Hello, Tom,' said Tunney.

Tom weighed 203½ lb. Bernard Mortimer said he wasn't worried as his fighter would lose weight under the hot arc lights during the bout. The boxers were examined by Dr William Walker, Commission physician and brother of Mayor Jimmy Walker. 'In all my experience I have never examined a boxer with such high blood pressure as Tom Heeney, nor one who was in such a highly nervous state on the eve of a bout,' the doctor stated. 'On the other hand, I have never examined a man who was in such perfect physical and mental condition as Gene Tunney.' Tunney's blood pressure was normal, he had a resting pulse of 66 and 73 after exercise and good reflexes. 'Heeney impressed me as exceptionally nervous, highly excitable and justified the conclusion that the fight was very much on his mind,' the doctor said. Tom's blood pressure was very high, his resting pulse was 74 and 83 after exercise and his reflexes were very slow.

The mercury hovered between 75 and 80. Tunney was driven to a hotel on the Grand Concourse where he slept for several hours and had to be woken to go to the stadium. Tom slipped out the rear gates and went back to his Bronx hideout, thought to be Eddie Harvey's home. He wasn't feeling right. The combination of the newspapermen interfering with his training and rest, his broken thumb — he was still finding it hard to get the idea of not using his right out of his head — and a fractured left rib that he'd had to protect with a ribbed steel patch while sparring, meant he 'was all in the day of the fight'. Perhaps it was also the fact he hadn't achieved his best fighting weight and that his nervousness had been made public. Or it may simply have been that he was about to fight the heavyweight champion, the man Norman Mailer once described as 'conceivably the most frightening unarmed killer alive'.

The Rocking Statue of Pain

Ivan O'Meara lived a few miles out of town. It was the day of the fight and Ivan owned a radio. His guests of honour were Hugh and Eliza Heeney and various other members of the clan. Dressed in their Sunday best, they sat and chatted in the sunshine until the fight was about to start. Tom's parents wanted to stay at home until someone brought them news. But they agreed to listen to the broadcast because 'it's just possible that Tom may speak over the wireless', Eliza said, 'and if he does it's our duty to be there to hear him'.

As Tom's fights got bigger so did the crowds rushing over to the Heeney home. Hugh had to start shutting his door to people, something he'd never expected to do. 'I don't like all these things going in the paper, but there is one thing I would like to ask: Will you tell people to leave us alone on Friday night?' They wanted to absorb news of the Tunney fight in peace and to spend quiet time with a few specially invited family friends.

If there wasn't a knockout Tunney would win, was Hugh's prediction. If there was a knockout it would be Tom's victory. 'I am a proud man to have reared a son who is the second best boxer in the world,' Hugh said. 'If he gets no further than second best nothing can lessen my pride in him. If it is that he is to be champion of the world, then I shall be very happy, but if he fails in this final test I shall not be disappointed.'

'If Tom gets a beating he gets a beating, and that's all there is to it,' said Eliza. 'All the worry in the world isn't going to make any difference.' So they weren't worrying. 'I don't think we are even excited about it. Tom's a good boy — one of the best a mother ever had — and he deserves success. If he wins no one will be more pleased than we will. Tunney is a clever fighter, there's no doubt about that, but our Tom must have a chance or he wouldn't be matched with him. I know this much: Tom will do his best, and what else matters?' Eliza was nothing if not rational. 'They can't both win, and if Tom is beaten he knows how to take a beating. He's just as good a loser as a winner, and that's how it should be. Anyhow, if a Heking's coming to him he's got to take it whether he wants it or not,' she added with a smile, 'and it won't be the first either.'

Ivan O'Meara was one of three Gisborne radio pioneers. Ivan, Percy Stevens and Bob Patty had experimented with a crystal set to listen for Morse signals, which they picked up from Western Samoa, during the war and the trio established two-way shortwave links with amateurs around the world. In 1923 Stevens and O'Meara set up what was believed to have been New Zealand's first two-way radio-telephone circuit and the three established the Gisborne station 2YM, later 2ZM, after they secured one of the first broadcasting licences. Stevens was the owner before becoming director, operator and owner.

The Heeney–Tunney fight would be relayed to the world 'by the most ambitious radio station hook-up in the history of broadcasting' and Gisborne had several experts ready to receive it. If the weather was good the largest ever radio audience would be listening, probably more than 50,000,000. Republican presidential nominee Herbert Hoover had a brand-new radio set installed the day before the fight. At ten o'clock in New York WEAF's network of 48 stations in the United States and Canada, together with two shortwave transmitters of the General Electric Company of South Schenectady, 2XAF and 2XAD, would send out the ringside description from veteran sports announcers Graham McNamee and Phillips Carlin. The BBC and broadcasters around the world would intercept the shortwaves and attempt to carry the fight.

Percy Stevens was to relay the fight to radio-owners and to crowds outside 2ZM in Gladstone Road over two loudspeakers. If the ringside announcers couldn't be heard there was a back-up plan. A boxing expert would describe the fight to a colleague at ringside, who would dictate it to telegraph operators, who would tap the report in Morse across a thousand-mile landline to the *Montreal Star*, whose staff would phone the report over five miles of line installed by the newspaper to a radio amateur, who would transmit it to Patty in Gisborne, who would decode it and, with the help of *Gisborne Times* staff, send it over another mile of special phone line to 2ZM when it would finally be sent 'over the air'.

'GISBORNE GOES TO NEW YORK FOR HEENEY FIGHT', read one headline. Farms and businesses were abandoned. More than 3000 people gathered in front of 2ZM and a large crowd stood outside the *Poverty Bay Herald*. The newspaper was putting out an early edition soon after the result was known. 'The roads that converged on Gisborne rattled with traffic as weird and wonderful and as picturesque as ever turned out for any circus parade,' wrote one scribe. 'Gisborne lost its identity in the mist of hope and melted through a mirage into a stadium somewhere in New York.'

At four in the afternoon at the Yankee Stadium there were only a couple of people at the ticket booths selling the most expensive tickets. The hordes hadn't turned up. The policemen had nothing to do. Hundreds were there to handle the expected congestion and confusion outside the stadium. Across the 40 entrances were 250 gatemen and inside were hundreds more officials: ushers, ticket-takers and special police of the Garden. When Paul Gallico arrived he was surprised to be 'admitted instantly without having to argue with any one'. He looked at the golden clock on the scoreboard above the 'Batting Order' sign that read seven minutes past five and then scanned the stadium. There were a few people in the five-dollar seats that had been reduced to three dollars the previous day. Rickard's officials with red hats and armbands were the only people in the upper stands. Staff were still working on the ring in the ballpark somewhere near the pitcher's box and second base. The ringside seats stopped many yards before the running track that circled the outfield.

The first man to buy a ticket predicted a draw. The first woman to buy one said, 'I think Tunney is beautiful.' It was fine and cloudy and fresh breezes tempered the sultry heat. Ushers and special policemen cheered the first two customers as they headed for their seats. When the first preliminary began at 7 p.m. there were around 20,000 in the stadium. It would be another half hour before any ringside seats were occupied, by which time Rickard admitted he'd be lucky to get a crowd of 60,000.

Tom arrived in his dressing room a little before Tunney reached his. 'A fellow with a crooked nose came into the dressing room,' said John Mortimer, 'and he says to Harvey, says he, "Tom's bandages are too long." I know what he was in there for, to get Tom's goat, and he got it, too.' Harvey was furious and burst into Tunney's dressing room and insisted on measuring his tape bandages. 'Tunney merely grinned,' wrote Grantland Rice, 'and finally kidded Harvey out of the argument.'

At 9 p.m. there were still many gaps at ringside. It began to rain a little. The odds were 3 to 1 for Tunney and the Mortimers bet $11,500 on Tom. Last-minute crowds spilled through the entrances, but bare patches remained. In all, some 45,000 people came. In the first six rows around the ring were hundreds of newspaper correspondents, shouting over telephones, dictating to telegraph operators and tapping on typewriters. Over the ring two large platforms were filled with newspaper and motion picture photographers. Under it, the grass was littered with telephone equipment, radio control boards, brooms, buckets, chairs, boxes, blowtorches, steel wire, rope, saws and cables. The New Zealand flag fluttered beneath the Stars and Stripes. Among the spectators were Jim Corbett, Theodore, Kermit and Archie Roosevelt, Vincent Astor, Cornelius Vanderbilt Whitney, and the Governors of Maryland, Massachusetts, Michigan and New Jersey. Red and white lights illuminated the seats in the galleries but the spectators around the ring were in semi-darkness. Shadows fell from two dozen arc lamps over the ring.

Jack, Artie and Pat Heeney were 'ringside' 26 rows back and struggled to hear the announcer. Two others in 'row 26, section G, ringside' complained to the ushers that their neighbours were talking too loudly. One was deaf and the other was shouting in his ear about crops and business problems. A scribe in row 35 — still 'ringside' — had rows of empty chairs behind him and complained of loneliness. A volley of shots broke the silence. He wondered at first if it was Rickard trying and failing to commit suicide, but it was the 101 Ranch Wild West Show across the street.

In the three-dollar seats sat the members of the 'Le Blang Cut Rate Splinter Absorbing and Distant Gazing Society'. Joe Le Blang was known for selling cut-rate tickets in large numbers. Some had queued since sunrise for their seats. The 'bleacherites' perched on a plank with the lights of the ring so far away the fighters looked like insects. Other fans tried to watch the fight for free from Bronx rooftops and windowsills, but they were blocked by blindingly powerful searchlights on the stadium roof, there to stop movie cameramen bootlegging the fight.

The last preliminary was over by a quarter to ten. The cheering increased until the announcer, Joe Humphreys, stepped into the ring to introduce the 'distinguished visitors'. A cordon of police was posted along the aisles from the boxers' dressing rooms. Jimmy Hennessey climbed into the ring carrying a bucket. Tom was close behind and he got a brief cheer. Draped over his left shoulder was the Maori cloak, described by one writer as 'the strangest garment ever worn in the ring by a prizefighter'. Another said it looked like 'a Gypsy blanket for a Ford roadster and was trimmed with hair from Charlie Harvey's moustache'. Tom wore the official trunks of the boxing commission: black and red seamed and red belted. Eddie Harvey stood behind Tom as he sat, head bowed, listening to last-minute advice from his trainer. The Mortimer brothers sat close to Tom's corner.

The champion wore a dark blue robe trimmed in red with the Marine insignia on the back. Under his robe he wore purple trunks. The first New Yorker to hold the world's heavyweight title was defending it for the first time in his home city. He walked through the cheering crowd, head bowed, talking to people he recognised.

As soon as Tom saw Tunney coming up the steps he rushed across the ring and met the champion in his corner. They shook hands and moved to a neutral corner to pose for photographs, hands clasped. As the cameramen got ready Tunney asked a rather self-conscious Tom about the cloak.

'Where did you get it?' he asked, smiling.

'I got it from home.'

Knute Hansen, Johnny Risko, Tommy Loughran and Jack Sharkey were introduced. The crowd paid little attention to the perfunctory business, however, until the arrival of an idol. Jack Dempsey emerged from the crowd in a bottle-green suit and green tie just as Humphreys was about to introduce Tom and Tunney. He climbed through the ropes, strode across to each corner, shook hands with the fighters and bowed in the centre of the ring with his straw hat in his hand. The crowd thundered. Joe

Humphreys introduced him as 'The greatest and most colourful fighter of all time'. Tunney smiled; Tom remained stony-faced.

Tom and Tunney stood together in the centre of the ring with their seconds while referee Eddie Forbes gave his instructions. Forbes was a Brooklyn newspaperman with nearly 50 years' experience as a fighter and manager, known as 'Square Eddie' because of his honesty. The judges were cigar merchant Tom Flynn and veteran New York boxing writer Charles Mathison. 'When I say break, you break and step back a yard,' instructed Forbes. Tom had been training for six weeks to hit coming out of the clinches and he'd just been told he couldn't do it. They returned to their corners.

The bell rang. Punches were thrown and the men wrestled to the ropes. As they broke Tom smashed in a solid right to the head. He looked apologetically to the referee and was warned for hitting on the break. They traded punches to the jaw and clinched. In an early clinch the Mortimer brothers claimed Tunney whispered 'Let's fight as gentlemen, Tom.' They broke. Tunney danced around looking for an opening and repeatedly went for Tom's jaw. A sweeping left hook almost had Tunney off his feet. Tom had been trained to expect a left jab followed by a right cross. He was to smother the jab and land his own left before the right got under way. But a right to the side of his head flashed in before he could raise his left shoulder to block it. It was one of the hardest blows of the fight and when Tom stayed upright Tunney knew the fight would go on for some time. Tom said the lefts bothered him the most. Tunney 'kept shooting left hooks like a machine-gun'. Years later he recalled that the champion 'had the most perfect straight left I ever saw. Every time it landed it jarred you to your back teeth.' They were slugging toe to toe at the bell.

Tom kept moving forward but the champion waited for him to come in, jabbing with his left. 'Tunney blasted left and right into the sturdy head of the Hard Rock without causing a flicker of Heeney's eyelashes,' wrote one commentator. They 'mixed it hotly' and often clinched. Forbes ordered them to break several times. 'In the second I had staggered him with a sharp right to the jaw. At that moment I had visions of the championship coming to me,' said Tom. But he took a lot of punches to the head and one of Tunney's rights opened a small cut on his lip. 'Tunney sparred as Tom ripped in,' wrote another. 'When Gene's left hook dropped low, Tom mentioned it, and Gene smiled and asked forgiveness. A second later they were crashing each other all along one side of the ring in a slugging exchange of head clouts that rocked both on their heels.' The bell to end the second stopped an exchange of blows and people stood up to cheer.

At Ivan O'Meara's house the description of the early rounds was barely audible. In other places around New Zealand the reception was so poor the news was clearer in Morse. Tom's parents sat silently side by side and whatever the news they acknowledged it with a nod and smile. Eliza was slightly flushed, her lips tightly closed and her eyes a little misty. Hugh stared at the radio. He strained forward as the rounds progressed and put his much-loved pipe in his pocket.

> . . . *There's the bell* . . . came the announcer's voice at the start of Round Three.

The fighters came together and Tom hooked Tunney on the nose. Tunney crashed a right to Tom's jaw. There was more clinching, more of Tom rushing in and of Tunney dancing away. Tunney fired rat-a-tat punches at Tom's nose but Tom went after him, swinging rights and lefts, and made him back away. Tunney took several telling blows in the early rounds, but from the fourth onwards the outcome seemed inevitable. The champion kept landing punches, and when Tom gathered the energy to rush in Tunney stopped him with the crushing rights to the heart he'd perfected at Speculator. 'One of them thudded against Heeney's ribs with such a resounding smack that it sounded like the booming of a Maori drum even to the people in the upper tiers,' wrote McGeehan. Sometimes he varied the onslaught with stinging rights to the head. One of Tom's punches almost made Tunney lose his footing again. A small cut appeared under Tom's chin, his nose started bleeding and then his right eye.

> . . . *Heeney's nose is not so good* . . . said Graham McNamee whenever there was a lull in the fighting.

> . . . *Gene's left again finds that sore nose. That sore nose of Tommy's is considerably sore* . . . he said when the punches started again.

Tom fought back. He launched a savage onslaught, forcing Tunney to the ropes. The crowd sympathised with the challenger. One particularly loud supporter kept yelling, 'How do you like that, Gene?' and 'Get in there, Tom!' The bell broke his attack and Tom went back to his corner with his face covered in blood.

Blood streamed from Tom's nose as the bell tolled for the fifth. He kept on moving forward, but really only had one punch, a looping right to the head. Invariably he telegraphed it five seconds before it came across by jockeying his legs into position and dropping his shoulder. When the punch finally arrived Tunney wasn't there. 'In the fifth round he came on with a spurt, launching looping lefts and rights to my head,' Tunney said. 'That was my chance to make him miss by drawing my body back and leaving me in position to catch him with a left hook to the face.' Tunney kept targeting his opponent's heart. Tom slipped to the canvas and Tunney stepped back, but he scrambled up without a count. The referee rubbed off Tom's gloves. The New Zealander looked in a bad way but was still fighting viciously at the bell.

Tom caught Tunney now and again, despite his short arms, and this got the crowd excited. But after the fifth Tunney's punches to the heart weakened the New Zealander. By the sixth Tunney seemed to be punching Tom at will, wearing him down, cutting up his face and drawing fresh blood. Tom kept charging. Tommy Loughran wrote that Tom won the first half of the sixth round, 'the only one in which he made any kind of a showing'. They were standing up close hammering each other to the head when the bell sounded.

In the seventh Gallico counted Tom miss eight consecutive punches. Tunney missed none. In the clinches Tunney had Tom tied up, holding his glove as Tom struggled to break free. Tunney punched and then danced away. 'It was so much one-sided that it was getting monotonous,' wrote one scribe. Tunney had gradually slowed Tom down using two main punches: a left poke in the face and a heavy right to the heart. During the break the champion was doused with half a bucket of water. Between rounds Tom's seconds poked glass tubes with some sort of astringent fluid into his nostrils. It didn't stem the flow of blood. Harvey rubbed ice on Tom's neck.

During the eighth Tom retreated for the first time. He suddenly staggered back from Tunney as if half-blind, blinking furiously and shaking his head with the pain.

> *... Something's the matter with Tom's left eye ... it's blinking ...*

Tom said it felt as if his upper lid had been torn away. He wiped the eye with his glove but couldn't clear it.

> *... and now Gene's following Tommy ... Gene gets a right and a left to Tom's body ... and a right to the jaw as Tom is trying to blink something out of that eye ...*

There was confusion at ringside. Had Tom's seconds got collodion in his eyes? Had dye got onto Tunney's gloves and into Tom's eye? Tunney claimed he stepped back to give Tom a bit of time to recover. He had seen his friend Gene Delmont hit with a powerful right-hand punch that seemed to land on his forehead during a bout in Hollywood. After the fight Tunney found his friend crying in the dressing room and asked him what had happened. Delmont said he was punched over the left eye and he couldn't see so when he went back to his corner he told a second he had an eyelash in his eye that needed turning out. His second told him his eye was open and Delmont realised he was blind in that eye. Tunney said he was scared he might do the same to Tom.

> *... Now Tommy smashes a left to Gene's face, but Gene follows with a left and a right to the jaw of the Hard Rock Down Under ... Heeney is still blinking that eye ... somehow or other he's blind in that eye ...*

Phillips Carlin sometimes took over from McNamee.

> *... The only thing the matter with that eye is that it's a black eye ... Several gloves were thrown into the said optical attachment ...*

Partially blinded, Tom tore into the champion as a thin stream of blood trickled from his nose. Tunney pumped lefts and rights to the body. The crowd cheered Tom loudly as he went back to his corner. Tom apparently claimed that Tunney had stuck the thumb of his glove into his left eye. Hennessey squatted in front of Tom on his stool and bathed the eye.

'What happened to his eye out there when he began to blink?' asked John Mortimer.

'Thumb,' said Harvey. 'Thumb in his eye.'

Westbrook Pegler didn't see a thumbing from ringside, but disputed that Tunney had refrained from hitting Tom. Tunney said he looked over to Tom's corner and saw a boxing writer rush over to Harvey to ask what had happened. He saw Harvey make a jabbing motion with his thumb. 'I was furious,' Tunney said. 'For the next two rounds I gave Heeney a terrible beating — the worst beating of his life, and all because of his manager.' Graham McNamee told the world Tom's supporters claimed he'd been thumbed.

> *. . . but the referee says no . . .*

Tom's troubled left eye was still bleeding when the bell rang for the ninth. Hennessey urged Tom to butt Tunney in retaliation. 'Use your 'ead in the clinches, Tom, use your 'ead on 'im,' a scribe heard him say. But Tom wouldn't do it.

Radio reception improved at Ivan O'Meara's as the fight went on. 'I'm afraid that's the end of it,' Eliza said after she'd been told of the cut over Tom's eye. Hugh remained silent.

Tom moved towards Tunney, still blinking. They slugged and blood oozed from his eye and his nose. The claret poured down his face but still he bored in. 'Tunney hit me a million times, I guess, but he has not a knock-out punch; but when any bloke hits you that many times, it is bound to do damage,' Tom said.

> *. . . I don't think that Heeney will be calling on any of his girl friends tomorrow . . .*

'Punch in close!' Harvey shouted at Tom as the tenth began. Tom tried but took hit after hit. At each of Tunney's thrusts, left, right, left, blood spurted onto the canvas and onto the journalists' notepaper. But he stayed standing. He spat blood but kept plodding. 'Heeney's fighting style of always coming on in the face of punishment made the ideal situation for my left jab to the face,' Tunney said. The crowd watched silently. The end of the round was near and Tunney battered Tom to the ropes.

> *. . . Tommy caught a terrific left to the body. Tommy's half out of the ring . . .*

Tom struggled to straighten up. 'Heeney came out of that exchange ready for the work of a killer, and Tunney cocked his body just the way Demspey used to do,' wrote Gallico. 'Tunney stepped back. Heeney straightened, and then slid onto the south ropes, facing Tunney. He was wide open. He was ready for it. Tunney let him have that right, and he cocked his leg for the follow through the way a golfer does to lend power.' Tom crashed onto the canvas and his head cracked against the floor.

> *. . . I think it's going to be all over now . . . he took a terrific right to the side of the jaw . . . there's the count . . . but the bell sounded before the count . . .*

The crowd roared and only those near the ring heard the bell. Joe Humphreys thought Forbes had stopped the bout. He climbed the steps and clambered through the ropes at Tunney's corner and tried to grab the champion's hand. Tunney waved him away. Spectators got up and started for the exits thinking it was all over.

Tom's seconds were in the ring shouting, 'Tom! Tom!' Harvey hobbled over and grabbed Tom's head. 'Heeney's ears were wet and slippery both from the gory lather smeared by Tunney's pounding fists and from water sprayed on him with a sponge and as Harvey lifted, the unconscious man's head slipped out of his grasp and banged on the wadded floor with a dull sound as of a bowling ball dropping in the pit,' wrote Pegler. 'Tom! Tom! Ginger goodness, Tom old boy . . . Get up boy, the bell.' Tom stirred and the Harveys and Hennessey half-carried him back to his stool, propping him there while they worked frantically: wiping some of the blood away, rubbing him, putting ice on the back of his neck, dabbing iodine on a cut on his right eyelid, splashing him with cold water, shaking his head and prodding his limp body. 'It wouldn't have done any great good if they had thrown the Atlantic and Pacific Oceans on the broken challenger, now approaching a shambling wreck,' wrote Grantland Rice.

Gallico sat directly beneath Tom's corner. 'I like Tom and it sent that choking feeling high into my throat to see what they were doing to him after the dreadful tenth round, where he was smashed to a quivering pulp. With all my heart I despised those who were trying so desperately to bring this stricken animal back into the semblance of a human so that his indomitable courage could again function and drive a battered body still further into destruction. The carcass was beaten, they knew, and so, with all the slobbering greed of jackals, they strove to awaken that which is stronger than the flesh. They pawed with their filthy hands at the bloody head and rattled away at a frame already racked with dreadful pain. They bawled at him the way a herder bawls at his swine.'

. . . Tommy's taken back to his corner after laying outside the ropes . . . it may be over . . .

Forbes looked set to stop it but gave Tom one more chance.

. . . no . . . the contest will go on . . .

A boy climbed through the ropes with a large card showing '11' and everyone knew the fight was still on. Tunney's chief second urged his man to finish Tom off straight away. Tom's head was between his knees and blood and water poured onto the canvas. His left eye 'seemed protruding from its torn socket'. His right was swollen and cut. Blood streamed from his lips, but he was conscious.

. . . I don't think Tom will be able to continue . . .

Gallico wrote that despite everything that had been said about mild, sweet-looking Harvey, when the test came he was just like every other fight manager. He had neither the courage nor the decency to stop the fight. 'For that ghastly ten seconds awaiting the bell for the eleventh round, when he sat bowed and abandoned in his corner, Heeney was a figure to stir compassion, a rocking statue of pain,' wrote Gallico. 'Left alone by his tormentors, his boy's head slumped forward on his chest and he rolled forward as though he were about to spill from the stool and bury his head in the little lumps of powdered resin in the corner.' Gallico involuntarily raised his hand as if to break his fall, 'and then felt myself thrill as I have rarely thrilled before, when the bell sent him miraculously charging his foe, winging punches harmless, unguided blows, a brave youth with not even a wooden sword charging a steel armed foeman'. Tom punched harder than he had in the previous rounds. Unconscious a few minutes earlier, 'How he ever came to know what was wanted of him not even he will ever know. It was an epic of courage.' Runyon wrote that

Tom 'came out for the eleventh like a gallant old fire horse responding to an alarm, flourishing his gloves around with astonishing courage'. Marion had tears in her eyes when Tom got knocked down so she shut them tight. 'When I opened them he was still fighting. It was wonderful.' The crowd stood and roared.

Harvey told Tom to crouch when he went back in, but he stood up and was wide open. 'When he came out for the eleventh round he was like a baby in my hands,' said Tunney. 'I got in rights to the heart that were like hitting a heavy bag in training.' Tom landed a few blows but reeled as he took four times as many from Tunney. A left to the jaw made Tom's mouthpiece fly out. Rights under the heart forced his mouth to drop open and lefts to the head sprayed blood around the ring.

'Stop it!' the crowd shouted. Tom was helpless and groggy and his face was gory. He staggered in Tunney's corner and the champion was poised when he glanced at the referee and claimed to have told him, 'If you want me to go on hitting this man, I won't be responsible for the consequences.' Forbes stepped in and stopped the bout after two minutes and 52 seconds of the eleventh round. Tom weakly protested, choking from the blood. The referee pushed Tunney back and held up his right hand. Tunney hit his opponents so many more times than they hit him that they eventually crumpled under the cumulative effect. With Tunney's glove on his elbow Tom 'reeled and staggered back to his corner, not quite certain whether he was in New York or New Zealand', wrote Rice.

The fighters complimented each other's performance and wished each other luck. While Tunney was talking, Tom bowed his head, and one observer thought his eyes were teary. Tunney put his soggy gloves on Tom's shoulders, they parted and the champion greeted friends at ringside. When the last photographs had been taken, ambulances hired as mobile developing rooms raced downtown with a police escort. Tunney was still the heavyweight champion of the world 'by a margin as wide as the gap between New York City and Gisborne, New Zealand', according to Rice.

Every word could now be heard at Ivan O'Meara's. Eliza sat up straighter as if the tension had eased and Hugh pulled out his pipe and lit up again. 'Well, a man can't do more than his best. Tom was a trier and he went down fighting,' he said. 'We're sorry, but it can't be helped.' He was proud of Tom for getting as far as he had. 'Well, one of them had to lose,' Eliza smiled. 'Of course,' she said, 'we would have liked him to win, but we're not disappointed. He did his best, and that's all we could expect. We still have every reason to be proud of him.'

Then they heard their son's voice for the first time in four years. 'I did my best,' he said. 'Tunney beat me fairly and squarely, and I want to congratulate him on his victory.' John Mortimer said that after a rest Tom would make another bid for the title. 'Tom's parents away in New Zealand have been listening to the description of the fight, and he wants me to tell them that although he has been beaten he is quite all right, and that he has not sustained any injuries which are in any way serious. Tom's message to them is "Kia ora".'

'What does kia ora mean?' asked someone by the microphone.

'Kia ora', explained Mortimer, 'is good luck in the language of the natives of New Zealand, where Heeney's home is. I have in my hand an historic Maori cloak sent to Tom Heeney by native admirers in his own country, and which he wore on going into the ring. "Kia ora."'

Back in his dressing room Tom was stripped, his face washed, blood stemmed. He looked very different to the pitiful figure that had left the ring. He walked around the room eating oranges with his battered left eye taped up, trying to dismiss the 'sympathetic advices' of Charlie Harvey and the brothers Mortimer. He felt like he could have continued. The controversy was over the thumbing incident. In one version of the story Tom blamed a mosquito or bug attracted by the glare of the ring lights. In another he confirmed Tunney had stuck his thumb in his eye; and in yet another a clean punch had driven a lash into his eye. Later he repeatedly denied foul play. But some sports writers were convinced Tunney had thumbed him and so was Tom's team. 'Tom fought a wonderful fight and I know he would have won had not Tunney's thumb poked him in the eye,' said Harvey, adding that when the eighth round opened Tom was fresh and kept saying he 'never felt better in his life'. John Mortimer claimed the evidence was in the movie of the fight. It happened in a clinch. Tunney's back was to the camera and there was no sign of a blow. Tom emerged from the clinch rubbing his eye. Mortimer also said one of the Commission doctors told him straight after the fight the injury wasn't caused by a blow. He said Sammy Mandell was standing nearby when Tom denied foul play and said, 'You know it wasn't an accident, Tom. I saw it, and I have written for several papers that you were poked with a thumb.' Tunney insisted he'd paralysed Tom's optic nerve with a hard right just above his eye.

'I am very gratified to have won,' Tunney said when he arrived in his dressing room. He was unmarked, but concerned about Tom's condition. Messengers were dispatched to the New Zealander's dressing room. John Kieran of the *New York Times* wrote of an incident few people witnessed. Most of the well-wishers had gone, Tunney was chatting with a few friends and the lights of the stadium were being turned off, when the door opened. In came Tom.

'Tom, listen!' said Tunney as he rushed over. 'Take care of that eye. Gosh, don't let it get infected.'

'Never mind me eye,' Tom said. 'Gene, I just came in here to tell you that you're a square fighter and a great fighter. Here's my hand. The best of luck go with you wherever you go.'

Only after Tom had gone did Tunney manage a few words. 'Wasn't that great of Tom?'

Later that night Tom telephoned a message for his parents to an American radio amateur. 'I am very sorry that I was not able to win,' he said, 'but all the folks at home will know that I did my best. I have been defeated but I am not hurt.' His parents were still at the O'Meara's. They'd been having afternoon tea and invariably answering any questions with a smile and 'Oh, well, they couldn't both win' or 'Someone had to lose'. They were about to leave when Tom's message was received. Asked for a reply they said, 'Just tell him we're not disappointed; that we have been listening to the fight, and knowing that he did his best we are very proud of him'. More than a hundred friends gathered for supper at the Heeney home that night.

There was a story that one of two Maori who'd been 'celebrating a little' near a loudspeaker in town said, 'Gorry, I let Tunney bash me to death for twenty thousand quid'. It was assumed the money would have to be paid before the fight. There were a couple of brawls in the back streets. The hotels did a phenomenal bar trade. 'Just as the merry-makers in Gisborne rolled their uncertain way home — probably while Tom was having breakfast before slipping along to Tex for his cheque — so, too, throughout New Zealand was the official eye shut to the little alcoholic faux-pas that might be perpetrated,' wrote one newspaper, and that Gisborne pleaded mitigating circumstances. 'The child of her soil had tussled with gladiators; and she had merely embraced a trier.' The

Prime Minister cabled Tom: 'We are all very sorry success did not come your way. However, you have the satisfaction of having put up a splendid fight against the champion. Kia Ora. — Coates, Prime Minister.' 'EVEN GREATER IN DEFEAT — Whole Nation Applauds Tom Heeney — FOUGHT FOE TO LAST GASP' ran the *Poverty Bay Herald*'s headline on Saturday.

At the luxurious Ansonia Hotel on Broadway a sports writer from the *Port Washington News*, the paper of Marion's home village, interviewed Tom. He reported that Tom had just found out that his father was very ill — reportedly at the point of death. His brothers had chosen not to show him cables they'd received until after the fight. 'The writer further wants to state that Heeney is a person of wonderful personality and a delightful person to converse with and is willing at all times to discuss any matter or nature other than pertaining to boxing.'

Tunney awoke the next day a more popular champion, who'd destroyed his challenger with a scientific, textbook performance. 'Gone, apparently, is the Tunney who always was content to outscore his foe. The evolution of Tunney, the boxer, into Tunney, the fighter, is complete,' wrote one scribe. 'The fight with Heeney, I believe, was the most skilful performance of my career. It was the most satisfactory, personally. Everything clicked in unison,' the champion wrote.

Tex Rickard awoke to his first big financial failure. A fight without Dempsey hadn't worked and the Madison Square Garden Corporation lost $155,719.77. Rickard blamed the radio, Tunney's lack of box-office appeal, staging the fight in July instead of September, and the choice of Tom as challenger. 'I thought any heavyweight fight would draw. But Heeney couldn't draw — I've been sure of that for three weeks.' He also said he didn't think Tom could have won if he had 'trained in heaven'.

Tom awoke with a bruised and battered face, one eye partly closed, and sore ribs. Thanks to his $100,000 guarantee he was also much richer. But the cheque lay unclaimed in Rickard's office all day. He was recovering from the fight in the uptown house of friends and no one called to pick it up. The newspapers reflected on his bravery against Tunney. McGeehan's words pretty much summed up the general opinion: 'Too much could not be said in praise of the stubborn, stolid courage of Tom Heeney, the stout man of the Anzac. He showed the fighting heart of his breed, which produced some of the finest troops that were raised for the World War.

In the ring he showed the spirit of the men of the Anzac in Gallipoli and on all the bloody fields of the war.' Boxing writer Nat Fleischer believed Tom could return to New Zealand with pride. 'He can go back to his Fatherland with the knowledge that he accepted the chance America offered but was whipped by a better fellow. He can go back with that modesty, manly-bearing, that extreme frankness and ever-beaming smile that has endeared him to American fandom, and tell his folks that he has earned not only American dollars which will make him comfortable for the rest of his life if he invests them properly, but with them, popularity such as no other foreign fighter with the possible exception of Bob Fitzsimmons ever carried back with him.'

From Tiger to House Cat

'Our wedding was too funny for words,' said Marion. 'We dashed off to Ladentown, the tiniest town I was ever in . . . and got married there.' Tom, brother Pat, Marion and Marjorie Irvine drove upstate. They left Spring Valley, where Marion had been living, and headed north towards the edge of the Ramapo Mountains. On the way they stopped in the town of Ramapo to see Mrs Grace Ronk. She promised not to talk about the meeting. After arriving in Ladentown they went to a general store selling shoestrings and colic remedies run by Pincus Margulies. Later that night in the parlour of Margulies' home, in front of Pat and Marjorie and a few local residents, Tom and Marion became husband and wife. Afterwards the wedding party motored back to Spring Valley. Word of Tom's kayo by Cupid soon got out. Justice of the Peace Margulies fielded dozens of phone calls from New York.

'Are you sure it was the prizefighter you married?' asked one reporter.

'Yes, that was the man all right. I've seen his pictures lots of times.'

Grace Ronk refused to admit she had issued the marriage licence. Marion had given her parents' names as John Dunn and Anna Scherer, so a Mr John Dunn of Spring Valley was tracked down. He didn't know any Marion Dunn. A Mrs John Dunn said she didn't have a daughter

Marion and didn't know of any other Dunns in the area. Tom's friends were called. Eddie Harvey knew nothing but thought it must be true. 'Tom and Miss Dunn have been going together for some time,' he said, 'and the marriage is no surprise to me.' John Mortimer confirmed the union and said the newlyweds were driving to New Jersey.

The couple was rumoured to be hiding out at a luxurious apartment at 1 West 85th Street, which was listed under the name of Isaac Rosenblum. The Upper West Side boasted some of the finest apartment buildings in Manhattan. An *Evening Journal* reporter phoned the apartment. A man with a broad English accent who sounded suspiciously like one of the Mortimers answered. 'Mr 'eeney used to live 'ere,' he said, 'but at present I think 'e is on 'is wy to the Coast.' The newspaper dispatched a reporter and photographer to the apartment. They asked whether Tom was in. A laughing 'coloured maid' strenuously denied Tom was there. Whispers and muffled giggles could be heard inside. 'Why, of course Mr Heeney ain't here,' she said. 'Never has been here. Don't know anybody named Heeney.' Jack and Art Heeney hurried through the door and dashed into a car. The reporter quizzed other tenants in the building. He found out that Tom was a tenant; had left the previous day with a woman and returned early that day.

'Tigers of Ring Transformed Into House Cats by Marriage' ran one newspaper headline. Tom had been the last of the eligible bachelors among the challengers and now it was official that the champion was also taken. Tunney announced he was to marry 21-year-old Greenwich society girl Mary Josephine 'Polly' Lauder. A very rich boxer was about to marry an even richer heiress. Once a fighter got a girl or got married, he was through, went the old adage. He was said to lose 'the indefinable ache inside' that got him through torturous training and punishment in the ring when there was everything to gain and nothing to lose; when he wasn't used to the comforts of a family home; when he only had to look after himself.

The champion formally announced his retirement at a luncheon for newspapermen and friends. The former Greenwich Village shipping clerk had earned an estimated $2 million in the ring and became only the second heavyweight champion to retire since the introduction of the Queensberry rules. The first, James J. Jeffries, made a comeback only to get knocked out by Jack Johnson. So, unsurprisingly, some people wondered if Tunney was really through with the ring. Tom believed he was, that he didn't like the game and just used it to make a fortune. 'I have not spoken a dozen words with him in my life,' Tom said. 'He is looking for riches in millions, and maybe he will get them. Anyway, he's got no use for the ----- working class.' He thought Tunney's Shakespearean studies were a publicity stunt and that it was only in the last couple of years that he had talked of Shakespeare, wanting to 'high-hat it over all creation'.

Tunney's retirement created a scramble to find his successor. Risko claimed the heavyweight championship in a letter to the Commission, posting a cheque for $2500 as proof he was willing to meet anyone who challenged his right to the crown. Phil Scott also laid claim to the title, citing his victories over Risko and Tom and other prominent heavyweights. He issued a challenge to any boxer in the world that disputed his claim.

There was talk of Tom fighting Knute Hansen in the middle of September, but he didn't seem keen. The most likely match looked like another fight with Scott. Tom knew there'd be big money in London for it. If Harvey got the match he'd go to England and then go home to New Zealand. But the Scott negotiations fell through. Later, Tom said he asked for £8000 (about $40,000), win, lose or draw.

On 15 August Tom, Harvey and John Mortimer met Rickard in private at the Garden. 'Heeney just wanted to see me before he left for home,' explained the promoter. 'He's going back Friday and will not return to this country until January, when he'll come back ready to resume fighting. I think he'll be welcomed back, too, for I expect him to be one of the biggest cards in our heavyweight title eliminations.' The following evening Tom hosted a farewell dinner at Billy La Hiff's Tavern for friends and newspapermen, and the day after that he left for Vancouver with Marion and his three brothers. It was reported that Tom had departed New Zealand with about $40 but in the 'land of opportunity' he'd gathered $125,000 and a bride. It was generally thought Tom had made about $200,000–250,000 and saved about half. For the Tunney fight alone, after paying tax, his managers and expenses, he was left with roughly half the $100,000 guarantee.

A few hours after Tom's departure Tunney left New York on the *Mauretania* bound for Europe. He was to be married abroad and Tom sent him a wireless message wishing him good luck in his wedded bliss. He said he'd been through the same recently himself and he should know what it meant. Crowds waited at every station as Marion and the Heeney boys made their way across the United States to Seattle and north to Vancouver. On board the Canada–Australasia liner *Aorangi* there were sports, motion pictures and fancy dress balls; there was canoeing on Waikiki Beach at Honolulu and a great welcome for Tom at Suva from the crew of the warship *Dunedin*. And there were candid comments. 'I was beaten from the start,' Tom told one passenger. 'I think the only round I won was the fourth, despite what the reporters said about me.'

It was dusk on Sunday 9 September 1928 when the *Aorangi* sailed slowly around North Head towards downtown Auckland, her shape just visible in driving rain. Officials ran alongside in a launch and climbed a steep gangway over the ship's side. Tom was found in a corner of the first saloon stateroom. Marion was enveloped in a luxury fur coat over a smart black dress. Dark brown curls peeped from under her black toque decorated with a cluster of black grapes, and slender high-heeled shoes adorned her feet. The only ring she wore in addition to a narrow gold band was a sparkling solitaire diamond. Tom still had a slight scar above his left eye. He took a cigar from his mouth as he greeted the party.

Tom spoke to reporters and opened telegrams. He denied claiming that Tunney had thumbed him. He planned to fight for the title again and thought he had an even-money chance. He had turned down all offers to lecture and give boxing exhibitions except for a request from Gisborne. He had refused £50 a night to appear at Auckland's Regent Theatre. 'Money doesn't matter to me,' he said. Marion spoke with a husky, American drawl. The Americans loved Tom so much there was talk of a big manufacturer producing a 'Kia Ora' silk. She had always been interested in boxing, but of course more so since marrying Tom. As the ship was about to weigh anchor to move to her berth Tom and his wife went below for tea. Meanwhile, trouble was brewing on shore.

Despite the rain, people had gathered behind the barricades on Princes Wharf in the afternoon and news that the ship was in the harbour had swelled the crowd to more than two thousand. The wharf gates were closed and in Quay Street, buffeted by a chilly sou'west wind and bitter rain squalls, another two thousand without admission tickets gathered. Inside the wharf gates people climbed over the shed and up the cranes, risking electrocution by the high-power electric wires. The liner moved into her berth and her lights fell upon a sea of faces. 'Where's Heeney?'

Father and son reunited in Gisborne.

All Blacks legend George Nepia with Tom at Te Araroa Beach, on the East Coast, a few months after Tom's title fight in 1928.

A Heeney family group with Guide Bella Papakura in Rotorua.

Visiting the 'Star of Canada', Gisborne.

The rematch with Max Baer, San Francisco, 1932.

Marion reminds Tom to cut the grass, Miami Beach, 1935.

Tom's house, Miami Beach.

Boxing referee Tom Heeney meets Commander Gene Tunney, Guadalcanal, Christmas Day 1943.

Sparring with Hawke's Bay boxer Maurice Donovan in New Caledonia, c. 1944.

Tom in his Miami Beach bar.

In Miami with Marion (far right) and others.

Tom returns to Gisborne to see his mother.

An interview with famous New Zealand rugby commentator, Winston McCarthy.

Visiting Ruatoria.

Tom's final days are spent in a North Miami nursing home.

they cried. A saloon passenger on B deck raised himself on the rail, apparently to wave to a friend on shore.

'Get down! You're not Heeney... We want Heeney... Where is he?'

The castigated passenger might well have been the author John Marshall, although he remembered the incident a little differently in *Vagabond Deluxe*, an account of his 21-month trip around the globe. 'Many small craft loaded with men and women, and one with a band, circled the ship. "We want Heeney... we want Tom... Raise your hand, Tom, we want to see you." Their idol was nowhere about. The more the crowd was made to wait, the more they yelled. "Raise your hand, Tom, so we can see you." I was standing amidship at the starboard rail. Hoping to give satisfaction to the throngs below, I raised my hand and waved. There was a great cheering and screaming. Now the crowd was content.'

When the gates were opened to allow a mail van onto the wharf a near-riot ensued. A dozen constables and Harbour Board officials couldn't restrain the mob and punches were thrown. A few gatekeepers sported knuckle marks on their faces the next morning. Several women fainted and were trodden on. Some were plucked out by officials; others were rolled in the mud. 'The women fought worse than the men,' said one gatekeeper, 'and I have bruises all over my ribs from trying to stop a party of elderly ladies.' 'No such scenes have ever been witnessed on Auckland wharves within recent years,' said a Harbour Board official. 'The mob went almost mad, and the only wonder is that there was no one killed. Fortunately a heavy shower of rain shortly after 6 p.m. dispersed some of the crowd or I don't know what we would have done.'

Tom finished his tea and came on deck. There was a burst of cheers.

'Take off your hat and wave,' someone urged him. He did and the crowd on the wharf roared.

'Good Old Tom... Good Old Heeney,' they cried. Tom went up to the boat deck and appeared under a floodlight. He was home.

'Where's Mrs Heeney?' demanded a youth on a crane. The crowd called for her. She appeared at Tom's side and there was more cheering.

Tom filed down the gangway, helping his bride. A flashgun serving a battery of cameramen perched on the wharf shed exploded loudly overhead. Arms reached out for Tom, but he was looking for his parents. Policemen cleared the way. Tom was reunited with his mother and other relatives in a waiting taxi and gradually the car was forced through the crowd and onto Quay Street. It continued up Queen Street and to a hotel where Tom met his father.

The number of people to welcome a passenger ship that night stood as a record for many years. New Zealand wasn't used to the celebrity culture of Manhattan. Tom's welcome was a 'clear indication of New Zealanders' devotion to sport and their propensity for hero-worship', wrote one reporter. 'In this case it is not because Heeney is gifted intellectually, or is possessed of personal magnetism, or has done anything particularly elevating, or contributed to the advancement of civilization or, yet again, been a successful leader of men. There are hundreds of great statesmen, soldiers, sailors, discoverers, scientists, and giants in the learned professions who might have stepped from the *Aorangi* on Sunday evening, and not received so cordial a reception as did this now world-famous pug.'

The new, famous Tom seemed a bit too outspoken when he talked on the radio that night. 'Perhaps it was in the excitement of the moment that Heeney was led to intersperse in his radio message . . . certain references to Prohibition in the United States . . . This questionable taste and obvious play to the gallery is so foreign to broadcasted messages in general that it will be surprising if more is not heard about the subject. Anything of the nature of a controversy, it is hoped, will be avoided, but one would have thought that his recent experiences would have given Heeney a more sober sense of responsibility,' wrote the *New Zealand Pictorial News*.

Tom's trip was bookended by a couple of small controversies, but mostly it was one long, enthusiastic celebration of flowers and gift giving, visits to hospitals and schools, photographs, handshakes, autographs, speeches and banquets. So many bouquets of daffodils, freesias and other spring blossoms were heaped on Marion that Tom later joked she was becoming spoiled and might expect flowers for the rest of her life. In one of his speeches Tom was applauded when he said that although he'd married an American girl it didn't make him an American and they would return to settle in New Zealand. In Vancouver he said he might settle in New York as he had many friends there, but in New Zealand he said what New Zealanders wanted to hear.

In Hamilton there was such a throng that traffic in Victoria Street had to be stopped. In Cambridge they were greeted by about a thousand people at the steps of the Town Hall and swarms of children engulfed their car. Outside the Lake House Hotel overlooking the Maori village of Ohinemutu Tom was welcomed with a haka. The party was met about 30 miles from Gisborne on the morning of Thursday 13 September and all the way in crowds at every village, mostly children, blocked their passage, demanding to hear from 'Our Tom'. The party was driven in a Whippet car similar to one Tom had used in America and decorated with bridal ribbons. 'Here they come,' someone yelled. Two Maori men performed a haka that could be heard above the din. Tom and his family were given a welcome on a scale never before seen in Gisborne. It was a carnival with flags and bunting and a band. Hardly had Tom got out of the car when one of his sisters rushed forward and kissed him. He was soon enveloped in a seething mass, shaking hands and grinning.

No building would have been large enough to cope with the crowd so the guests of honour made their way to the balcony of the Coronation Hotel on the main street. People covered the road and footpaths. Every vantage point was filled, and dozens peered from the parapets of buildings and second- and third-storey windows. 'Ake, Ake, Kia Kaha! Good Old Tom . . . Our Tom!' they chanted. The Mayor welcomed him and Mr Clayton of the Gisborne Boxing Association said that Tom was the embodiment of the spirit of the people — a Britisher to the core, imbued with grit, courage, pluck and determination. Lady Carroll delivered a speech in Maori which was then translated. 'Greetings to you, the people of Gisborne who have assembled to do honour to our Tom Heeney. Though he was unsuccessful in obtaining the world's boxing championship, he was more successful in another venture, in that he has brought back an American wife to our midst. I think this is a greater honour than the world's boxing championship.'

Then it was Tom's turn.

> You've got me stuck up here today and I don't know a thing to say. All the kind things have been said and I don't know if I'm supposed to hit you on the back and say something nice about you too. I thank you very, very much for all the kind words about me. I can't find the words, but I want to say that since I've been in the limelight I've been to several 'kick ups' but they've never been attended by such a crowd. It's a great delight to meet you all again and receive such

a reception from the town I was born in. I don't suppose you want to know much about boxing — I don't know much about it myself. (Laughter.) I thought I did — then I met Tunney. (More laughter.) I was after the championship and did not get it, but now Tunney's going to be married so that leaves a chance for me. I'm going back to the United States in December to fight for the championship, which is to be decided by an elimination series of the four leading contenders, of which I am lucky enough to be one. In my training, and when I step into the ring, I will think of all the good things you have said about me, and the whole-hearted reception, and it will make me put a bit more snap into my work. I don't know how to thank you all for all you've done for me.

Americans were considered in New Zealand to be bad sports, but Tom praised their sportsmanship. He'd gone there unknown and was treated as one of them. 'It's a hot day down there,' he said, 'and I suppose you're all thirsty. I've seen America under Prohibition and it's a joke, nothing more.'

'There's plenty of good water,' came a voice.

'I don't think,' said Tom amid more laughter.

The crowd called for the new Mrs Heeney. She concluded with the words, 'I feel all choked up today'. Much was made in the local newspapers about Tom's loyalty to his home country and that he hadn't changed. He was still genial and obliging.

Mr and Mrs Heeney spent their first night in Gisborne in Tom's old room in a bungalow on his parents' farmlet. Marion, used to the sounds of Manhattan, awoke to crowing roosters and lowing cows. Tom's father was too sick to go to a local banquet of 300 people in his son's honour, but he listened to the proceedings on the radio. Tom reiterated that he had not accused Tunney of putting his thumb in his eye and he regretted the absence of the late Sir James Carroll. On Friday he gave a sparring exhibition with brother Jack in the Opera House. On Saturday he refereed a charity rugby match between the Fire Brigade and the *Gisborne Times* at the Childers Road Reserve. The fire brigade's fullback, by virtue of his chairmanship of the Gisborne Fire Board, was the Mayor, D.W. Coleman. Coleman seemed a bit too small and old, even for a charity match. A plan was devised and Tom obliged. The Mayor, who hadn't even touched the ball, was ordered off a few minutes into the game for 'rough play'.

There were more cities, more banquets, receptions, dinners, lunches, boxing tournaments and functions, more haka, more 'For He's a Jolly Good Fellow's, more gifts and more bouquets for Marion. Tom said it seemed as if 99 per cent of the people of New Zealand were interested in him and his career.

Back in Gisborne, Tom visited his old schools Te Hapara and St Mary's, which had moved further along Childers Road. Mouths open and staring, the St Mary's boys were in awe of Tom and his huge fists. In honour of his visit a half-holiday was declared. Tom told the students to obey the Sisters and eat vegetables to grow strong like him. A confession that he'd written down the answers before an exam didn't go down so well with the Sisters, though. One of the pupils at the time was his nephew Darcy Heeney, Jack's only son. Darcy would win his father's old title of New Zealand amateur welterweight champion in 1937, '38 and '39, become a silver medallist at the 1938 British Empire Games and a fleet champion during the Second World War. While serving with the Royal Navy he was reported missing presumed dead in December 1941.

Tom had been away from New Zealand for four years and in New York for more than a year and half. He'd seen the way things were done elsewhere and he was determined to dispel a few myths while he was back. He laughed long and loud when a *Gisborne Times* reporter asked him about Prohibition. He said the reason Americans didn't vote for 'Restoration' even though Prohibition had failed was because they could get all the liquor they wanted, and the rich bootleggers who could buy votes didn't want Restoration as they'd be out of a job. 'Prohibition is a curse that personally I should never like to see in force in New Zealand,' he declared.

Prohibition in the United States had helped to swing opinion away from the movement in New Zealand, after it had been an influential political force in the late nineteenth and early twentieth centuries. But Tom's statements infuriated J. Malton Murray, the Executive Secretary of the New Zealand Alliance, who wrote a long letter to the *Gisborne Times* in which he suggested, 'if Mr Heeney has been doing all the drinking that he leads us to infer whilst he was in the USA it is small wonder that he was defeated by the total abstaining champion'. Tom was up for the fight. He replied with his own letter arguing that Prohibition was a 'pitiable failure'. He wrote that he'd be leaving the country shortly so he wouldn't be able to 'keep up a controversy' with Murray but that there were other New Zealanders who'd been to America who could back up what he said.

Although he'd hoped to go to Australia to see the Melbourne Cup, the heavyweight eliminations and New York were beckoning again. Tom decided to return earlier than planned to enter the elimination tournament during the semi-final stages and thought he'd meet either Sharkey or Paulino. He left Gisborne on 11 October. 'Please tell the Gisborne people that Tom Heeney will not forget that he is a Gisborne boy, and that he owes a great deal to the people here who put him on the way to make a name for himself,' he said in a farewell message. 'If I had known how greatly my fights interested New Zealand people and what an opportunity I had to advertise the good features of this country abroad, the welcome given to me would have been better deserved . . . When I get into the ring again, I will make a supreme effort to win the championship for New Zealand. Nothing else can repay my many friends here for the way in which they have treated me, and for the confidence they have shown in my ability.'

Marion liked the people and the scenery but not the roads. 'I have never experienced anything like it in the way of rough travelling,' she remarked in Auckland before sailing. It was a quiet departure: a little group of friends and family sheltering from the rain on shore; Marion carrying a bouquet of pink roses and sweet peas in one hand and waving a tiny handkerchief that was almost carried off by the wind in the other as the *Niagara* moved out into the stream; Tom's burly frame eventually becoming indistinguishable from other passengers waving their final goodbyes.

During a brief stopover in Honolulu Tom weighed himself in the lobby of the bank where he went to get some American money. After weeks of feasting and celebrating he came in at 230 lb. He wasn't concerned though; he thought 18 to 20 lb would come off easily when he started training. 'I think I will be the next champion,' Tom said in Toronto. 'The bout I had with Tunney taught me a great deal. I made a lot of mistakes in that fight that I'll never make again.' He would begin training on his arrival in New York and hoped to be fighting by January or February.

Most of all he wanted to meet Dempsey in the ring. 'He is the greatest of them all, and I will never consider myself a really experienced fighter until I have had a go with Jack.' Marion was quoted as saying she would never try to persuade Tom to give up fighting. 'That is his life, so why should I want him to change?'

Throughout the trip Tom talked the talk and promised his supporters he'd be champion one day. But he was away from the daily grind of training and it was easy to ignore the inner voices that told him he was past his best. Shortly after arriving in New York he admitted he was considering retirement. Marion wanted him to quit and start a business with the money he'd saved instead of risking injury. The first interview Tom granted following his return took place in Harvey's office on Broadway. The reporter didn't think Tom understood how much more money he stood to make and that he didn't realise how popular he was. 'I want to fight some more and then again I don't,' Tom said.

> My wife wants me to get out while I am sound in body and mind. She doesn't want me to expose myself to danger of injury through further fighting. That's one side of it.
>
> The other is the way I feel myself. I've fought them all. There's no new ones around for me to tackle. I've got a little money and I feel I'd like to get into some business which would bring me a satisfactory income. That's the situation the way it stands right now. I don't know whether to retire or keep going.
>
> Yet I'd like to keep on if it were possible for me to fight men suited to myself and my style. I don't mean that I want to pick opponents. That's furthest from my mind. When I'm going I don't care who or what they are. If they're better than me that's all right. If they are not, well, that's all right, too.
>
> But what I mean is to fight men near my own size and more closely related to me in style. Fellows like Sharkey, Risko, Paulino and Dempsey... Of course, it's all right for people to talk about the amount of money that is to be made through fighting. The tendency, though, is to exaggerate. I suppose I could earn about $40,000 in a year's fighting, which would include five or six matches. That would be my net earnings, not the gross. Against this, however, is the idea of exposing yourself to injury.

> Another thing is the loss of privacy you experience. It's hard on me to accustom myself to the attention I attract after the obscurity that once was my lot. For instance, I went home to enjoy a holiday and some rest and found that I was the centre of a continuous round of celebration.
>
> Of course, that's all part of the game. I don't resent it. Don't get me wrong. But, at the same time, I haven't yet become accustomed to it and I don't know as I ever will. At any rate, I haven't quite made up my mind on the future.

There was one type of business that particularly appealed to Tom: diamond importing. Two of the friends he'd made in South Africa in 1925 had made fortunes in diamond mines and wanted Tom to handle their uncut stones in the States. Meanwhile, Tom was mentioned as a possible opponent for San Francisco fighter Armand Emanuel and Sharkey. But all fight talk was soon put on hold. After an exhausting and emotional year Tom came down with a severe attack of pneumonia. He walked around with the illness for a week refusing to rest until he finally gave in to doctor's orders, took to bed in his uptown apartment and agreed to be treated.

His health improved, slowly, and there was talk of a match with Sharkey in February. But with his fragile health, not even his manager seemed to know what Tom was thinking. Harvey told one reporter his man would be ready for the eliminations in February, another that he wasn't sure whether Tom was definitely going to continue fighting. It seemed that if he came back it wouldn't be to meet any old boxer. 'If Tom wants to keep on fighting I'm going to try to match him with Dempsey,' said Harvey. 'They're the two men who fought Tunney and they ought to fight for the title.' On 20 December Tom went for a short walk for the first time in weeks. Harvey announced his man would soon be ready to meet Jack Dempsey for the title. 'Tom takes the stand that if Dempsey can be held in reserve for a big shot, so can he. Laugh that off if you can,' wrote Jack Farrell in the New York *Daily News*.

Rickard announced that Sharkey, Young Stribling, Paulino, Jack Dempsey and Tom would be in his 1929 elimination tournament. Sharkey and Stribling would fight a 10-round bout in Miami on 27 February. Next he hoped to match Tom with Paulino. The winners of those two bouts would meet and the survivor would meet Dempsey — if he returned — in August or September to decide Tunney's successor. Rickard travelled to Miami to finalise arrangements. Harvey met him there several times and expected Tom would soon announce his return to the ring to meet Paulino in late March.

And then something happened that shocked the New York boxing world. At 8.37 on the morning of 6 January 1929 at Miami Beach Tex Rickard died. He'd fallen ill after dinner on New Year's Eve and was operated on for acute gangrenous appendicitis. It was an unspectacular exit for the man whose name was synonymous with gambling, gold and guns. His body was laid out with lips and cheeks rouged and his best suit on, in a glass-covered bronze coffin amid flowers at the west end of Madison Square Garden. A seemingly endless line of people filed past. Tom and Harvey attended his funeral. Rickard's private box at the Garden was pictured empty and draped in black.

The eliminations went on without Rickard and Tom finally chose between rings of the diamond and pugilistic type. Harvey talked him out of the diamond business. 'You can peddle diamonds any old time,' he said. 'Tom, I want you to fight Paulino,' Rickard had said. 'The winner gets Sharkey or Stribling, and then the big shot with Dempsey will be waiting for the victor.' So Tom went back into daily training for what he hoped would be a match with Dempsey in September.

'I've got to get started in some other business some time, and if I can't lick Paulino I haven't got any business fighting any more,' said Tom. 'The quicker I get into the ring again the better I'll like it. This bloody training gets my goat. I don't like it.' Paulino was ready to fight as soon as Tom agreed, but Garden matchmaker Tom McArdle said the demands of the managers of both men were exorbitant. January turned to February and Tom said he'd only return to the ring to fight Dempsey for the title, while Harvey was doing his best to give the impression that his man was still at the centre of things. He claimed the championship of the world on Tom's behalf and announced his fighter's willingness to defend it against all-comers.

Scott's backer, W.J. Ward, offered to post side stakes of $10,000 for a battle for the 'world's' heavyweight title between Scott and Tom in England in May. Bernard Mortimer cabled Tom in New York and Harvey told a reporter, 'Heeney would be glad to meet him. I am not much interested in the side bet laid by Scott's backer, though. What I am interested in is the gate. Provided the terms are all right for Heeney, the fight may be arranged.' It never eventuated. Finally, on 8 February Tom was matched for his first bout since Tunney. After all the talk about Paulino and Dempsey and other leading heavyweights, his opponent seemed a strange choice. He was to fight Jimmy Maloney for 10 rounds in Boston in March. After losing badly to Sharkey and Tom, Maloney had given up boxing for a while and gone into the gas station business and trucking. Newspapers speculated that the Hard Rock wouldn't be the same man after the beating by Tunney, but for now at least he was still a drawing card.

It was reported that Harvey demanded $30,000, but in the end Tom signed for something in the region of $15,000. And he'd also get a substantial sum for a bout afterwards in Chicago with Norwegian Otto von Porat. Von Porat signed straight away but it took Chicago promoter Jim Mullen a month to agree terms with Tom. And perhaps Tom could yet become champion. 'When Tom had been carved into a gory replica of a side of beef by the murderously scientific Gene Tunney it was universally agreed that he might as well quit the racket for good and all,' wrote Jack Kofoed. 'Tom didn't need the money. He was well set on the financial side, but the lure of the thing kept pecking at him.'

Under a Tottering Tower

There was shouting, screaming, grabbing, collapsing — the culmination of five days of panic and frenzy. On the trading floor of the New York Stock Exchange the get-rich-quick, decadent, excessive twenties were coming to an end. It was the twenty-ninth day of the tenth month of 1929: Black Tuesday. On this day 16.4 million shares were traded and $15 billion was lost. The United States' economy was falling apart and its people would be subjected to unimaginable suffering. Those who found their losses too much to bear hurled themselves from New York's skyscrapers. The Crash destroyed the hopes and dreams of many Americans, and it put a resounding end to what Gallico called the 'wildest, maddest, and most glamorous period in all the history of sport'.

The year hadn't even started well for Tom. He arrived in Boston at midnight on 26 February, with Marion due to follow. In the morning a 'beastly' reporter found him before he'd even had breakfast. He yelled for Harvey, who didn't appear, and then resigned himself to the interview. After a few monosyllabic answers, conversation turned to the speedy knockout of Maloney in 1927.

'Surprised? I'll be doggoned if I knew what happened, that fellow Maloney went down so fast. Well, it's liable to happen to anybody.'

The reporter asked if he should quote Tom as planning to do the same thing to Maloney again.

'No, no, not a bit of it. I have never in my life promised to knock a fellow out. I just go into the bloody old ring and do my best, you know. Dammit. That's all a chappie can do, isn't it? — do your bloody best, what?'

Later the reporter remarked that the Tunney fight must have been the hardest of Tom's career.

'Not so,' he replied, remembering Colin Bell.

Tom talked of how his parents wanted him to be a businessman, that his brother Jack had the middleweight championship and Frank had been on his way to the welterweight championship when he was killed.

'Plumbing! Bah!' said Tom. 'We are all in this world for the sugar; now . . .'

'He means money,' interjected Hennessey.

'Sure, sugar means money,' Tom continued. 'It's the ambition of every bloody boxer to quit the ring when he gets enough money. But they never do. I'm like all the rest. When I get enough money I want to throw the beastly gloves away. I like boxing, and then, again, I don't like it. Like all the rest, I'll probably stay in the game until I'm knocked silly, eh, what?'

'What would you do if you did throw your gloves away?' asked the reporter.

'Eh, what? . . . Well, now, what beastly job could I do?'

They discussed Tom's future.

'If I get past von Porat, I'll probably get another chance in New York, at this man Paulino who held me to a draw once and won the other time. After that it's Sharkey again, and Schmeling, perhaps, if I live that long.'

The reporter had been dealt with; now there was the usual sparring exhibition before the big event. Tom entertained a crowd of 300 at Harry Kelley's new gym on Hanover Street, giving 'the impression of a big boy who likes the work of fighting, so earnestly did he go through training stunts mapped out for him by his trainer, Jimmy Hennessey', wrote a local paper. Tom said the Maloney battle was the first of a series of bouts that would take him to the world's title. He didn't spar at the gym and Harvey said most of the time in Boston would be spent sightseeing.

On the day before the fight Maloney was still in the gym doing light exercises while Tom had a complete day of rest. Tom hadn't fought since

Tunney, and Harvey admitted he would have preferred the match to be held at a later date after a few easy fights. The psychological effect of Tom's beating by Tunney, his recent attack of pneumonia, a new wife who wanted him to quit, the fact he was carrying excess weight, and the apparent transformation of Maloney from a pushover to a fearless fighter made this a dangerous fight.

In New Zealand Tom had been teased by 'an old Maori' who said he'd lost to Tunney because the cloak he'd worn was a woman's garment and not for a fighting man. The gods were angry and caused him to lose. The man gave Tom a whale bone, a token of battle, and said it would bring him luck in the rest of his fights. It didn't.

'Finely Trained Maloney Wallops a Flabby Heeney' ran the headline in the *Boston Evening Transcript*. Tom was out of condition and seemed very tired even after three rounds. He was several pounds above his best fighting weight, and even though it was well known that Tom was 'careless' about his training, the newspaper reported, it seemed 'almost suicidal' to attempt a comeback after an eight-month layoff without trying to reach his best form.

'Keep off the ropes, Jim! Keep off the ropes!' the crowd yelled at Maloney in the early rounds and it looked as though the South Boston man was a bit scared of Tom — until he realised his opponent was a shadow of the man who'd fought Tunney. Tom kept walking forward, but Maloney won walking away, or with his back to the ropes, moving from side to side and never giving Tom the chance to get in the right-handers that were used in their previous meeting. The pace never slackened. In Tom's corner Harvey complained to the referee about Maloney's tactics: using the heel of his glove and the way he used his elbows, for which he did get one warning.

Blood trickled from Tom's mouth and he had a scratch on his left cheek and a bloody left eye. It had been a severe beating. Maloney was virtually unmarked. 'Tonight's bout proved that Tunney took everything he had out of Heeney but his stout heart,' wrote Jack Farrell. Harvey thought Tom won on aggressiveness and Maloney was allowed to use his elbows too freely. Tom lost his place in the heavyweight eliminations and Maloney had muscled his way back in.

The word was Tom was finished. But on he fought and was a slight favourite due to his experience and weight advantage over Otto von Porat. He said he'd be happy with nothing but a knockout. After a stint in a New York dentist's chair to repair the damage from the Maloney bout, Tom took the New York City–Chicago train 'The Twentieth Century' to another beating. This one was so serious he ended up in hospital. He'd started well, scoring punches at close quarters and showing his characteristic gameness, but von Porat dominated. In the tenth and last round von Porat smashed a right into Tom's face, cutting a deep gash in his lower lip. Suddenly his face was smeared with blood and he was backing away or hanging on desperately. Tom sat stoically as doctors probed his wounded lip. Harvey stroked his moustache and looked on and said he had nothing to say as he packed his bag.

Tom went to hospital to have a V-shaped gash inside his lip closed with 18 stitches. The cut had become infected and could cause disfigurement and Tom was told to stay in bed for several days. The doctor told Harvey plastic surgery would be necessary if the infection spread. They both thought Tom would never fight again. Harvey admitted Tom was in bad shape; his confidence was shaken, his morale withered. The New Zealander still earned an impressive $17,500 for meeting von Porat, but he would now find it harder to attract large purses. He and von Porat had passed each other: one on the way up, the other on the way down.

By the end of May Tom was back in a ring, winning on a foul against the local French-Canadian Elzear Rioux in Montreal in the eighth round after leading all the way. For his next match he headed back to New York. The towering Argentine Victorio Campolo had signed for three matches at Ebbets Field and Tom was to be one of his trial horses. Campolo, 6 feet 7 inches tall, was a contender. He'd fought only once in the United States, winning on a foul over Arthur DeKuh. Tom was still grappling with health problems, although he claimed to be in great shape, 'renovated by the removal of his tonsils after a recent illness'.

Tom had fought Maloney and von Porat against doctor's orders and as a result narrowly escaped with his life and was confined to bed for several weeks. Now it was Charlie Harvey's turn to fight for his life. He went for a drive with John Pollock and Sarah Dennen, partners in a real estate and contracting business. The three were heading north in Brooklyn when another car crashed into them. Both cars overturned and all the occupants were thrown out. Harvey suffered three fractured ribs and a fractured skull and ended up in a critical condition in hospital. It was his second serious car accident and both times his skull was fractured.

Tom had a special wire installed at the Pioneer Club gym to get updates on Harvey's condition. 'If it was up to me I would stop work right now and postpone the Campolo fight until Charlie gets better,' he said. 'There never was a finer fellow in the world. It was due to him that I got the crack at the title against Gene Tunney last year. It was not his fault if I lost. But I've decided it will be best to carry on for Harvey's sake. Charlie is a liberal fellow — never saves a cent, and he'll need plenty of money now to help him back to health and strength. This unfortunate accident has made me more determined than ever to win, more for Charlie's sake than anything else.'

There was talk of Tom fighting the German Max Schmeling, one of the most exciting heavyweights around at that time, but the Commission ruled Tom wasn't good enough. They did approve his meeting with Campolo, however, and for Tom it was a chance to get back in the running for the title. As the fight neared, the betting was 8 to 5 on Campolo. 'I'll win or quit the game for good and I don't want to quit,' Tom said. Gallico wrote that while he wished Campolo no ill, 'I kind of would like to see old Dommas come through because of . . . well, just because of old times at Fair Haven, N.J., where he was training for Tunney'. The fighters looked ridiculous standing next to each other at the weigh-in, and even the grim Muldoon couldn't stifle a grin. The Argentine was taller by half a foot and had a much longer reach. And then there was the weight.

'Campolo 223!' announced Bertie Stand as he obliged a photographer. 'Without his horse,' he added. Much guffawing followed.

'Heeney 204½!' he said.

'Just a shell of his former self,' someone joked when it was realised that Campolo had lost three pounds in three weeks.

After rain forced a day's postponement a large crowd gathered in the National League ballpark, producing a gate of around $21,400. Tom and Campolo would each get $5362.20. Tom 'turned himself into a human battering ram', wrote McGeehan, 'and made some desperate efforts to wreck the altitudinous structure. He rocked the tower, but he could not make it topple.' Gallico was sitting next to Fugazy, who gave him a strange look when, excited by the first decent action he'd experienced at ringside for months, he screamed, 'Come on, Tom!'. Gallico explained to Fugazy that he always supported the underdog and Fugazy said he understood. 'Nevertheless, I could detect from the look in Il Duce's eyes that he was fervently hoping that I would drop dead or burst a blood vessel while I was thus crying encouragement to the brave New Zealander.'

In the eighth Campolo slammed a right uppercut that lifted Tom off the canvas. Marion wept into her handkerchief. The fight was stopped with just seconds to go in the ninth as Campolo stood poised to deliver a blow on a helpless Tom who 'lay sprawled in a neutral corner, knocked down by a long, piston-like right to the jaw', wrote McGeehan. 'He got to his feet and reeled toward the tall tower, but referee Crowley pushed him back and he sagged into his own corner.' Tom seemed to be a 'pugilisitc guinea pig' and he had reached the end, McGeehan wrote. After the knockout by Campolo it was unlikely he'd even be used as a trial horse again. Gallico thought Campolo was the leading heavyweight contender in the country. Tom was so bashed at the end Gallico feared he would never again fight efficiently. 'No one ever hit me as hard as that giant did with those right hands. I think he'll be the next heavyweight champion,' said Tom. The following month, in the 'battle of the leaning towers', Campolo's rise in the heavyweight ranks was checked by Phil Scott.

Tom had vowed to quit, but once again he came back. McGeehan wrote that when Tom met Tunney it was the pinnacle for him because he had always been a second-rater at heart. He'd often said in confidence he didn't think he was in the same class as the likes of Tunney. Tom was now battling the second- and third-raters and his next fight must've brought back memories of the Tunney defeat and a realisation of how far he'd dropped since then. On 26 September he was back at the Yankee Stadium with referee Eddie Forbes, this time in a 10-round supporting bout for the main event between Jack Sharkey and Tommy Loughran. It was thought Tom would triumph over George Hoffman, a former ironworker. As Tom did his best to fight off the youthful Hoffman, Phil Scott entered the stadium in a dinner jacket. Tom got the decision but the crowd howled in protest. The scribes agreed Hoffman had won — and so, apparently, did Tom.

The following day he turned down an offer to fight Gerald Ambrose 'Tuffy' Griffiths in the Garden on 18 October. He was disgusted with his performance against Hoffman and had finally had enough. As an amateur

Hoffman used to call at St Nick's to test himself against the professionals including Tom. 'When young squirts like Hoffman can lick me it's time to quit and that's just what I have done,' he declared. Pegler wrote that Tom was never much of a prizefighter. 'Licked by Tunney in a fight that was more an execution than a contest, he went home to Australia to reflect and count his earnings and then came back to the USA to sell off the ruins of his reputation as a burnt-out haberdasher does in a fire sale.'

It seemed as if Tom had recognised that he no longer belonged in prizefighting. Perhaps he might yet escape the curse of the boxer who was past his best but couldn't stop fighting; the boxer who convinced himself over and over again he had one good fight left in him; that he was just about as good as he used to be; that he couldn't possibly be a 'has-been'. And then came Black Tuesday.

Eight and Two and You're Out

The two years since he fought Tunney hadn't been kind to Tom. He was only 32 but seemed much older, especially as he stood alongside the blue-eyed Irish-American Tuffy Griffiths of Sioux City, Iowa. 'Heeney went up the steps on hairy, pool-table legs,' wrote Westbrook Pegler. 'There was manly fur on his wishbone and his sandy dome was frosty with years. Maybe Heeney was forty years old. The records are lax about the vital statistics of pugilism, but this dogged campaigner had a roll of slack tissue undulating above the margin of his purple trunks, and his ring shoes, with the toes bursting through and laced up with grocer string, were the practical working apparel of an old journeyman who has no romantic notions as to his future.'

Griffiths was considered one of the best of the new crop of heavyweights. Tom said he knew a defeat would end his career and he had only signed when he felt sure he was on top form. 'My wind is better and I'm punching faster,' he said. 'I know Griffiths is a tough youngster and one who can hit. But I'm satisfied with my condition and feel sure that I'll beat Tuffy.' But this was a last, desperate attempt by Tom to regain his old standing and become a contender for the heavyweight championship now held by Max Schmeling. Schmeling had won it on a foul against Sharkey. The heavyweight ranks desperately needed another ring great.

EIGHT AND TWO AND YOU'RE OUT

It was a cool and starless night in July 1930 when some 8000 people gathered at the Queensboro Stadium. On the weathered boards sat friends of Tom and Marion from Port Washington. The drivers and passengers of the elevated trains that ran past the stadium peered out at the drama unfolding in the distant ring.

Tom showed glimpses of his old self in the first as he 'spread his big, meaty feet with the toes straining almost out of his shoes in the effort', wrote Pegler, and sent Griffiths sprawling hard into the ropes. But Tom was pounded to the head and body by lefts and rights from the younger and lighter man. Near the end of the ninth he was left doubled over from an onslaught. His left eye was swollen shut and he had bloody welts on the left side of his body. He was on his way to the canvas when the referee grabbed him and the bell rang. Tom groggily retreated to his corner. 'Up on the steps to meet him, leaning on his cane, aged, infirm, crippled and defeated, with moth-eaten bristles of his frayed mustache twitching in excitement, was his manager, Charlie Harvey,' continued Pegler. 'There was a lot of age and ruin in that corner. Old Charlie stomped on the ring floor with the butt of his limping-stick. Old Thomas waggled his graying head drunkenly. Arthur Donovan, the referee, leaned over Heeney, searching him for signs of hope and strength.'

The bell tolled for the tenth and final round. Tom moved towards his opponent. He could barely see as blood oozed from his left eye and his mouth. The crowd yelled and Donovan stopped the fight before a punch was thrown. He helped Tom to his corner. Griffiths shook Tom's hand and Tom wished him the best of luck. Tom was cheered loudly when he left the ring.

Tom had turned down a Griffiths fight the previous year and he should have turned this one down as well. Back then he said he wanted to spend the rest of his days in a pub with lots of boxing photos behind the bar. He had often talked of settling in South Africa and of his desire to hunt big game. While training hard for one of the Paulino fights he'd relaxed with a visit to a big game exhibition. And when asked what he'd do if he won the title he once said:

> There's just one thing I want to do, and that is to travel. I've always longed to see things, to watch other people. Big game shooting in East Africa — that's my greatest desire. There are all kinds of

animals, more than any man could want. Gosh, what I wouldn't give to get out there, and really live, and I could do my own cooking, and wouldn't have to shave or put on a clean collar. Do you think I'd monkey with vaudeville or try to make money in other ways, if I won the title with all that waiting for me? Gosh, no! I want to see Africa. I want to see China, where they don't have chairs or forks.

The stock market crash didn't alter Tom's plans and by the beginning of December he and Marion were on their way to South Africa aboard the *Eastern Glen*. They arrived in Cape Town on 2 January 1930. 'I like South Africa,' said Tom, 'and I like the people. They have always treated me very well, and I should like to stop here. But my wife was born in New York, and she may not like it. If she does, we will go back to America to fix up our business and come back to settle down here.' Tom caught up with old friends in Johannesburg, keen to show that despite his success and money he hadn't changed. 'Nobody can accuse me of "high-hatting" like Tunney, and I'm still "with the boys," he insisted.

Just two months later the South African dream was over and they were on their way back to New York. The talk was Primo Carnera's rise had encouraged Tom to return. A reporter in Cape Town found the New Zealander in the saloon of the *Eastern Glen* collecting his refund on his cinematograph camera from customs officers. Marion was doing the Charleston to a new gramophone record. 'Shall I fight again?' Tom smiled. 'Well, that depends entirely on what offers I receive. I should like another fight, and I've cabled my manager in the States to that effect; but I won't fight under a thousand pounds. The Wall Street smash hit me pretty hard and on paper I figure I lost £19,800 [about $100,000]. That's a tidy sum for anyone to lose. Perhaps some of my holdings will recover a bit and the loss may not be as much after all.' He threw some silver to the customs officers. 'Have one on me, boys,' he said and then continued, 'I lead a very quiet life and am never really out of training. I shall begin to work off the superfluous fat as soon as we get to sea, so that I can be in some sort of shape when we get to Boston.' Where did Tom intend to settle for good? the reporter asked. Marion stopped dancing and answered for him. 'New York. That's where I have a say in the matter.' 'Yes,' agreed Tom. 'I guess it'll have to be New York. Somehow one gets more out of New York than anywhere else in the world.' Tom chatted a bit more and then went to help his wife unpack. The reporter asked one of the *Eastern Glen*'s officers what he thought of the Hard Rock. 'A regular guy,' was the reply.

Back in the United States Tom said hunting had given him an appetite to get back in the ring, though he didn't think much of lion hunting. 'Why you might just as well hide behind a barrel in a Broadway alley and pot a tabby cat. That's all the kick I got out of it, anyway.' Tom talked of trekking back on the veldt a couple of hundred miles from Johannesburg, of pitching camp near a waterhole and of bagging eleven lions inside a week. 'I got most of my fun in the long hikes over the veldt looking for waterbok, antelope, giraffes and zebras, which are the hardest of all animals to approach. Those long hikes put me in trim again. They got me feeling fit as a fiddle and longing for action, real ring action.' Sharkey and Schmeling had been matched for the world title and Tom said he'd fight Sharkey if anything happened to Schmeling. 'I should have got that fight for the world championship with Sharkey, anyway. Didn't I hold Jack to a 12-round draw? You bet I did. And most of the critics claimed I was robbed of the decision. Anytime that Mister Sharkey wants to prove I am wrong or thinks he can whip me, here I am, ready and willing to clamber through the ropes against him.'

The lure of the ring might play a part, but for most prizefighters it's more about the prize than the fight, and Tom needed a prize because most of his savings had gone. Between December 1929 and March 1930 the market recovered well and the Great Depression didn't really set in until the second half of 1930. The stock market surged in March and continued improving into the first half of April. So perhaps Tom did initially recover some of the value of his stocks. But even the best fighters lost money in the Crash and the subsequent Depression. Dempsey said he lost $3 million. It was reported that most of Harvey's money was wiped out. In 1930 and '31 it seemed everyone was broke. As the Depression took hold in New York there would be desperate hunger, hundreds living on the street and others moving into shacks in 'Hooverville' in Central Park.

Tom still had enough money to buy a house and he set up home with Marion not far from Port Washington on the north shore of Long Island where she grew up. The property was in Munsey Park, a few blocks from the Long Island railroad station at Manhasset where commuters could travel by electric train to Penn Station in the heart of Manhattan. A decade previously Munsey Park had been an open meadow and now it was a high-class community of about 300 acres with more than 400 residents. The site of beautiful rolling woodland, grand old trees and wide meadowlands was part of the estate left by prominent newspaper publisher Frank Munsey to the Metropolitan Museum of Art in New York. Before construction began museum officials were involved in house designs and street plans. Houses were built as colonial American reproductions with woodwork, stairways, corner cupboards and fireplaces modelled on historic examples on display in the American wing of the museum. Winding streets were designed to complement the rolling topography and preserve the natural wooded environment. The Park resembled a quaint old English village.

Paradoxically, the Wall Street Crash boosted the sale of property in Munsey Park. Agents for the village, Garden Estates, reported an increase in 1930 summer sales over the total for the same period in 1929. 'Strange as it may seem,' Sales Manager John S. Withers said, 'a part of the summer sales activity may be traced directly to the Crash in Wall Street. Money, for several years tied up in stocks, became available at reasonable rates for mortgage financing and a considerable number of people have decided to build their own homes at this time because of this ready finance money.'

In early May 1930 Tom started light training at his new home and said he'd use a local gym when he needed to do heavier training. But he was half-hearted about a comeback. Several bouts were postponed but finally Tom was booked to fight Griffiths. He vowed to hang up his gloves if he was badly beaten. 'It looks as though Heeney's gloves will be dangling from a nail in his Manhasset mansion by this time tomorrow,' wrote one scribe. Jack Kofoed hoped that if Tom got a terrible beating he'd quit for good. 'But it will probably take an injunction from the Supreme Court to make Heeney do that. He is like Johnny Dundee and a lot of other fellows who never admit that age had a sting. They think they can go on forever.'

Kofoed was right. Tom took a lacing, but of course he fought on. The Griffiths fight had put a couple of thousand in his bank account so Tom figured he could punch his way through the hard times. But a win on points over George Panka and losses to Frank Cawley and Emmett Rocco did little to change the perception that Tom was now washed up.

A knockout by Max Baer seemed to confirm it. Tom had been matched with Baer to 'build up' the young curly-headed California heavyweight for more serious matches. After killing an opponent during a match in San Francisco the previous year Baer had lost a few fights but now he was on his way up again. He was a 9 to 5 favourite and one reporter questioned why the Commission allowed the match to go ahead as it didn't 'figure to be anything but a massacre'. But everything was not as it seemed in the curious story of the Max Baer fight.

'Here y'are, getcha mornin' papers. Baer knocks out Heeney. Here y'are, Heeney knocked out, fight extra, Baer knocks out Heeney in the third,' the newsboys at Broadway and Seventh chanted to passers-by in the cold Manhattan air. 'MAX BAER KAYOS HEENEY' declared the papers. Baer had officially knocked Tom out on 16 January 1931 and that's how the result would always be remembered. At eleven o'clock Paul Gallico emerged from the Newsreel Theatre to hear the shouts of the newsboys. 'Ironic, unjust, untrue,' he wrote. 'Everybody on Broadway was hearing this ... Now the cries of the news vendors happened to impress me even more because I was in Madison Square Garden an hour and a quarter before and saw what happened. And Heeney wasn't knocked out. He wasn't even knocked down.'

A relatively small crowd of about 10,000 had gathered at the Garden that night. The real attraction of the evening wasn't Baer or Tom, it was the appearance of the highest-paid referee in the business: Jack Dempsey. At the opening gong Tom went for Baer. He never took a backward step. In the clinches he plugged away with left and right uppercuts to the chin that Baer tried to laugh off with a silly grin. In the third Baer crouched low and started throwing short left hooks. In trying to get away, Tom was knocked out of the ring and onto the press table with a left hook and a shove. Tom grinned as he found himself inelegantly sprawled over the outstretched arms of the newspapermen. He had landed on Jack Kofoed's neck. 'It is unpleasant having 208 pounds draped around your Adam's apple, so I and William Morris, my co-worker at the ringside, propped Mr Heeney into a more perpendicular position. He then crawled back through the ropes,' wrote Kofoed.

Gallico wondered why, as Tom 'snuggled to the manly bosoms of the representatives of the press', knockdown timekeeper Arthur Donovan just gaped at the spectacle instead of beginning a count with his wooden mallet. It was only after Tom was helped back into the ring and had crawled onto one knee that the hammer came down with the shout of 'One!'. Dempsey guided Baer to a neutral corner and picked up Donovan's count over Tom around 'Three' or 'Four'. Tom wasn't badly hurt. He was resting on his hands and knees, watching Dempsey's swinging arm. 'Eight!' yelled Donovan and Dempsey. Tom stood up ready to continue. But then timekeeper George Bannon piped up, 'Ten, he's out.' Dempsey rushed across the canvas to Donovan, who confirmed the fight was over. As Donovan had pounded 'One' with his wooden mallet Bannon had counted 'Three'.

Dempsey proclaimed Baer the winner on a knockout. The crowd protested. Joe Humphreys raised Baer's glove while spectators and scribes bustled around ringside. Donovan blamed Dempsey. Dempsey blamed Donovan. Tom was upset. Harvey came into the ring and Dempsey shrugged as if to say, 'What can I do?'. Baer apologised to Tom as Tom's second took off his gloves. As Donovan was escorted out by police he said, 'Heeney was out of the ring for two seconds and in the ring on the floor for eight seconds, a total of ten, and a knockout count.'

Gallico said Tom was the victim not of Baer but of 'Muddled Artie', an incompetent official of an incompetent prizefight commission.

> I do not suppose that the Three Suspenders will suspend knockdown timekeeper Arthur Donovan but it was 'Eight-and-two-makes ten Artie' who spoiled the show. Artie can't kid me. I heard him count. He counted — 'One-two-three-four-five-six-seven-eight yer out.'
>
> 'Whaddya mean, eight yer out?' queried Referee Dempsey and a couple of newspapermen who sat next to Muddled Artie.
>
> 'Well,' welled Artie, 'Eight and two. Eight and two make ten, see. And that's out.'
>
> This established a precedent which I am sure will add much to the hilarity of our so-called prizefights. 'One-two-three, and thirty minutes in the dressing room. Yer out!' Or — 'One, two, multiply by four is eight, subtract three for a correction in the timekeeper's watch is five and five is my lucky number makes ten and out.'

The Commission took no action over the timekeeping fiasco and said the referee had supreme power in the ring and Dempsey could have waved the fighters back together. Anyway, Tom was automatically disqualified when he allowed himself to be helped back into the ring, the Commission said. It ordered all ring floors to be extended by two feet, so that the floor from the ropes to the ring edge measured three and a half feet.

Gallico did the maths. Bannon claimed he counted two before Tom got back into the ring, which added to Donovan's eight made ten. But at least five seconds went by while Tom was getting back in the ring. So what was the timekeeper doing for the other three or more seconds? 'Actually, while they confessed to only ten seconds, Heeney was down about thirteen or fourteen. So he owes us three or four. Thus, according to a new ruling that the Three Suspenders will doubtless pass within a day or so, the next time Heeney is knocked down the count will be started at four or five instead of one in order to catch up with the officials and make everything come out even.'

Fading with the Platinum Blondes

The Brookdale stock farm at Lincroft was just a short drive from Tom's training camp at Fair Haven. There, Tom had met another battler with a reputation as a game competitor: a pampered 28-year-old racehorse named Broomstick. 'I 'ope they take just as good care of me when I have outlived my usefulness in the ring,' Jack Farrell from the *Daily News* heard Tom say as he left the once great steed in its rustic and peaceful surroundings.

It was now March 1933, almost five years since that visit. And to have seen Tom larking around at the Legion show at the Manhasset school, it might've seemed that whatever remained of his boxing career was just one big joke. Tom and Nassau County Police champion Frank Carpenter were staging a burlesque boxing show. Afterwards there'd be Moorish and Spanish dancing and a comedy skit. Tom entered in a silver bowler and tights. After the first round he fanned the exhausted referee with a towel and later the referee took the count instead of either of the boxers. The audience roared with laughter.

Ten days later Tom was back in a real ring and no one was laughing. The setting was his old Manhattan haunt St Nick's. His hair was severely short, so the grey was less obvious. But Jersey City heavyweight Stanley Poreda still looked young enough to be his son. From early in the second, bloody wounds appeared on Tom's face. His left ear streamed blood after it was pummelled with a succession of rights. Poreda had opened up an old cut and kept jabbing at it.

'Why don't you lay off that ear, you big bum,' someone shouted from the gallery.

A cut opened on the bridge of Tom's nose and a gash over his left eye oozed blood. Tom got in a few good blows and just as the bell sounded to end the seventh he landed a 'wild overhand swing'. Harvey sent him out in the eighth to go for Poreda's chin. But Tom couldn't do it; his left eye was clouded with blood. Marion wept openly near Tom's corner. In the tenth and final round another cut under his eye streamed blood so badly the referee stopped the fight. Tom wanted to keep going — but neither the referee nor the crowd could bear it any longer. It was just too gruesome. The fans were on his side and Poreda was booed in victory.

Tom needed to fight again, and soon. But how bad were the injuries? And more importantly, what did Harvey think? The severe cut under his left eye and the slash to his left ear were obvious. 'You'll be all right soon,' his manager pronounced. 'You know,' Harvey addressed the onlookers, 'Tom has been through this before.'

Tom had indeed been through it many times. He'd continued travelling around the States, as was the lot of the boxer no longer good enough to fight where the big money was. In March 1931 Charley Retzlaff, a rangy, hard-hitting boxer from Duluth, won a technical knockout in the seventh of a 10-round fight in Detroit in front of 15,400 people. Tom went down under a succession of swinging rights and lefts to the jaw. He got up after 'Seven' only to hit the resin again. At 'Ten' he staggered to his feet, but as he reeled around it was obvious he was in no fit state to go on and the referee stepped in.

'The Heeney finish shows how fast they can travel down the soapy chute, once they are on the skids. Only a short while ago Heeney was more than holding his own with the Sharkeys and the Paulinos and such, and later was out there fighting for the heavyweight championship. Now his chin is hanging in the open air and unless he retires at an early date the back of his heels will be worn to the bone,' wrote Grantland Rice.

Johnny Risko avenged his 1927 defeat by 'decisively outpointing' Tom in a gruelling 10-round bout in Toronto. Locals had waited two years for a heavyweight fight in the city, but the crowd was more enthusiastic about the semi-final. Rice wrote that both Risko and Tom had been 'up under the roof' a few years ago but in this fight they had come from the 'roof to the cellar'.

Tom was matched with Jimmy Slattery in Buffalo, New York. He had a 39½-lb advantage over Slattery and dazed his opponent in the first round with two right hands but was ultimately outpunched and outpaced. Both he and Marion were hurt because of this fight. Tom was cut on his nose and over his left eye by Slattery's gloves and Marion was slightly injured when a Delaware Avenue bus she was riding crashed into a tree.

In Tiverton, New Jersey, ticketless fight fans gatecrashed Mark's Stadium by tearing away a large section of the fence when Tom fought giant Portuguese boxer José Santa in September. Santa had notched up a string of wins on the Pacific coast. Tom, the 'old-timer', now weighed 222 lb. Santa was the favourite but Tom ground out the decision to a mix of boos and cheers. The 250-lb Santa was continually warned about low punches and he emerged from the fight with a cut and swollen face.

Santa generally did better in return bouts and was predicted to win when the pair met again, this time in Providence, Rhode Island. 'Heeney will be in there to win,' said Harvey. 'Old Tom is in line for the main bout in the season's opener of the St Nick's club in New York on October 19, where he is booked to met Giovanni Bergomas, young Italian heavyweight; he has a long-standing engagement to clash with Max Baer in a return fracas, this one to take place in San Francisco, and Billy Ames, matchmaker of the Boston Garden, will be at the fight tonight with an offer for Heeney to meet Charley Retzlaff at the Hub palace in November if he repeats his win over Santa. Heeney can't afford to lose.' In a similar bout to the Tiverton one, Santa ended up with both eyes almost closed, his left cheek split and swollen and his mouth battered. It was ruled a draw but one report had it that Tom lost a well-earned decision.

Finally able to ply his trade in a Manhattan ring for the first time since the Baer fight, Tom battled Italian heavyweight Bergomas at St Nick's to a draw. 'The verdict was a moral victory for Heeney,' wrote one observer. 'The veteran demonstrated that he retains enough of his old fighting strength and determination to discourage the pretensions of such ambitious young heavyweights as Bergomas.' Indeed, the following month Tom was one of the opponents offered to Dempsey by Jimmy

Johnston, the new head of the Garden's boxing department. There was talk of a tune-up bout for Dempsey ahead of a possible comeback. On 8 February 1932 Harvey left for the East Coast hoping to finalise a Baer–Heeney match for later in the month. A couple of days later Baer and Tom were signed for a 10-round bout in San Francisco.

After a four-day train ride across the country Tom was in the gym. 'Just off the train, after a tiresome trip,' trainer Dutch Shurneman said. 'He's a bit stiff-ended up, is Tom, but he'll be all right in another day.' Tom wasn't going to do any boxing that day but a big crowd had gathered and he didn't want to let down the fans and boxing scribes.

Harvey was in Los Angeles watching another of his fighters. While he was alone in his hotel room with the $5000 guarantee for the fight two racketeers held him up at gunpoint. Hampered by a broken back, Harvey knocked the gun from the smaller man's hand and hit him so hard he sprained his right thumb. The bigger man punched Harvey on the chin but he yelled and the pair ran off. The bigger man had rented a room adjoining Harvey's and that's where police found his sidekick. The gun had been tossed out the window, landing on an awning. It seems the thugs knew about the money and waited until Harvey was alone. 'It was a good thing I was an announcer in my day,' Harvey said. 'When things were going good, I yelled at the top of my voice and you could have heard me from Los Angeles to San Francisco. Why did I hit the chap? Impulse, I guess. Sober second thought would have made me hand over the "poke" and tell him to get out. Money isn't everything.'

Odds of 3 to 1 with even money Baer would knock Tom out had stretched to ringside odds of 3½ to 1 on a sunny and warm Monday afternoon in Seals Stadium. Betting had opened at 2 to 1 but had lengthened due to a lack of support for Tom. 'Heeney rates better than that,' Harvey said, 'and some of the boys who like to have a bet down are apt to have their fingers burned.' Baer got the decision in 'a rousing battle from start to finish', went one report, 'with the veteran Heeney putting up unexpected opposition to force his younger opponent to the utmost'. Tom got about $2500 for his troubles.

Tom eventually won a fight when he beat Hans Birkie at the Oakland Auditorium. He was in much better condition and there was talk of another match with Baer. Other fights were discussed but never eventuated as the summer when stock market prices finally hit their lowest point came and went. There was more disappointment in September when Ray Impellittiere cancelled a fight because of a chipped elbow. In October Tom drew with John Schwake in Saint Louis and both ended up with bruised and battered faces.

When Tom arrived in Cleveland, Ohio, on 4 December he was still talking about a comeback. He said he wanted another crack at Risko and a good victory over Patsy Perroni was the best way to get it. He wanted one more 'big shot'. Perroni was younger but had only fought once since a motoring accident more than a year before. Tom revealed something that looked suspiciously like a beer paunch when he took off his robe. He gave a 'pathetic exhibition' according to the *Cleveland Plain Dealer*, winning only two rounds narrowly. He was warmly welcomed when he stepped into the ring but given the old 'Bronx cheer' as he headed for the dressing room after the decision went to Perroni.

> 'Where do you get that Honest Tom stuff about this old Heeney guy?' a fellow asked me yesterday. 'How can a guy be honest and accept dough for a fight like he put up there at Public Hall? Why he ought to be arrested for taking money under false pretenses.'
>
> 'Oh, Tom's all right,' I said. 'Just a well-meaning old gent trying to get along. And do you mean to tell me that you didn't get YOUR money's worth at those fights?'
>
> 'No, it's not that. I got more than my money's worth — on the four of the six scraps that were so good. I'm only talking about Heeney. I can see now why Tunney picked him — and why Tunney should make a swell politician. I don't imagine the guy was much better than that when Tunney took him, was he?'
>
> 'Why, he could punch a little then,' I said. 'He was a fair puncher to the body.'
>
> 'Yeah?' was the skeptical response. 'But say, tell me — who was that old bird in Heeney's corner? The bird with the cane.'
>
> 'That was his manager, Charlie Harvey.'
>
> 'It was? Why, somebody was trying to tell me it was Heeney's son.'
>
> James E. Doyle, *Cleveland Plain Dealer*, 8 December 1932

A Los Angeles match with Primo Carnera looked possible, but the idea was abandoned. A match with Isadore Gastanaga at the Garden in New

York was cancelled when the Spaniard said a cold prevented him training properly. A return match with Retzlaff did come off, however. Retzlaff won a newspaper decision in a 10-round bout on 7 March 1933 in Saint Paul, Minnesota. 'It was merely a question of how many right hands Retzlaff could throw and how many the amazing durable Heeney could take,' wrote a Minneapolis scribe. And then came Poreda.

Tom got just $200 for his terrible beating by Poreda. His value in the ring had plummeted so drastically Ed Hughes wrote an article in the *Brooklyn Daily Eagle* entitled 'Failure in the Stock Market Keeps Heeney in the Sock Market'. Win, lose or draw with Tunney it was assumed Tom would be able to live comfortably for the rest of his life. But then came the stock market failure. 'The Hard Rock was soft picking for the investment market. It could have picked on a much less deserving fellow than honest Tom Heeney,' wrote Hughes. Tom had always given his best and still did in a 'desperate, feeble way'.

Hughes' words were reprinted in Auckland and the story got around that the rich and famous boxer who'd returned with his glamorously dressed wife to a near-riot in New Zealand five years before was now poverty-stricken. 'I wonder if there is a sportsman in New Zealand today who does not feel sorry at heart for our old champion, Tom Heeney,' wrote R. Craig in the *Auckland Star*. Tom displayed 'to the whole world such courage and bulldog pluck that made every true New Zealander tingly with pride', he continued. Craig advocated a collection for Tom and Marion. Not if 'Sel Himself' had anything to do with it. 'If Heeney is still big and strong, let him come back home and get on with the same job as his less fortunate countrymen — folk who never had the money or chances he has had — and who yet find it necessary to work hard to start again.' Craig responded. 'How many millions of people the world over asked the questions "Where is Heeney from? What country does he represent?" In advertising New Zealand alone, Heeney did more than a hundred men could do in ten years — why, the whole world was getting out maps and geography books to find this practically unheard of land that could produce such a man.' 'Wanderer' also objected to a fund for Tom. 'Tom Heeney's fame seemed to me to be a wave of hysteria that overcame a few of our New Zealand "sports." He had beaten only a few second-grade men in a lean time of good fighters. His only strong point, to my light, was his ability to take punishment.'

'Sportsman' pointed out that by wearing the Maori cloak Tom brought 'before the eyes of the world, through the medium of newspaper reports, etc., our country and our Maori population' and he deserved financial help. But surely Tom wore the cloak more for luck than to advertise his home country, wrote 'Sel Himself'. 'And the only "luck" it brought that day was good, kind judgement on the part of the referee, who interfered just in time to save Heeney from looking like a doormat.' Some advertisement. And what about returned servicemen surviving in relief camps or by selling shoelaces on the streets — would Tom's supporters give so readily to those men? Mention of New Zealand's soldiers brought forth a few words from 'Anti-Humbug'. Surely it was their 'undying heroism' and the achievements of such eminent New Zealanders as Lord Rutherford and Katherine Mansfield that put New Zealand on the map and not 'the meteoric, flash-in-the-pan pugilistic career of Tom Heeney'.

Paul Gallico saw Tom a few rows back from the ring at the featherweight title fight between Kid Chocolate and 'Seaman' Tom Watson at the Garden in May 1933. The Garden wasn't the same as it had been in the heyday of boxing when Jimmy Walker showed up surrounded by cops, Ruth Elder sat behind him, and a row of bootleggers sat at right angles to 'Gangsters Row' on the Eighth Ave side with 'a lot of good-looking janes'. There were still as many platinum blondes in the first six rows but they were fading. And of Tom he wrote: 'He looked sad and sullen and more gnarled and seamed than ever. The fight game was kind to him for a while and then abandoned him. I don't suppose he has much of the money he made in his best years. I don't suppose he ever really made a lot of money. His shot with Gene Tunney was the biggest purse he got but, then, money doesn't last forever. That is what is so treacherous about a fighter's career. Even if he is thrifty, wise and careful and saves his money when he is making a lot, he has nothing to fall back upon when his fortune is wiped out as most of them were in the last financial disaster.' Men who lived by their wits or who had a profession could make another start but a fighter wasn't good for anything else, and 'most of them are broken in mind as well as body when the ring is through with them', he wrote.

Things weren't quite as bad for Tom as they may have appeared. He wasn't broken in mind or body, and whatever his bank balance, he still had a nice house. It seems Munsey Park was a good place to have bought property during the Depression. Realtor Ernest G. Blaich wrote in the *Manhasset Mail* in May 1933 that although sales and rentals were being made at prices far below 1929 values, he thought most of the properties being sold at distress prices would soon be cleared and normal sales values would return. He didn't mean, however, that a property bought for $30,000 in 1928 would sell for $30,000 in the near future, as even in good times a house could depreciate in value. Whenever a list of foreclosed properties on Long Island was offered there was rarely any mention of Manhasset, Plandome or Munsey Park. Eighteen years later it was revealed that an 'Emergency Committee of Munsey Park' had been formed in 1933 to collect funds from villagers to aid 'Munsey Parkers' on the edge of mortgage foreclosures.

Tom denied being embarrassed financially and after the Poreda fight he finally stopped looking to his gloves for income. He had to accept he would never again become a contender. He'd been unable to recover his form. Gallico still blamed his manager for allowing Tom to start the eleventh round of the Tunney fight. Harvey was unable to say 'enough' and spare Tom from the 'last smashing punches that finished him and his ring career', he wrote. Back then Gallico claimed that beneath Harvey's appearance of a sweet old gentleman lay greed and cruelty. It was not a popular view and friends swore he was mistaken. But in 1935 he would call Harvey a 'cruel and heartless second' again, when he let another of his fighters, Steve Hamas, continue 'long after mercy and decency indicated that he should surrender his pretensions'. For five years the Hard Rock had been crushed, cracked, splintered, pulped, chipped, pulverised, blasted, battered and ground into a powder. He had finally had enough.

'GOOD NEWS!' began a piece by Ike Gellis in the *New York Evening Post* on 13 May 1933. '"Ole" Tom Heeney has decided to quit.' Tom was to 'enter the real estate field in Florida in the immediate future'. Many of Tom's friends had visited South Florida and he said he had 'never seen one fellow knock it. So I said by God, it must be a little bit of heaven.' Tom and Marion left Manhasset to spend the summer in Florida. Tom insisted he had finished with boxing and was ready to spend the rest of his life with Marion in their Miami Beach home.

Miami Beach was a place of cool breezes, turquoise waters, blue skies and breathtaking sunsets. While the rest of the country was still reeling from the effects of the Depression, Miami Beach was at its height.

Society flourished even in the darkest days, as the rich in Miami were rich enough to lose money and keep on partying. Would-be residents and holidaymakers continued to fuel a demand for schools, hotels and apartment buildings. So many gaming ventures started up, Miami Beach became a gambler's paradise. What started as a mangrove swamp had become the 'World's Winter Playground'.

There was a rumour that Tom was planning a comeback. In March 1934 at Florida's first heavyweight championship fight since 1894, between Tommy Loughran and Primo Carnera, Tom was spotted sitting not far from Tunney and 'occasionally casting a wistful glance at the former titleholder'. It was common for fighters to announce their retirement and then a comeback. Tom had done it himself several times. But Tom picked up some refereeing work and later ran a fruit stand. In late 1935 he was pictured in a newspaper happily basking in the sun while Marion stood beside him with one hand ruffling his hair and the other on a lawnmower, as if to remind him the grass needed cutting. It seemed this time he had *really* retired.

Boxing with Hemingway

The ring was squeezed between the tall coconut palms and the white sand, and beyond the white sand was the blue sea and the darker blue of the Gulf. The late-afternoon breeze had blown the mosquitoes and sandflies away and the boats had all come in and were lying tied up in the slips of Brown's dock. The BBC's Empire Service whistled from the radio set perched on the old liquor barrels that supported the bar at the Compleat Angler. A writer lived in the room above the bar and he worked at the window that overlooked Brown's dock and the boxing ring he'd built. When the tuna run was over and the game fish had gone he'd given $250 to any man who could stay on his feet for three rounds. His body was tanned and strong after weeks of fighting marlin, giant tuna, sharks and all-comers.

The summer days were too hot when the trade winds occasionally failed. But when the nights were cool from the breeze that came chilled from the sea across the banks and then faded it would be time for 'trying him'. His bare-fisted 'Sunday punch' sent the head of a wealthy New York publisher slamming into the wood of the dock. Joseph Knapp was carried to his yacht and taken back to Miami for treatment while the writer drank whisky sours and replayed, each time with greater speed and ferocity, the three left hooks and two right clubs behind the left ear that had caused his opponent to 'hit ass and head at almost same time on planks'. He'd 'gotten what was coming to him' for chiding the writer about his fishing prowess. That night a calypso band composed 'Big Fat Slob in the Harbour, Tonight's the Night We Got Fun' in his honour.

'Since the Knapp thing when anybody is tight here or feels dangerous they ask me to fight,' he wrote a friend. Big Willard Saunders, a man so strong it was said he could carry a piano on his head, approached him while he was drinking in the heavy calm before the wind rose. Saunders wanted to try him for the two-fifty and a dawn bout was suggested, but the challenger wanted to try him straight away on the dock without gloves. He remained standing for one and a half minutes. Another lasted two rounds, not long enough for the two-fifty but long enough to throw a right hook that paralysed the writer's face for half an hour.

It was the summer of fishing and drinking and fighting people who wouldn't believe him. It was also the summer that an old prizefighter landed on Bimini, in the Bahamas. The writer and the prizefighter donned the salt-stained gloves for a few rounds after the sun had just dipped below the coconut palms. The first punch was thrown on a deserted beach where land crabs scuttled among fallen coconuts, but then a crowd gathered and they kept the two men surrounded but gave them plenty of room. They carefully and respectfully prodded and jabbed at each other for a few rounds until the writer looked up and saw a line of spectators on the path above them. 'We've got to quit now, Tommy, any charity would give anything to pass the hat here,' he said and they disappeared into the hut made from abandoned liquor boats and barges that was the Compleat Angler.

Tom Heeney was 'way out of condition', as even Ernest Hemingway admitted, but he took great pride in the bout and the 'event loomed larger in his imagination every time he told about it'. George Brown, who had a New York boxing gym where the writer used to work out, thought the only way Hemingway could've hit Tom was if the New Zealander got bogged down in the sand and couldn't move.

Ernest and Tom were friends. They were big, strong, macho, barrel-chested men born a little over a year apart with shared passions. There was Africa, big game hunting, drinking, the sea and fishing. Tom had fished in New Zealand for trout and even though he didn't read much he read about fishing. Tom said of Hemingway: 'He was a great boxing fan.

I wasn't much of a fisherman.' The author Enrique Cirules says that by the late 1920s and early '30s Hemingway and Tom spent time together in Havana. The trips weren't well publicised but fishermen, turtlemen and old residents remembered Tom. One story involved a secret trip Tom and Hemingway made on the north coast of Cuba. They arrived at the port of Nuevitas and visited an American colony in the valley of Cubitas called La Gloria City.

Hemingway watched boxing, wrote about boxing, and boxed so he could write about boxing better than someone who hadn't. He boxed because he liked it and because he could be a brute and a bully. Boxing for him was a metaphor for life and he liked to use the language of the sport. Of his literary prowess he said: 'I trained hard and I beat Mr de Maupassant. I've fought two draws with Mr Stendhal, but nobody is going to get me in any ring with Mr Tolstoy unless I'm crazy or keep getting better.'

Hemingway knew and admired Gene Tunney. He once dreamed about fighting him. When Tunney went to Cuba he'd visit the writer and they'd have frozen daiquiris. Hemingway would try to get Tunney to spar with him barefisted and Tunney would refuse. He'd once hurt the president of the New York boxing commission in a sparring session after Eddie Egan sneaked in a punch that hurt him. But one day Tunney gave in and demonstrated a move his friend 'Fingey' had shown him.

'Try it again,' Hemingway urged.

Tunney did. Hemingway saw an opening and couldn't resist. He shot his right elbow into Tunney's mouth, cutting it.

'I shoved Ernesto back against the wall — quickly — and threw a short left which I pulled at the last fraction of a second and laid against his chin,' Tunney said. 'Then I did the same with my right. Bang! Bang! Hemingway went white. It was the only time I ever saw the man flustered.'

After that Hemingway would sometimes get out of his chair, look at Tunney and move around as if about to ask him to spar, but never did. Roy Bosche fished with Hemingway in Bimini and heard that when Tom and Hemingway sparred Tom had been warned the author might try to sneak in a Sunday punch, and that when it came he was ready. Tom leaned back to make Hemingway miss and then dropped him with a sharp left hook, teaching him a lesson just like Tunney did.

Hemingway must've harboured a certain fascination for the New Zealander who fought Tunney for real. But above all, Tom had guts. Hemingway always demanded that from his friends. He was in Italy, badly wounded in the Great War, when he 'picked up a fear of his own fear and the lifelong need to test his courage' — although Hemingway didn't talk of 'courage' because he preferred the word 'guts'. Someone once asked him what he meant by guts.

'I mean,' he said, 'grace under pressure.'

Hemingway wrote about Tom in letters and articles. 'We are on the air tonight through the courtesy of the Kansas City Star and associated newspapers. Oh my this really is a fight,' he wrote F. Scott Fitzgerald from Piggot, Arkansas, in October 1928. 'I wish you all could see Tommy Heeney's left eye. Now they are at it again.' Hemingway was probably referring to one of the first radio stations in the city, WDAF, founded by the *Star* in the 1920s. 'Try to find out how old Tom Heeney really was when he first hit New York for what he thought was to be a single fight on his way home across the country to New Zealand, a fight to get passage money home, but which turned out to be the first in a series which led to a chance to fight for the championship of the world,' he wrote in 'My Pal the Gorilla Gargantua' in 1938. In December 1953 Hemingway wrote to Robert Ruark from Kenya that killing buffalo with a spear would be like boxing Tom Heeney.

Other well-known authors wrote about Tom. In his classic novel *Man Alone* John Mulgan created a Maori musician named in tribute to the prizefighter.

> They sat round there as the sun went down and one of the Maoris [*sic*] — Tom Heeney, they called him, though that was not his real name, he was fat and called after the prizefighter . . . Some of them were growing a little noisy and one boy was sparring in front of 'Tom Heeney', challenging him to fight. The big man stopped playing for a moment and pushed out his hand with the fingers extended, hitting the boy in the chest so that he staggered across the room and sat down heavily on a bale, while everybody laughed, and 'Tom Heeney' began playing again.

Mulgan took the title of *Man Alone* from a line in *To Have and Have Not*.

Hemingway's tale of rum-running, gun-running and man-running from Cuba to the Florida Keys during the Depression was written when the author was fishing these waters with Tom.

'This rain is no friend of mine. It's no friend of mine and these other gents (four of whom must go). Maybe it's a friend of Katharine Hepburn's, or Sarah Palfrey Fabyan's, or Tom Heeney's, or of all the good solid Greer Garson fans waiting in line at Radio City Music Hall. But it's no buddy of mine, this rain,' said Vincent Caulfield, J.D. Salinger's character in 'This Sandwich Has No Mayonnaise', whose younger brother Holden was missing in action. It was one of a group of stories related to Salinger's later work *The Catcher in the Rye*.

In his baseball novel *The Veracruz Blues* Mark Winegardner created a scene between Hemingway, Tunney and Jorge Pasquel observed by the narrator Frank Bullinger Jr. It was February 1946 and Bullinger was a guest at Hemingway's home in Cuba.

> 'Up on your feet,' said Hemingway.
>
> I stood. But Hemingway was talking to Jorge Pasquel.
>
> Pasquel had taken off his holster. His pearl-handled pistols lay on a coffee table, on top of a copy of *Look*. He also had taken his shirt off. He was not fat, but neither was he thin. Hemingway was more muscular.
>
> 'You know, I sparred with Heeney in '35,' said Hemingway, referring to an Australian meatbag Gene Tunney had carved up in the Polo Grounds in '28. 'Gave him all he could handle.'
>
> 'Right,' said Tunney. 'I know. We all know.'

It's likely that Tom was a source of literary inspiration for Hemingway too. The summer of 1935 at Bimini inspired part of Hemingway's novel *Islands in the Stream*. There was the character Rupert Pinder, 'a very big Negro who was said to have once carried a piano on his back' and 'fancied himself as a fighting man'. And there was a fight on Brown's dock between one of the main characters Roger and a man who called him a slob.

'Roger stepped quickly over to where the man stood and raised his left shoulder and dropped his right fist down and swung it up so it smashed against the side of the man's head. He went down on his hands and knees, his forehead resting on the dock. He knelt there a little while with his forehead against the planking and then he went gently over on his side.' The crew of his yacht carried him on board and there was a lot of concern about his condition, just as Ernest worried he might've hurt Joseph Knapp and told friends at dinner about the fight.

After the fight Roger talked to the central character in the book, the painter Thomas Hudson, and it was revealed that he almost killed a man in a fight. Could it be that over drinks in the Compleat Angler on Bimini, Tom told Ernest of the night his gloves ended the life of Cyril Whitaker back in Auckland and how Brian McCleary nearly suffered the same fate in Christchurch?

> Thomas Hudson went to the icebox, mixed the drink, and came back out to the screened porch and sat there in the dark with Roger lying on the bed.
> 'All fights are bad.'
> 'I know it. But what are you going to do about them?'
> 'You have to win them when they start.'
> 'Sure. But I was taking pleasure in it from the minute it started.'
> 'You would have taken more pleasure if he could have fought.'
> 'I hope so,' Roger said. 'Though I don't know now.'

Hemingway leapt to Tom's defence in the winter of 1936 when *Washington Herald* columnist Bob Considine claimed the author had floored the New Zealander. He'd written the column from a hotel in Orlando, Florida:

> Around the bar, one night, we heard a traveller from Key West tell a story about Ernest Hemingway, the man who didn't come back after writing "Farewell to Arms." The author, who is more than 40 now, has become amazingly adept at using his dukes. He was always a good bar room fighter (although he was cooled completely in such a brawl when last in New York), but of late he has gone into the matter scientifically. He has old Tom Heeney with him in Key West and had the one-time challenger for the world's championship on the floor the other day.

Hemingway rattled out an angry response on his typewriter:

Dear Mr Considine;

Refering to your column of February 22 which I have just seen:

I am not over forty, nor was I recently 'cooled completely in a brawl when last in New York'; nor was I in any brawl of any kind in N.Y. nor is Tom Heeney with me in Key West; nor did I ever have Tom Heeney on the floor.

If you write everything you hear around the bars you want to be pretty careful you do not write libel.

Tom Heeney made plenty of money and hung on to plenty of it and has a fine home in Miami Beach. He does not have to act as a sparring partner to anyone. He and I sparred a little last summer in Bimini where he fished a day with us as my guest and no one was on the floor at any time. If you ever saw Tom Heeney you would know that it would take a better man than me to put him on the floor even if he were sixty. I have great admiration for Tom Heeney both as an intelligent and upright man and as a great game fighter and it disgusts me to read the statement you make in your column.

As for me being cooled in a brawl in N.Y.; I have had several fights in my time none of which was of my own seeking, and I have never been cooled in any of them.

If you wish to be fair you will publish this letter in full, exactly as written, in your column.

Yours very truly,
Ernest Hemingway
(© Hemingway Foreign Rights Trust)

Next he wrote to Tom, enclosing both the offending article and a copy of his letter to Considine. Hemingway was angry, and wasn't ready to let the 'hyenas' write any 'crap' about him or his friends. He told Tom if Considine didn't publish his letter he'd have his lawyer write to the newspaper. He enquired after Tom and Marion's health and wrote that his wife joined him in his regards.

The letter was duly delivered to Considine, who wrote he was 'ducking under the superior thrusts of a notably abler member of the great happy writing family . . . The vexed subscriber is Ernest Hemingway, who has done me the great honour of objecting by mail, to something that I now see was nothing but the base repetition of a baser canard and a custard pie heaved at the head of dignity.' An apology, of sorts, followed:

> I don't understand how Mr Heeney managed to get himself insulted in that February 22 bit of hackery, but deeply appreciate that he has been defended warmly and well by his friend. As a matter of truth I have always been a great admirer of Mr Heeney's, and sympathized heartedly with him when Gentleman Gene Tunney, unable to "cool him completely," had to thumb Tom in the eye in order to hit him in the lug.
>
> The column was not a story about Heeney, but an idle yarn about Hemingway, told me in apparent good faith by one who represented himself as near to Mr Hemingway as Mr Hemingway's socks. So few writers of hard brave words can even attempt to back up their letters with their dukes. That the discovery of one literarteur [sic] gifted with good knuckles made me want to record the miracle.
>
> If this poor attempt on my part to humanize one of our great men of letters has done anything to harm a figure firmly entrenched enough to have overcome some of those Esquire pieces and "Death in the Afternoon," then I apologize pretty abjectly. For I would that no harm ever come to a guy good enough to write 'The Sun Also Rises,' and 'Farewell to Arms' and short stories like 'Fifty Grand' and 'Today is Friday.'
>
> I treasure his fine blunt letter highly, not only because of the autograph and the indubitable honor of becoming a correspondent with such a great writer, but also because it bided me over what promised to be one heluva dull 20 minutes for the daily readers of this column.

Considine later revealed that Quentin Reynolds, who'd spent a weekend as Hemingway's guest, was the one who said Tom was working for the writer as a sparring partner. He also said that by the time he met Hemingway in New York the incident seemed forgotten.

Hemingway was probably right when it came to Tom's money. In early

1937 Tom opened a fashionable bar in Miami Beach. Tom Heeney's Bar was on Washington Avenue, a bustling strip of delis, kosher butchers, bakeries, greengrocers, fish shops and cafés and souvenir shops and shops selling beach bags and coconut suntan oil to tourists. A couple of blocks over was the wide public beach. Miami Beach was booming in the thirties as block after block of Art Deco apartment buildings, hotels, shops, bars, theatres and nightclubs blossomed.

'Tom Heeney, "The Hard Rock From Down Under", Here to Greet You Every Night' read Tom's postcards; 'Try Tom Heeney's Punch' invited the matchbox covers. But even as the owner of a celebrity hangout, Tom still welcomed customers wearing a polo shirt. 'I don't own a dress suit.' Tom now weighed around 240 lb and swimming was his main exercise. 'I'll never go back into the ring,' he said. 'I'm too old for one thing. I'm 38 now. No, I won't fight again, not unless some mug takes a slug at me, or unless it's just a show for charity.'

There was a tradition of retired pugilists running bars, and since Prohibition was over this was now a legitimate enterprise. Many of the ventures failed. But Tom knew of the danger of ending up on the wrong side of the bar. 'I like to take a drink as well as anyone, but if I drank with everyone that came in I'd soon be standing on my ear. So I just say "no" to everybody,' he said. Tom didn't get to bed until 3 a.m. He liked it, but fighting was simpler. 'My manager would come up to me and say, "You're to fight so-and-so on such-and-such a date." All I had to do was get in touch with my trainer and from then on it was just a matter of form. All the headaches, all the grief, went to my manager. "See Charlie Harvey," I used to say. Now all the headaches are on me. It's "See Mr Heeney." This is lots better than working for someone else, though, and you meet some interesting people.' Although he did have a secret arrangement with the waiters in case he needed to escape a particularly tedious patron.

In later years Tom was especially proud of two pictures on the far wall. They were of an old friend and were inscribed 'To Tom Heeney, wishing him the best always. Ernest Hemingway.' 'Now that fellow is a real man, and he's a writer too . . . He always comes straight here when he's over from Cuba,' Tom said. Hemingway liked to impress his women by visiting Tom and his bar. In January 1937 Martha Gellhorn, future wife number three, wrote to wife number two Pauline of dining with

Ernest and Tom in Miami. 'I had a very fine time with Ernestino eating the most superb steak somewhere and then quietly and sleepily digesting and admiring the vast head of Mr Heeney.' Pauline, referred to in *Green Hills of Africa* as 'POM' or 'Poor Old Mama', and Ernest inscribed a copy of the book to Marion:

> To Marian [sic] Heeney
> With love from POM
> and her friend
> (I hope)
> Ernest Hemingway

Wife number four, the petite and blonde Mary, accompanied Hemingway to Tom's bar after they'd driven up from Key West. 'He was an absolutely *vast* man,' she recalled. 'I didn't think he could have walked on a beach without dropping in. I had a trick at the time of being able to heft quite big men off the ground — sneaking up behind them, locking my arms around their middles, and hoisting them up an inch or so off the floor. I tried it on Heeney — he was deep in conversation with Ernest — but I couldn't budge him . . . not even a millimetre. He was like a tree rooted to the floor. I'm not sure that he even noticed.'

Tom fished with Hemingway in the Florida Keys and Ernest enjoyed potent pitchers with Tom in his Miami Beach home. But the days of fishing and beaching and eating and drinking in good company soon came to an end as the world faced another crisis and Ernest and Tom went to war.

'When that moment arrives, whether it is in a barroom fight or in a war, the thing to do is to hit your opponent the first punch and hit him as hard as possible,' wrote Hemingway. 'But we were a great and noble power and they relied on our nobility and kept men talking to us while they prepared to hit. They had hit once before against Russia without warning. In Washington they seemed to have forgotten that. We kept on talking. As a matter of fact, I believe we were talking to them at the moment when it happened. So we had Pearl Harbor.'

On 21 August 1942 Tom, now an American citizen, took the oath in Miami as a second-class seaman in the Naval Seabees, an overseas naval construction division. He was shipped to New Caledonia, with visits to Guadalcanal and New Zealand. In March 1943 he was interviewed at 'an advance base in the South Pacific' where he was on special service with an athletic unit. He said Sharkey was the best man he'd fought. What about Tunney?

'Mister Tunney is a commander and my senior officer. It wouldn't be policy for me to say anything about him.'

Tunney served as a lieutenant commander and later as a commander in charge of the Navy's conditioning programme. Tom was offered a chief's rating in the Navy's athletic branch but preferred to be an ordinary seaman.

'I didn't know then how the Navy operated, or I would have taken the rating,' he said.

When he went back to New Zealand he saw his mother for the first time since 1928. On Arbor Day he visited his old school, Te Hapara. He planted a pohutukawa tree in the school grounds and spent half an hour with the children.

'Did you hurt Gene Tunney?' asked one student. Tom said he didn't know but that 'Gene didn't do me any good!'.

'How heavy can you be when you're fighting?' asked a standard four lad.

'Up to a couple of ton,' Tom joked.

'Are you going to stay in Gisborne?' asked a little girl. Nothing would suit him better, Tom replied. 'Of course, you have to remember that I am classed as a foreigner now, and I have to go along to the police station to find out if they will let me stay,' he added and his audience laughed. The children didn't understand how Tom could be a foreigner.

In October Tom met Tunney in the ring for the first time since that night in July 1928. Tunney was on a tour of the Pacific, mostly to check up on the fitness of sailors and marines. They exchanged handshakes and a few playful sparring punches. They were together again at Christmas 1943, when 7500 servicemen at Guadalcanal watched 24 young fighters in a boxing tournament. Tom had taken his New Zealand and New Caledonia fighters to 'the Canal' for the Southwest Pacific Championship matches and Tunney was presenting medals donated by Hollywood movie stars. Tunney thought Tom was doing a lot for morale by putting on weekly boxing shows. He got him promoted, which tripled Tom's pay.

By September 1944 Chief Specialist Heeney was home in Miami Beach. 'I've never seen such enthusiasm for boxing as those boys have,' Tom said. 'At my camp we had a show every Saturday night, rain or shine, and we always had crowds of 10,000 or so . . . they were in the trees and all over the place.'

After the war Tom resumed his position behind the mahogany counter of Tom Heeney's Bar. Miami had men who'd never seen war and men who'd seen the worst of it. Veterans of the Pacific and the China/Burma/India theatres were brought to Miami to recuperate in the luxury hotels and on the beaches. There was talk of the impending gold rush; of the city of millionaires, film stars, grand houses, women dripping jewellery, neon-lighted nightclubs and palm trees. 'Men with pockets full of war profits, men with war nerves, and women with nothing to do are all bound for this "gem on the Florida coast", it was written.

One day a very rich and famous person came into Tom's bar. It was Gene Tunney. He'd run into Hemingway who'd said, 'Tom Heeney tells me you were a dirty fighter.'

'Tom Heeney said that? Do you mind if I ask him about it?'

Hemingway didn't mind. So the next time Tunney was in Miami he went to see Tom. He ordered a martini but Tom wasn't in the bar. Marion came over and introduced herself and called her husband. He came in and they had a couple of drinks. Tunney repeated what Hemingway had said.

'I didn't thumb you, did I, Tom?'

'Yes, Gene,' Tunney recalled Tom saying. 'You *were* a dirty fighter.'

'Tom, I don't understand you. Would it be reasonable for me to try to maim you, and then immediately step back and allow you to recover?'

Tom agreed and they parted friends, but Tunney wasn't convinced. 'I don't know even today if that man believed in his heart that I was telling the truth.'

Tom recalled saying to Tunney: 'That's in the past, we can forget that now', and then telling him how great he was and meaning it. Tom still seemed in awe of the former champion. 'I didn't see Gene for years after our fight,' he once told a reporter, before explaining how Tunney jumped his rating during the war. 'Then, a few years ago, he came by the place here just to say hello. How many multi-millionaires would do that?'

'Heeney's Bar is famous in Miami,' Anton Vogt wrote in the *New*

Zealand Listener in 1960. He described the curved bar with its swivel stools and the enormous old Bowery-style sideboard with mirrors, bottles and trophies behind it. There were half a dozen small tables and chairs, skittles, a television, a jukebox and a piano. The walls were covered with photographs, mostly of boxers. John L. Sullivan was up there, as were James Braddock, Jack Dempsey and Tommy Farr. Most of them were signed with 'Wishing you the best, always . . .'. And there were the valued pictures of Hemingway with his fishing rods and his prize tuna. But there was no photograph of Gene Tunney.

Epilogue

> I loved this country and I felt at home and where a man feels at home, outside of where he's born, is where he's meant to go.
>
> Ernest Hemingway, *Green Hills of Africa*

Miami Beach was Tom's little bit of heaven. That's how he described the subtropical holiday playground with its constant partying and its warm and inviting waters all year round. Tom liked the American way of life. 'I always liked Aussie. Now New Zealand is where I come from, and I like that too; but you've got to admit that it's a bit like a cemetery. Now here people are *alive*!' he told a journalist visiting from New Zealand in 1960. He remembered not being able to play rugby on a Sunday back home. But in America you could go to church on Sunday morning and to a ball game in the afternoon. 'If you can't say enough prayers on a Sunday morning to get to heaven, then you'll never make it,' was Tom's theory. He enjoyed the licensing laws in Miami and recalled six o'clock closing in New Zealand where a man would gulp down six or eight beers in an hour 'like a pig'.

For three decades Tom greeted the clientele of Tom Heeney's Bar with his mixed accent, tanned skin, clear eyes and white hair. In his early seventies he said he felt great and was enjoying life. 'I don't know what a headache is. I suppose that's because I never had any brains to give me a headache,' he joked. His father would probably have attributed his good health to a good choice of jobs. 'If you enjoy your work, are keen about it, you'll get on, and your health will be right,' Hugh wrote. 'It's no good working on at something that doesn't agree with you. Life's too short for that.'

A reporter once asked Tom how he managed to stay away from

boxing after he'd retired from the ring. 'Never cared much for fighting and fighters,' Tom said. 'And I never particularly wanted to stay around boxing after I hung 'em up in 1933.'

Someone in the bar suggested maybe Tom was too honest for boxing.

'Ha!' laughed Marion, 'a chipper little lady'. 'He crooked me out of a game of gin rummy the other night.'

'No, no, not a matter of honesty,' Tom said. 'I never cared to imply dishonesty to anyone. The only reason I'd have gone back into boxing would have been to handle a good young prospect. I never ran into one.'

Tom talked about New Zealand affectionately and encouraged Americans to visit. He made several trips back himself and was very much the returning celebrity. He saw family, refereed the odd boxing match and enjoyed the Gisborne beaches. 'That's the only thing wrong with Miami — there's no surf,' he said. 'The Gulf Stream kills the waves. It's okay for the wife, she doesn't want to get her hair wet. But I prefer the surf.' In 1947 he wrote: 'Everyone knew me. I can't understand why a loser is standing on a pedestal.' He'd gone back to see his mother for a few months and still talked about the possibility of returning with Marion to live in New Zealand if he found the right work.

Eliza Heeney died two years later after her first real illness of just a few days. She'd lived alone since Hugh's death in 1936, refusing to be dependent on her children and still milking her cow morning and night. Family legend has it that when she broke her wrist in a fall she denied having a problem. She had to be persuaded to go to hospital by one of her sons and her wrist had to be rebroken. She was so worried about the milking not being done properly she grabbed her purse that she was never seen without and sneaked out of hospital. Failing to notice a brick had been put in her handbag (to stop her picking it up) she trudged back to her house. 'Mrs Heeney died full of years and Irish wit, highly respected by all who knew her and proud — in her scornful Irish way — of what her sons had done to make the family name a by-word for courage and tenacity — qualities which her own life had exemplified so markedly,' the *Gisborne Herald* wrote.

Tom attended the national boxing championships as part of Gisborne's bicentenary celebrations in 1969. He was besieged by autograph hunters and wrote to his friend Mario Castricone of the welcome he received.

Friend Mario,

I'm back in my home town and the people treat me like a king, every one thinks it was very nice for me to come back, but getting here was not so hot, it took two nights and a day on the plane, when you sit down that long the old can gets sore, you can bet I'll never come again on a plane, there is nothing like the old boat for pleasure, it may take 3 weeks on the boat but I'm going nowhere so why should I be in such a hurry to get here. Hope everything is going well back home at the next meeting give all the boys my regards.

Good health
Tom

The pair had met as members of the Veteran Boxers' Association of South Florida, Ring No. 31, an organisation for those involved in boxing to help their own by assisting boxers who'd fallen on hard times. Mario, who would look after Tom in his last years, was just a teenager devouring copies of *The Ring* magazine in a basement when he read about Tom and the big fight. Close to 40 years would pass before he'd finally meet his idol.

As the decades passed, new generations of heavyweights captured the public's imagination. There was Joe Louis, Rocky Marciano and Mohammed Ali. Tom belonged to an increasingly distant era of boxing. There were traces of regret in some of his later remarks: that he had never learned how to box properly; that he might've felled Tunney if he'd been allowed to continue; that he hadn't won the Australasian title from Colin Bell. But he didn't dwell on past failures or successes. Tom Heeney's Bar had given him a good living and a comfortable retirement. He'd built a house with three bedrooms, each with its own bathroom, and the modest investments he'd made along with his Social Security every month meant he'd never go hungry. At 76, a decade or so after he'd retired from the bar business, he joked that he was 'doing nothing, just living like a millionaire'.

Tom's name still appeared in the pages of the local newspaper. In 1951 a *Miami Herald* scribe wrote of Tom's supporters calling him at three in the morning to argue that Tom should fill an empty place on the boxing

EPILOGUE

commission. He wondered if Tom shut his place at three. And there was the mystery of Tom's burglar alarm. As he closed the door of his bar at two in the morning the alarm went off. He couldn't work out why but he was in a hurry to get home so he disconnected the system. When he reopened the bar at a quarter past nine he discovered $106 and three and a half quarts of whisky missing. A 25-year-old 'Negro handyman' he employed was later arrested and charged with vagrancy and suspicion of grand larceny. A cleverly positioned thumbtack had short-circuited the mechanism in the alarm system. And there was the time when Tom found a dead body. In 1950 real estate operator Hugo Ernest Brandt lived at 8345 Atlantic Way, a house Tom once lived in. Brandt's wife returned from a movie to the sound of water running in the bathroom. She asked Tom to investigate, who found Brandt lying in a bathtub full of water and the shower faucet still running. He reached into the water and found a rusty pistol near the drain. Two bullets had lodged in the wall and one had gone into the man's right temple.

Over the years, Tom kept in touch with old boxing friends. Johnny Risko used to look him up when he was in Miami and had arranged a dinner date with him on the day in January 1954 that he collapsed and died. Tom outlived most of his New York team from his best fighting years. Jimmy Hennessey succumbed in hospital to a ruptured appendix in 1931 at the age of 32. Charlie Harvey made it to 79, collapsing on his way to Madison Square Garden in 1944. Many of Tom's ring foes had gone too: Delaney died at 48 and the 1970s finally claimed Maloney and Tunney.

After Marion died in 1980 Tom found life harder. He was quiet now too; when he was a famous boxer Marion said he could barely keep still he talked so much. But with age he became increasingly subdued until eventually he preferred to talk only when spoken to. A stroke in 1982 put Tom in a North Miami nursing home and that's where he stayed. He was confined to a wheelchair but meticulous about answering his fan letters. On 23 May 1984 he suffered a second stroke and slipped into a coma. Tom died at 2 a.m. on 16 June 1984. His death certificate shows 'boxer' as his usual occupation and 'fighting' as his kind of business or industry. He had been the oldest living man to fight for a world heavyweight championship. Now that honour passed to an old adversary, Jack Sharkey, who was sad to hear of Tom's death. 'Tom fought like the Rock of Gibraltar,' he said. 'He gave me a tough fight.'

Four days after his 86th birthday and the day before he slipped into the coma from which he never recovered, Tom received a fan letter. As the letter was read to him he smiled and sat up straight.

Dear Mr Heeney:

I am somewhat of a fan of yours. I say somewhat because I never have seen you fight (I am too young — 22 this year). But I have read a lot about you. I'm wondering if you would autograph this enclosed card and send it to me.

Sincerely,
Nikki Neville
Los Angeles

Tom scribbled a final autograph before he departed forever the little piece of heaven he'd found on the south-eastern tip of the United States. And that's where his story ends. As another of Tom's fans, Ernest Hemingway, famously wrote in *Death in the Afternoon*: 'Madame, all stories, if continued far enough, end in death, and he is no true story-teller who would keep that from you.'

Bibliography

Books

Akenson, D.H., *Half the World From Home*, Victoria University Press, Wellington, 1990.
Armbruster, A., *The Life and Times of Miami Beach*, Alfred A. Knopf, New York, 1995.
Atkins, J., *The Art of Ernest Hemingway*, Spring Books, London, 1952.
Baker, C., *Ernest Hemingway*, Penguin, Harmondsworth, 1972.
Baker, C. (ed.), *Ernest Hemingway: Selected Letters 1917–1961*, Scribners, New York, 1981.
Cavanaugh, J., *Tunney*, Random House, New York, 2006.
Considine, B., *It's All News to Me*, Meredith Press, New York, 1967.
DeLisa, M.C., *Cinderella Man*, Milo Books, Preston, 2005.
Fitzgerald, F. Scott., *The Crack-Up With Other Pieces and Stories*, Penguin, Harmondsworth, 1971.
Fleischer, N., *Gene Tunney*, F. Hubner & Co., Inc., New York, 1931.
Gabrielan, R., *Rumson*, Arcadia, Charleston, 2003.
Gallico, P., *Farewell to Sport*, Alfred A. Knopf, New York, 1938.
—— *The Golden People*, Doubleday, New York, 1965.
Gallimore, A., *Occupation Prizefighter*, Seren, Bridgend, 2006.
—— *A Bloody Canvas*, Mercier, Cork, 2007.
Griffin, M., *Wise Guy*, The Vanguard Press, New York, c. 1933.
Heeney, Mr and Mrs H., *Our Tom*, The Brett Printing and Publishing Co., Auckland, c. 1928.
Hemingway, E. (ed.), *Men At War*, Wings Books, New York, 1991.
Hemingway, E., *Death in the Afternoon*, Arrow, London, 1994.
—— *Green Hills of Africa*, Arrow, London, 1994.
—— *Hemingway on Hunting*, Scribner, New York, 2003.

—— *Islands in the Stream*, Scribner, New York, 2004.
Ingram, W., *Legends in Their Lifetime*, A.H. & A.W. Reed, Wellington, 1962.
Jarrett, J., *Gene Tunney*, Robson Books, London, 2003.
Kahn, R., *A Flame of Pure Fire*, Harcourt Brace & Co., New York, 1999.
Klein, M., *The Crash of 1929*, Oxford University Press, Oxford, 2001.
Kleinberg, H., *Miami Beach*, Centennial Press, Miami, 1994.
Lawrence, H. Lea, *A Hemingway Odyssey*, Cumberland House Publishing, Nashville, 1999.
Lummus, J.N., *The Miracle of Miami Beach*, The Teacher Publishing Co., Miami, c. 1940.
Mackay, J.A., *Historic Poverty Bay and the East Coast*, Gisborne, 1949.
Maguire, B., *Gisborne Catholic Education 1894–1994*, Logan Print for the author, Gisborne, 1994.
Mailer, N., *The Fight*, Penguin, London, 2000.
Marshall, J., *Vagabond Deluxe*, Kessinger Publishing, Whitefish, 2004.
Maxwell, A., *Tom Heeney*, H.E. Geddis & Co., Wellington, 1928.
Moorehead, C. (ed.), *Selected Letters of Martha Gellhorn*, Chatto & Windus, London, 2006.
Mulgan, J., *Man Alone*, Penguin, Auckland, 2002.
O'Brien, B.F., *Kiwis With Gloves On*, A.H. & A.W. Reed, Wellington, 1960.
Phillips, J., *A Man's Country?*, Penguin, Auckland, 1987.
Reynolds, M., *Hemingway: The 1930s*, W.W. Norton & Co., New York, 1997.
Reynolds, Q., *By Quentin Reynolds*, McGraw-Hill, New York, 1963.
Samuelson, A., *With Hemingway: A Year in Key West and Cuba*, Severn House Publishers, London, 1985.
Silverman, J. (ed.), *The Greatest Boxing Stories Ever Told*, The Lyons Press, Guilford, 2002.
Swan, A.C., *Rugby in Poverty Bay 1878–1964*, Poverty Bay Rugby Football Union, 1965.
Tunney, G., *A Man Must Fight*, Houghton Mifflin Company, Boston and New York, 1932.
Wagner, L., *A New Book About London*, George Allen & Unwin, London, 1921.
White, E.B., *Here is New York*, The Little Bookroom, New York, 2005.

Winegardner, M., *Veracruz Blues*, Viking, New York, 1996.
Life in early Poverty Bay: trials and triumphs of its brave founders: issued on the occasion of the golden jubilees of the Borough of Gisborne and the County of Cook, May, 1927, The Gisborne Publishing Co., Gisborne, 1927.
Long Island: The Sunrise Home Land, Long Island Chamber of Commerce, New York, 1929.
Manhasset: the first 300 years: a tri-centennial project of the Manhasset Community Liaison Committee, Manhasset Chamber of Commerce, Manhasset, 1980.

Articles

Bittner, J.R., 'African Journeys: Hemingway's Influence on the Life and Writings of Robert Ruark', *The Hemingway Review*, vol. 21, no. 2, 2002, pp. 129–145.
Davis, R., 'The Shamrock and the Tiki: Irish Nationalists and Maori Resistance in the 19th century', *Journal of Intercultural Studies*, vol. 1, no. 3, 1980, pp. 16–27.
Fenton, C.A., 'No Money for the Kingbird: Hemingway's Prizefight Stories', *American Quarterly*, vol. 4, no. 4, 1952, pp. 339–350.
Pope, S.W., 'An Army of Athletes: Playing Fields, Battlefields, and the American Military Sporting Experience, 1890–1920', *The Journal of Military History*, vol. 59, no. 3, 1995, pp. 435–456.
Weinberg, S.K. & Arond, H., 'The Occupational Culture of the Boxer', *The American Journal of Sociology*, vol. 57, no. 5, 1952, pp. 460–469.

Newspapers and Magazines

Australia: *The Referee*
Canada: *Maclean's*
Ireland: *The Anglo-Celt, Dublin Evening Mail, Evening Herald* (Dublin), *Irish Independent, Irish Times, Sport* (Dublin)
New Zealand: *Auckland Star, Auckland Truth, Budget and Taranaki Weekly Herald, Daily News, Daily Telegraph* (Napier), *Evening Post, Gisborne Herald, Gisborne Photo News, Gisborne Times, Manawatu Evening Standard, New Zealand Herald, New Zealand Sporting and Dramatic Review, New Zealand Listener, New Zealand Memories, New Zealand Observer, New Zealand Pictorial News, New Zealand*

Sports Digest, New Zealand Sportsman, New Zealand Truth, Poverty Bay Herald, The Press (Christchurch), *Southland Times, Sports Post, The Sun* (Auckland), *The Star* (Christchurch), *Taranaki Herald, The Weekly News* (Auckland)

South Africa: *Cape Times, The Star* (Johannesburg)

United Kingdom: *Belfast Telegraph, Boxing, Daily Mail, Sporting Life, The Times*

United States of America: *American Kennel Club Gazette, Boxing Blade, Boston Evening Transcript, Boston Globe, Brooklyn Daily Eagle, Brooklyn Daily Times, Boxing Illustrated, Chicago Daily Tribune, Chicago Defender, Cleveland Plain Dealer, Collier's, Daily News* (New York), *Daily Mirror* (New York), *Esquire, Evening Journal* (New York), *Everlast Boxing Record, Illustrated Boxing Record, The Leatherneck, Liberty, Life, Los Angeles Times, Manhasset Mail, Miami Herald, Minneapolis Journal, National Police Gazette, Newark Evening News, New McClure's, New York American, New York Evening Herald, New York Evening Post, New York Herald Tribune, New York Sun, New York Times, New York World, New Yorker, Philadelphia Inquirer, Port Washington News, Providence Journal, Red Bank Register, San Francisco Chronicle, Sports Illustrated, The Ring, Time, Washington Herald, Washington Post*

Index

Adelaide 48
Aislabie, Ben 61
Albertanti, Francis 145
Ali, Mohammed 242
All Blacks (Invincibles) 65, 67, 82
Ames, Billy 220
Anderson, Charley 96, 97, 98
Aorangi 192, 193
Archibald, Samuel A. 141
Ashburton 19
Astor, Vincent 175
Atlantic City 119, 136, 142, 147
Auckland 13, 17, 24, 49–52, 54, 93–4, 192–4, 223
Ayr 48

Baer, Max 54–5, 166, 215–16, 220, 221
Baillie, Jim 48
Baker, Walter 77
Baldwin, Joseph S. 113
Bannon, George 216, 217
Barry, D.J. 61
Bartlett, Bill 40–1
Batho, Tom 48
Beckett, Joe 59, 62, 78, 79–80, 81, 86, 93, 94
Bell, Colin 45–6, 47–8, 204, 242
Berengaria 88
Bergomas, Giovanni 220

Berry, Tom 79, 86
Bimini, Bahamas 228, 229, 231, 232
Birkie, Hans 221
Blaich, Ernest G. 225
Bosche, Roy 229
Boston 110, 112, 113, 202, 203–5, 212, 220
Braddock, Jimmy 159, 166, 167, 239
Brandt, Hugo Ernest 243
Brisbane 47
British Board of Control of Boxing 70
Britain. *See* Great Britain
Britton, Jack 165
Brown, George 228
Buckley, Johnny 108, 112
Buffalo 220
Burge, Dick 65
Burns, Frank 14, 49, 54

Cambridge (NZ) 194–5
Campolo, Victorio 206, 207–8
Cape Town 75, 212
Carlin, Phillips 173, 180
Carnatic 18–19
Carnera, Primo 212, 222, 226
Carpenter, Frank 218
Carpentier, Georges 39–40, 60, 78, 92, 104, 145, 148
Carr, Harold 51

249

Carroll, Lady Heni Materoa 42, 131–2, 154–5, 195
Carroll, Sir James 41–2, 60–1, 131–2, 196
Carter, Roderick Murray 49
Castricone, Mario 241–2
Cawley, Frank 214
Chandler, Ernest 134
Chapdelaine, Ovila. *See* Delaney, Jack
Chapman, John McAfee 118
Charles, François 79
Chicago 102, 147, 157, 170, 202, 206
Christchurch 51–2
Cirules, Enrique 229
Clabby, Jimmy 40, 60
Clarke, Jack 46
Clarke, Norman 70–1
Clayton, W. Lissant 60, 195
Cleveland, Ohio 222
Coates, Gordon 41, 84, 187
Coghill, Gordon 51
Coghill, Les 51
Cole, Jack 44–5
Coleman, D.W. 196
Complin, Jack 48
Coney Island Stadium 100
Considine, Bob 232–4
Cook, George 63, 68–9, 71, 78, 86, 152
Cook, James 19
Corbett, James J. 165, 175
Corbett, W.F. 47
Corri, Eugene 64, 66, 67–8, 86
Craig, R. 223
Crestmont Country Club 141
Coughlan, Eliza. *See* Heeney, Eliza (née Coughlan)
Cuba 229, 231, 235

D.J. Barry Limited 20
Davies, Frank E. 143
DeKuh, Arthur 96, 206
Delaney, Jack 98, 101, 107, 109, 113, 116, 117, 118, 119, 120–2, 123, 125, 126, 129, 130, 136–7, 138, 243
The Dell 80–1
Delmont, Gene 180
DeMave, Jack 99–100, 161
Dempsey, Jack 39–40, 90–1, 98, 100, 103, 104, 107, 108, 109, 110, 112, 113, 114, 116, 117, 118, 119, 122, 123, 125, 127, 128, 129, 131, 134, 138, 139, 145, 147, 148, 157, 159, 165, 166, 168, 170, 176–7, 182, 187, 199, 200, 201, 202, 213, 215, 216, 220–1, 239
Dennen, Sarah 206
Detroit 105–6, 137, 219
Deyong, Moss 83
The Dome 134
Dominey, Fred 43, 47, 48, 55, 57, 60, 61, 64, 71
Donovan, Arthur 211, 215–16
Donovan Bros 14
Dooling, Con 24–25
Dougherty, Jack 'Three-Fingered' 96
Driscoll, Jim 85
Dublin 81–4
Dundee, Johnny 214
Dunn, John 189
Dunn, Marion Estelle. *See* Heeney, Marion Estelle (née Dunn)
Durban 77

Eastern Glen 212–13
Egan, Eddie 229
Elder, Ruth 224
Ellery, Robert Henry Eric 37
Emanuel, Armand 141, 200

Fair Haven training camp 141–5, 146–9, 154, 156, 158–70
Faram, Frank 29, 30
Farley, James J. 122
Farr, Tommy 239

INDEX

Farrell, Jack 115, 119, 148, 156, 200, 205, 218
Firpo, Luis Ángel 92, 104, 145
Firrone, Johnny 133
Fitzgerald, F. Scott 230
Fitzsimmons, Bob 23, 99, 127, 134, 154
Fleischer, Moe 95–6
Fleischer, Nat 188
Flett, Jim 47, 51
Flynn, Tom 177
Forbes, Eddie 177, 182, 183, 184, 208
France 79, 132–3
Fugazy, Humbert 117, 128, 207–8

Gallico, Paul 72–4, 92, 108, 110, 111, 114, 115, 116, 120, 122, 126, 130–1, 137, 143, 145–6, 158–9, 162, 163, 166, 168–9, 174, 179, 182–3, 203, 207–8, 215, 216, 217, 224, 225
Galloway, Elizabeth 35, 36
Gans, Joe 91
Gastanaga, Isadore 222–3
Gaston, Charles 162
Gellhorn, Martha 235–6
Gellis, Ike 225
Gibbons, Mike 39
Gibbons, Tom 63–4, 68, 154
Gisborne 19–31, 33, 38–9, 40–4, 45–6, 48, 53, 55–8, 60–1, 71, 79, 131–2, 140, 149, 150, 151, 152–3, 154–5, 162, 163, 169–70, 172–4, 184–5, 186–7, 192, 194–8, 237, 241–2
Gisborne Boxing Association 15, 33, 39, 41, 45, 48, 50–1, 60, 61, 154, 195
Goddard, Frank 78–9
Godfrey, George 104, 129, 130
Goldman, Charley 96
Goodwin, Jack 80
Gorman, Bud 100
Gornik, Max 47
Great Britain 33, 59–60, 78–81, 84–9, 122, 125–7, 132, 133–4, 139
Greenhough, Percival 14, 17
Grenan, Jack 149
Griffiths, Gerald Ambrose 'Tuffy' 208, 210–11, 214
Guadalcanal 237

Hagen, Dugald Keith 13–14, 15, 17, 49
Hamas, Steve 225
Hamilton 194
Hannagan, Steve 145
Hansen, Knute 97, 109, 130, 176, 191
Harvey, Charlie 85, 86, 91, 94, 95, 96, 97, 98, 100, 101, 107, 108, 109, 110–11, 112, 117, 118, 119, 120, 123, 125, 128, 129, 130, 133, 134, 136, 137, 139, 141, 142, 143, 145, 147, 149, 161–2, 163–4, 167, 175, 176, 179, 181, 182, 183, 184, 185, 191, 199, 200, 201–2, 204, 205, 206–7, 211, 213, 216, 219, 220, 221, 222, 225, 243
Harvey, Eddie 120, 133, 149, 161–2, 163, 168, 170, 176, 190
Hastings 33, 40, 48
Hawke's Bay 33, 45
Hawke's Bay Boxing Association 153
Heeney, Arthur 'Art' or 'Artie' 21, 33, 43, 55, 144, 149, 163, 175, 190, 191–2
Heeney, Darcy 197
Heeney, Eliza (née Coughlan) 20–1, 23–5, 27, 29, 30–1, 32–3, 34, 63, 83–4, 89, 95, 112, 126, 132, 135–6, 140, 152–3, 172, 173, 178, 181, 184–5, 186, 193, 196, 237, 241
Heeney, Frank 21, 32, 33–4, 204
Heeney, Hugh (brother) 21
Heeney, Hugh (father) 19–23, 25–7, 30, 31, 34, 37, 40, 44, 45, 60, 66, 67, 89, 135–6, 151, 152–3, 172–3, 178, 181, 184–5, 186, 187, 194, 196, 240, 241

Heeney, Jack 21, 33, 34, 37–8, 40, 43, 44, 55, 60, 61, 144, 149, 150, 153, 162, 163, 166, 169–70, 175, 190, 191–2, 196, 197, 204

Heeney, Marion Estelle (née Dunn) 96, 164–5, 184, 187, 189–90, 191–2, 193, 194, 196, 197, 198, 199, 203, 208, 212, 213–14, 219, 220, 223, 225, 226, 233, 236, 238, 241, 243

Heeney, Pat 21, 24, 25, 144, 149, 163, 175, 189, 191–2

Heeney, Tom: childhood and education 21–31; death 243–4; golf 141, 146–7, 158–9; Hemingway friendship 228–36, 238, 239; holiday in England and Paris 125–7, 132–5, 139; holiday in South Africa 212–13; holidays/ visits to New Zealand 191–8, 237, 241–2; hunting 75–6, 211, 213; retirement, Miami Beach 225–6, 233, 234–6, 238–9, 240–1, 242–3; Royal Humane Society medal for bravery 35–7, 150; rugby 29, 34, 37, 45, 82, 84, 134; swimming 40, 132–3; war service 33, 34–5, 37–8, 154, 236–8

Heeney, Tom, boxing career: Cyril Whitaker fight 13–17, 48, 49–51, 53, 54, 58, 165, 232; early professional fights in NZ 40–7, 48–58; heavyweight champion of NZ 44, 60, 61, 66; in Australia 47–8; in Britain 59–60, 78–81, 84–9; in France 79; in Ireland 81–2; in South Africa 70–1, 72–8; in the United States 85–6, 88–125, 138–91, 198–212, 213–26; Tunney (world championship) fight 123–37, 138–88, 192, 198, 204, 205, 208, 237, 238, 239

Hemingway, Ernest 54–5, 227–36, 238, 239, 244

Hendrickx, Frans 67
Hennessey, Jimmy 91, 120, 146, 147, 149, 160, 168, 176, 180, 181, 182, 204, 243
Hennessey, William J. 149
Hoagland, John 149
Hoagland, Joseph 149
Hoagland, Raymond Jr 142–3, 149, 161, 167
Hoffman, George 208–9
Honolulu 192, 198
Hoover, Herbert 173
Howard, Walter 15
Hughes, Ed 223
Humphreys, Joe 103, 120, 176–7, 182, 216
Humphreys, 'Pop' 68
Hurst, Norman 68
Hyde, William 96

Impellittiere, Ray 222
Ingham, Thomas 36, 37
Ingram, Wallie 29, 30
Ireland 81–4
Irvine, Marjorie 189

Jacobs, Harry 71, 79
Jacobs, Joe 118
Jacobs, Mike 144, 145, 146, 162, 167
Jeffries, James J. 'Jim' 92, 103, 165, 190
Johannesburg 70, 72–5, 76–7, 87, 212
Johnson, Jack 92, 190
Johnston, James J. 'Jimmy' 108, 112, 116, 123, 220–1
Joyce, Peggy 136

Kahn, Roger 90
Kaiti 20, 21
Kelley, Harry 204
Kid Chocolate 224
Kieran, John 127, 186

INDEX

Knapp, Joseph 227–8, 232
Kofoed, Jack 116, 149, 202, 214, 215

La Hiff, Billy 139, 191
Ladentown 189
Lambert, Alec 68
Lauder, Mary Josephine 'Polly' 190
Lawless, Des 43
Lawless, Jay 159, 166, 167
Le Blang, Joe 175
Leahy, Jack 47
Leonard, Benny 39, 114
Leviathan 134
Levinsky, 'Battling' 39
Lewis, 'Strangler' 115
Lewis, Ted 'Kid' 70
Liguori, Mother 27
London 63–71, 84–5, 104, 112, 126–7, 132, 133–4
London Country Club 64
Los Angeles 221, 222
Loughran, Tommy 91, 114, 166, 176, 208, 226
Louis, Joe 54–5, 242
Lowe, Bert 44
Lucas, Charlie 68
Lyttelton 18

Mackay 47, 48
Madden, Bartley 81–4, 88, 95
Madison Square Garden 91, 94, 96–9, 100, 103, 104, 105, 107, 114–16, 118, 120–3, 124, 131, 139, 145, 165, 174, 187, 191, 201, 208, 215–16, 221, 222–3, 224
Mailer, Norman 154, 159, 171
Maloney, Jimmy 97, 99, 102, 103–4, 108, 117, 118, 126, 202, 203–5, 206, 243
Mandell, Sammy 185
Maori Haka Troupe 21
Marciano, Rocky 96, 242

Margulies, Pincus 189
Marshall, John 193
Martin and Swain 31, 38
Martin, 'Ted' 31
Massachusetts State Boxing Commission 109
Materoa, Heni. *See* Carroll, Lady Heni Materoa
Mathison, Charles 177
Maxwell, Alan 41, 44, 46, 55, 56–7
McArdle, Tom 201
McCleary, Brian 40, 48, 51–4, 55, 65, 232
McCormick, Boy 79
McFarland, Packy 39
McGeehan, Bill 78, 86, 92, 93–4, 97, 99, 100, 117, 119, 122, 123, 128, 129, 131, 138, 139, 141–2, 144, 147–8, 155, 161, 163–4, 165, 169, 178, 187–8, 207, 208
McGuirk, Charles J. 111
McMahon, Jess 96, 100, 101, 109, 123
McNamee, Graham 173, 178, 181
McQuarrie, Mrs Jack 150
McTigue, Mike 97, 104, 141
Menke, Frank 168
Mercurio, Phil 119–20, 143, 149, 158, 161, 167, 168
Mexon, Fonce 51
Miami/Miami Beach 84, 118, 128, 129, 130, 137, 201, 225–6, 233, 234–6, 238–44
Miller, George 'Blackie' 51, 76–7, 79
Modrich, George 41–3
Montreal 206
Morace, Nic 76
Moran, Owen 85
Morris, William 215
Mortimer, Bernard 59–60, 65, 66, 69–70, 71, 78, 79, 80, 84, 85, 112, 117, 118, 126, 128, 131, 132, 133, 134, 135–6, 142, 149, 160, 163, 170, 175, 176, 177, 185, 201

253

Mortimer, John 78, 80, 83, 84, 85, 86–8, 92–3, 97, 99, 126, 135, 136, 137, 140–1, 142, 145, 147, 149, 154, 155, 161, 163, 164, 165, 175, 176, 177, 180, 185, 190, 191
Muldoon, William 121, 122, 123, 207
Mulgan, John, *Man Alone* 230–1
Mullen, Jim 202
Munsey, Frank 214
Munsey Park, New York 213–14, 224–5
Murray, J. Malton 197–8

Napier 45, 62
National Sporting Club 59, 67, 84, 86, 97
Neill, Arthur 57–8
Nelson, 'Battling' 91
Nepia, George 82
New Caledonia 237
New Plymouth 13
New York 39, 84, 85, 91–104, 106, 108–24, 126, 127, 133, 134, 136–7, 139–41, 145, 149, 170, 172–88, 190–1, 197, 198–203, 206–11, 212–19, 220–1, 224–5
New York State Athletic Commission 98, 102, 109, 112, 113, 122, 123, 124, 128, 129, 133, 137, 145, 170, 176, 185, 191, 207, 215, 216–17, 229
New Zealand Boxing Association 38
New Zealand Boxing Council 61
Niagara 198
Nolan, Philip 127–8
Northern Boxing Association 13, 14, 16, 48

Ohinemutu 195
Olympia Stadium, Detroit 105
Olympic 126, 127
O'Meara, Ivan 172, 173, 178, 181, 184, 186
Osborne, Bill 138
O'Sullivan, Jim 51, 54–7

Pakirikiri Hotel 20
Palmerston North 57
Panka, George 214
Paris 79, 132–3
Parr, Sir James 134
Patty, Bob 149–50, 173, 174
Pegler, Westbrook 92, 111, 130, 137, 162, 167, 181, 182, 209, 210, 211
Peoples, Charlie 56
Perroni, Patsy 222
Pershing, John J. 'Black Jack' 39
Persson, Harry 79
Philadelphia 90, 137, 157, 170
Phillips, Jock, *A Man's Country?* 23, 26
Pollock, John 206
Pooley, Albert 43–4
Poreda, Stanley 218–19, 223, 225
Poverty Bay 19, 33, 45, 57, 60
Premierland, London 68–9
Preston, Harry 134

Queensboro Stadium 211
Queensland 20, 47–8

Retzlaff, Charley 219, 220, 223
Reynolds, Quentin 234
Rhodes, Elsie 35, 36
Rhodes, Vera 35, 36
Rice, Grantland 92, 99, 114, 117, 129–30, 131, 141, 165, 175, 182, 184, 219, 220
Rice, Jim 81, 88
Richardson, Jock 82
Rickard, Tex 91–2, 97, 98, 99, 101, 102, 104, 105, 107, 109–10, 112, 113, 115, 116, 117, 118, 119, 120, 122, 123, 124, 125, 126, 128, 129, 130, 131, 133, 134, 136, 141, 144–5, 146, 156, 162, 165, 166, 168, 169, 174, 175, 186, 187, 191, 200, 201
The Ring 65–6, 67, 79, 86
Rioux, Elzear 206

INDEX

Risko, Johnny 105, 107, 113, 116, 118, 122–3, 124, 125, 126, 128–9, 130, 131, 176, 191, 199, 219–20, 222, 243
Roberti, Roberto 130
Robinson, Eric 35, 37
Robinson, Lin 43
Rocco, Emmett 214
Roe, Thomas 21
Ronk, Grace 189
Roosevelt, Theodore, Kermit and Archie 175
Rose, Charlie 69–70, 71, 87–8
Rowell, Alfred Ernest 14, 16, 17, 49
Royal Humane Society of New Zealand 36, 37
Ruahine 62
Ruark, Robert 230
Runyon, Damon 78, 92–3, 101, 104–5, 119, 122, 125, 130, 139, 166, 183–4
Russell, James Wilson 14, 16, 49

Saint Louis 222
Saint Mary's Catholic School, Gisborne 26–7, 197
Saint Nicholas Arena, New York 91, 95, 98, 103, 119, 139, 143, 209, 218, 220
Saint Paul, Minnesota 223
Salinger, J.D. 231
San Francisco 220, 221
Santa, José 220
Saunders, Willard 228
Savage, Jim 55
Scherer, Anna 189
Schmeling, Max 204, 207, 210, 213
Schwake, John 222
Scott, Phil 59, 63, 64–6, 67, 68, 69–70, 71, 78–81, 82, 84, 85, 86–8, 104, 112, 127, 129, 191, 201–2, 208
Sharkey, Jack 84, 97, 100, 104, 107, 108–10, 112, 113, 114–16, 117, 118, 119, 122–3, 125, 126, 128, 129, 130, 131, 136–7, 138, 148, 176, 198, 199, 200, 201, 202, 204, 208, 210, 213, 237, 243–4
Sharkey, Tom 108, 165
Shaw, George Bernard 90–1
Sheppard, Charles Edward 68–9
Sheppard, Ern 51
Shurneman, Dutch 221
Sir William Wallace 20
'Six Hundred Millionaires' 97, 165
Slattery, Jimmy 220
Smith, Charlie 78, 79
Smith, Chris 168
Smith, Stewart 14
South Africa 70–1, 72–8, 87, 88, 104, 132, 200, 211, 212–13
Southland 13
Squires, Johnny 70–1, 74–5, 149
Squires, Tom 149
Stand, Bertie 207
Stanley, Jack 79, 84, 86
Star Athletic Club 85
Stevens, Percy 173
Stewart, Earl 'Mick' 59–60
Stribling, Young 200, 201
Sullivan, Con 47
Sullivan, John L 239
Swiderski, Paul 161
Sydney 47, 48
Syret, Julian 57–8

Taylor, Charlie 48
Te Hapara School 29–30, 197, 237
Te Karaka 44–5
Timaru 19
Tiverton, New Jersey 220
Tokomaru Bay 59
Tom Heeney's Bar 235–6, 238–9, 240, 242
Toronto 219–20

255

Towers, Mother Mary Bernard 27
Trentham Military Camp 37
Tunney, James Joseph 'Gene' 39, 81, 83, 90–1, 92, 97, 102, 103, 104, 105, 107, 109, 110, 112–13, 115, 116–17, 118, 119, 123, 125, 126, 127, 128–31, 132, 133, 134, 135, 136, 137, 138–48, 156–7, 159–60, 161, 164, 165, 167, 168, 169, 170, 172–88, 191, 192, 196, 198, 200, 201, 202, 204, 205, 207, 208, 209, 212, 222, 223, 224, 225, 226, 229–30, 231, 234, 237, 238, 239, 243

United States of America 38, 39, 64, 70, 78, 81, 85–7, 88–125, 128–31, 132, 133, 136–7, 138–91, 194, 196, 197–212, 213–26
Uren, Tommy 40
Uzcudun, Paulino 79, 97–9, 100–2, 104–5, 107, 116, 117, 118, 122, 123, 127, 129, 130, 131, 198, 199, 200, 201, 202, 204, 211

Vancouver 150, 191, 192, 194
Veteran Boxers' Association of South Florida 242
Vogt, Anton 238–9
Von Porat, Otto 202, 204, 206

Waddy, Ern 48, 51
Waikanae Beach 23, 27, 35–7, 57–8
Wakefield, Henry 80
Walker, Jimmy 170, 224
Walker, William H. 113, 170
Wallace, Frank 143, 157, 165
Wanganui 44, 55, 59
Ward, Wilfred 87, 201
Watson, Johnny 64
Watson, Tom 'Seaman' 224
Webb, Arthur 46
Webster, Tom 92, 125
Welling, Joe 149
Welling, Johnny 149
Wellington 62
Welsh, Freddie 39
Wembley Stadium 63, 112, 126, 133
West Coast 13
Whitaker, Cyril 13–17, 48, 49–51, 53, 54, 58, 165, 232
White, E.B. 95
Whiteley, William Eugene 36, 37
Whitney, Cornelius Vanderbilt 175
Wignall, Trevor 79, 135, 163, 165
Wilde, Jimmy 62, 85
Wilder, Thornton 146
Willard, Jess 39
Wills, Harry 81, 101, 104
Winegardner, Mark 231
Withers, John S. 214

Yankee Stadium 99, 133, 145, 161, 170, 174–86, 208
Young, Ern 59
Young, Jim 'Trooper' 67

Zukauskas, Joseph Paul. *See* Sharkey, Jack